JOE
LONGTHORNE MBE
THE AUTOBIOGRAPHY

WITHDRAWN

JOE LONGTHORNE MBE

Sugar in the Morning

THE AUTOBIOGRAPHY
WITH CHRIS BERRY

British Library Cataloguing-in-Publication Data:

A catalogue record for this book is available from the British Library.

Design by www.envydesign.co.uk

Printed in Great Britain by CPI Group (UK) Ltd

13579108642

© Text copyright Joe Longthorne and Chris Berry 2015

The right of Joe Longthorne and Chris Berry to be identified as the author of this work has been asserted by them in accordance with the

JOHN BLAKE

Published by John Blake Publishing Ltd,
3 Bramber Court, 2 Bramber Road,
London W14 9PB, England

www.johnblakebooks.com

www.facebook.com/johnblakebooks ❡
twitter.com/jblakebooks ❡

First published in hardback by Great Northern Books in 2010
This edition published in paperback in 2015

ISBN: 978 1 78418 718 7

A c   rary.

The rig   authors

Copyright, Designs and Patents Act 1988.

Papers used by John Blake Publishing are natural, recyclable products made from
wood grown in sustainable forests. The manufacturing processes conform to the
environmental regulations of the country of origin.

Every attempt has been made to contact the relevant copyright-holders, but some
were unobtainable. We would be grateful if the appropriate people could contact us

CONTENTS

Foreword – Ricky Tomlinson   ix
Foreword – Garry Bushell   xii
Foreword – Eric Hall   xv
Preface – Chris Berry   xvii

1. The Film   1
2. Last Orders   4
3. From Rifle Terrace to Hessle Road   8
4. Junior Showtime   17
5. Clubland   37
6. My Son Ricky   55
7. Jersey   57
8. My Personal Favourites   76
9. Search for a Star   80
10. Holiday Camps   85
11. Scarborough and Ravenscar   98
12. Television and the States   103
13. Turpin's   113

14. Favourites   120
15. My Own TV Show – The Start   122
16. Cancer   126
17. Living with It   130
18. My Own TV Show – The Series   132
19. Sydney Opera House   138
20. Stanley Kubrick   144
21. This Is Your Life   147
22. Drugs and Fights   158
23. Bankruptcy   163
24. Nervous Breakdown   166
25. Impressions   173
26. James and Pat   178
27. In Court   191
28. The Music Hall Tavern   204
29. Thailand   213
30. Musicians   217
31. Anyone Got Some Bone Marrow?   220
32. Reggie   230
33. Bone Marrow: The Prelude   232
34. Death's Door   238
35. The Comeback   246
36. Lifetime Achievement Award   251
37. Cyprus and Don Black   262
38. Benidorm   268
39. Forty Years   271
40. Bestseller and Silver Heart   274
41. Crash and Losing Pat   278
42. MBE   284
43. Teresa   289
44. Beating Cancer... Again   291
45. Left Ear   295

46.Back on the Road   297
47.James   300
Appendix I: Joe's Charities   302
Appendix II: Discography   304
Appendix III:Videography/DVD-ography   311

FOREWORD

RICKY TOMLINSON

It is difficult to know where to start when writing about Joe. His group of fanatical fans would describe him one way, fellow artistes would describe him another way and, of course, his faithful entourage would describe him their way.

I think the best way to describe Joe Longthorne is to use an old-fashioned expression my mother used when describing something which was far more than it looked: 'There's good stuff in little parcels.' I think this sums Joe up perfectly.

Offstage, talking to him or sharing a joke, he is Joe, the guy next door. Put him on a stage, under the bright lights and fronting his eight-piece band, you are watching a 'megastar'. I use that expression because his live show is simply breathtaking.

This man, who is probably 5′ 6″ or less, fills the stage with his amazing presence, wit and genuine love of his fans. He does, in my opinion, rank amongst the greatest performers we have ever produced in this country, and to this day I cannot understand why he is not topping the bill in Las Vegas or New York. I've just come back from Vegas, where I saw one of the biggest names in the world, a major US star, and the artiste (who I won't mention) was just not up to the standard that Joe reaches every time I have ever seen him.

His impressions are second to none, and his little schoolboy jokes are told exactly like a naughty schoolboy with a cheeky little grin at the tagline.

I have seen Joe perform many times, and indeed I've appeared on the same live show with him. His backstage demeanour is Mr Cool. This makes such a change from some of the prima donnas I have worked with over the years.

He appeared at Liverpool one time for a charity show on behalf of a famous Liverpudlian, Herbert the Hairdresser. Joe was on the same bill as The Real Thing and Claire Sweeney, but he stole the show, as he always does.

I recently appeared on The Alan Titchmarsh Show and Joe was at the same studio, getting ready to give yet another sparkling performance. When he knew I was in the dressing room, he stopped rehearsals and came to see me.

'Joe,' I said, 'get back and finish your rehearsal.' Joe replied, 'Friends are more important than rehearsals.' We sat in the dressing room and laughed as we swapped jokes and stories.

A short time ago, I had a four-way heart bypass and thought this would be the end of my performing career. Then I remembered the night Joe invited me to the Midland Hotel in Manchester. The Variety Club of Great Britain had arranged a gala benefit night in honour of Joe, who had recently undergone a bone-marrow transplant. I remembered the illness he had been through and how he had always bounced back. I said to myself that, compared to what Joe had been through, my operation was only like having a tooth out.

On that night, I was struck by all of the other show-business artistes who turned up to wish Joe well and show how much they loved and respected him. Needless to say, as frail as he was at the time, as he was just recovering, Joe sang and made a lovely, moving little speech in which he said the star of the evening was not him or any of the very many well-known faces from the world of entertainment in the hall. The star was, in fact, his surgeon and Joe thanked him publicly.

There is a saying about the phoenix rising from the ashes; I think this applies to Joe Longthorne in more ways than one. He has been up and down many times but never out. He, like many of us, has had money troubles; and he has let himself down on occasions by being led astray.

However, Joe always takes responsibility for his mistakes and never blames anybody else – and more importantly, he always comes good. The last time I saw Joe perform live was at the Floral Pavilion Theatre in New Brighton. My friend and I turned up on the night to see the 'House Full' sign in the foyer. The manager of the theatre knew us and sat us in an area reserved for wheelchair users (it was not being used at the time) with two deckchairs to sit on. The lights dimmed, music played and on walked a slight figure in an all-white suit – the audience erupted and he performed. It was electrifying. Joe sang, joked, played the piano, and it was the finest performance I had ever seen.

The story of Joe's life is the stuff that novelists couldn't make up. I am so pleased that he has got round to writing it with his good friend and fellow singer – as well as an excellent writer – Chris Berry. This book tells his amazing story, which has had more highs and lows than anyone I know. It is the best autobiography I have ever read!

Joe fully deserves his title of 'The Greatest British Entertainer' – as I said, there's good stuff in little parcels.

GARRY BUSHELL

Y eldest kids were teenagers when I first took them to see
Joe Longthorne. They weren't happy about it. My daughter
loved Shane Richie. My son was into Blink 182. They moaned
all the way to the Blackpool Opera House, and they carried on
moaning right up until the moment Joe started to sing. But they left
the show absolute converts to the Longthorne cause, just as I knew
they would.

Pretty much everyone who sees Joe is blown away by his range of
impressions; critics don't call Joe the 'Human Juke Box' for nothing.
But they're also touched by his humour, his vulnerability, and his
unique relationship with his adoring audience.

Man of the people, Joe Longthorne is more than just a class act.
He is, as I once wrote, the spirit of show-business decanted into a
suit. Pure variety.

Religious ecstasy is the closest parallel to the joyous intensity
of a Longthorne live show. His powers of mimicry are uncanny.
Close your eyes and he is Shirley Bassey or Tom Jones, or pretty

much whoever he chooses to be. Bassey says, 'Joe does me better than I do myself.'

Last year, as an experiment, I sneaked his David Bowie impression onto the indie rock-orientated Total Rock Radio. The musicians in the studio were amazed. Who was this hot new talent, they demanded to know. It was hot old Joe. A brand new, albeit small, audience was won over.

That is why it's a constant source of irritation to me that British television treats this incredible entertainer with such disdain. I'm not alone. The likes of Chris Evans, Peter Kay and Noel Edmonds have all sang his praises vocally over the years. And yet still TV bosses cock a deaf 'un. Instead of wining and dining each other at the Groucho Club or foisting the likes of Jedward on the viewing public, they might consider going to see Joe Longthorne live. Then they'd understand what a phenomenon the man is.

Interflora should give him shares for the amount of business his fans put their way. They leave his stage decked out like the Chelsea Flower Show.

You never know what to expect with Joe. The first time I interviewed him at home, his carthorse casually sauntered into the house and was left there until he fancied wandering out again.

Other journalists have been known to moan about Joe's laissez-faire attitudes, or his penchant for the odd medicinal 'Jamaican Woodbine'. I find it all endearing. How can a man this easygoing and seemingly disorganised off-stage be transformed into such a consummate pro when his band strike up?

The last time I saw Joe Longthorne in concert, he was headlining at Blackpool's North Pier. Joe promised my wife and I the royal box, which surprised me as I didn't think the North Pier had one. It hasn't. We were led up and over the roof of the venue to a very different box – the lighting box – where the scatty star had thoughtfully left us a bottle of champagne on ice.

Everything in Joe's life is touched with humour, even the tragedy – and he has had his fair share of that. As you'll read in these pages, Joe Longthorne has had priests read him the last rites more times than Tiger Woods has had hot girlfriends. The last time it happened Joe was ready to go.

'I'd been on the slab for six hours,' he told me. 'I was in agony and it was so cold I contracted pneumonia. My body had been weakened by eleven years of chemotherapy. I had food poisoning and my organs started shutting down. I heard one doctor say, "I wouldn't touch him with a bargepole."

'I had reached the point where I was thinking, "Please God, just let me go – I've had enough pain." And that's when it happened. Jesus came to me. I didn't see him, but I felt his presence and I heard a voice say, "Not just yet."'

Joe is not 'born again' and he hadn't gone mad either. But he assured me, 'In that hospital something came to me and my life has been different ever since.'

It's true. Joe performed at a Variety Club night in honour of Engelbert Humperdinck in Manchester, at the Hump's personal insistence. He was sensational, morphing from Tony Bennett to Willie Nelson via Barry Manilow and winning three standing ovations.

His TV career came and went, like his Bentleys, his swimming pool and his six-bedroom Berkshire mansion. The only things that have stayed constant are Joe's incredible talent and his army of fans.

'People are so kind,' Joe says. 'I get bundles of letters every day. The fans are what matter to me. Cars, houses, money…I do not give a s★★★ about all that. They're nice to have, but material things don't matter so much. What matters is when I'm on stage – that's when I LIVE.'

FOREWORD

ERIC HALL

I first heard Joe when he appeared on the TV show *Search for a Star*, although I didn't know it was him straight away as I was taking what is called a 'comfort break' in polite society today. I heard Shirley Bassey's voice and wondered what the hell she was doing on a talent show. When I came back in the room I saw this young man singing. He just knocked me out with his range of impressions and his fantastic voice.

At the time I was head of promotions for EMI and was responsible for plugging the likes of Queen, Cliff Richard and Cockney Rebel. I have also been responsible for promoting Tom Jones, Frank Sinatra and The Beatles, but what I can tell you is that there isn't anyone who can compare with Joe. He is the best male vocalist this country has ever seen and it's time more people became aware of him.

I wanted to work with him straight away but I missed out at the time. I fell in love with his voice, his character and, over the years, quite simply the man himself. Joe isn't just a talent, he's far more than that. He's a lovely human being and we are, finally, working together. It's a source of very real happiness to me and I'm sure that his career is set to flourish for many years to come.

PREFACE

CHRIS BERRY

I met Joe for the first time in March 2009. We share the same
birthplace, the wonderful but often unfairly maligned city of
Hull – or Kingston upon Hull, if we're being exact. When I worked
on the *Hull Daily Mail* in the late seventies and early-to-mid eighties,
the name Joe Longthorne was known by everyone in the city.

Joe's life has been the ultimate rollercoaster ride. It's perhaps
appropriate that he lives not too far from the Pleasure Beach.

His voice is captivating and, as we enter 2015, better than ever
in many of his fans' views. Joe's calling card throughout his career
has been his impressions. There are millions who are in awe of
his Shirley Bassey, Tom Jones, Barry Manilow, Barry White, John
Lennon, Engelbert Humperdinck, Frank Sinatra, Tony Bennett, Judy
Garland, Dean Martin, Sammy Davis Jr., Matt Monro, Ken Dodd
and literally hundreds of others. He is perhaps the world's leading
singing impressionist and they are still a great part of his show, his
own 'special guests', but Joe is so much more than a man who can
turn his art to others' voices.

When you consider some of the utter dross that is served up on our screens in the name of entertainment, it is hard to fathom the minds of TV producers and executives. *An Audience with Joe Longthorne* would be an ideal programme to show off Joe's unique, world-class talent and it would attract millions of viewers.

What I've learned about Joe is that he really does see himself as 'just Joe'. Don't get me wrong; he has had a star's lifestyle, he has had the world at his feet, he does enjoy the applause, the adulation, but when he's away from the stage he's just Joe. He was never bothered about the money; it's just what came (and went) with the territory because of his talent.

He cares very much about the people around him, whether those at home in Blackpool, his family over in Hull or his fans who he talks of so affectionately as friends. Helping others has always been close to his heart and he is constantly raising funds for various charities. In 2012, he was awarded the MBE for his efforts.

I do hope you find that this book is everything you hoped it would be. It is Joe's life. These are his words. There are parts of it where, for obvious reasons, others have had to fill a few gaps, but this is all Joe!

It has been not only an honour to write this book on Joe's behalf, it has also been a very real privilege.

CHAPTER ONE

THE FILM

I'm not a me-me-me person, I'm really not, but it's nice when you're asked whether you would like a film of your life to be made. I was approached recently and I started thinking of how I would like it to open. I'm feeling really positive at the moment, having just come through yet another cancer operation that I will talk about later, and I'm feeling better than I have in years. I still have ambitions and playing at the London Palladium, the Lady of Theatreland, once again this year is one of many I'm looking forward to. These ambitions also include two new albums: firstly, *The Great British Songbook*, which will include some of the best works of this country's songwriters and another album of my own new compositions.

It's that kind of spirit and inspiration that is providing me with a wonderful time of my life right now. I'm working on arrangements for new songs in my live shows such as Sammy Davis Jr.'s 'I'm Not Anyone', written by Paul Anka, and a great song called 'Make the World a Little Younger'. Jeffrey Archer is to introduce me onstage at the Palladium and I have one of the entertainment world's best-known publicists, Eric Hall, working with me. (Thanks for your kind words, Eric, at the start of this book – and Ricky's, and Garry's.)

Anyway, on with the film and how I see the opening; you'll see why as you read on in the further chapters: I can see it starting in a grainy brown colour, in the style of *The Sting* or something like that. The camera should be perhaps on a crane so that it shows the terraced housing of the 1950s, with washing hanging out in the street and kids shouting and playing. The music should be Johnnie Ray's voice singing, 'If your sweetheart sends a letter of goodbye…'

Coming down real slow, the camera then catches on the barrow that's outside our house before coming through the front door and into the kitchen. It's very nostalgic and evocative of the time and, while the music carries on playing, you see my mam, Teresa, and one of my two sisters, Anne. Their first words are about us having to move out of Rifle Terrace, but their second words are, 'Where's the bairn?' They mean me. The song comes back up again as they look for me.

I'm five years old at the time and where I am is in my granny's shop. This is all true, nothing made up. It's on the corner, packed with clothing and all sorts of hats, scarves, brassieres, dresses, shirts and shoes. It has a huge window and the camera gets there before my mam and sister do. I'm dressed up in all kinds of ways, as the camera does that thing where it flickers fast on each outfit, with me shown wearing frocks, wigs, the lot. I'm doing what kids do when they play in shop windows, posing and making faces. Then I see Anne and duck under the clothes rails behind me.

There's comedy as they find me. Then Anne tells me I need to go and get our dad out of the pub. It's on the same terrace and he's on the piano. This little fair-haired lad opens the pub door and there's smoke everywhere. There's a little scuffle going on at the back of the pub and someone gets thrown out just as I'm coming in.

Dad sees me and greets me with, 'Here he is, the next Al Jolson,' and sticks me on the piano where I go into a little song and dance routine wearing my big boots. I'm singing Alma Cogan's 'Sugartime'.

I'm supposed to be getting him back home for some reason. I really did all this, as well as singing in fish and chip shops and at two wakes. You see me next at my first talent contest, run by Hull Parks Department, including a little argument that Anne is having with the organiser about a form not having been filled in for me to take part. It kind of sets it all up, don't you think?

You'd see some fun and some action, that's for sure. Who knows when it will happen, but come and join me on the rollercoaster that has been my glorious life, where I wouldn't have changed a thing, ha ha. Well of course I would, who wouldn't, especially with some of the things that have come up along the way? Right, are we ready? Let's get going then. Roll the cameras! It's time for a bit of drama.

CHAPTER TWO

LAST ORDERS

This would make a good scene. I'm on the slab. They've given up on me. I'm on my way.

'He's going at six o'clock, we can't do any more for him.'

I'm laid there and I'm fighting, but they can't see that. They're talking about me as though I'm not here any longer.

'He's dead, he's dead, he's gone.'

I know they're trying to bring me back. I can hear them talking around me, so I know my brain is still alive. I'm saying to myself, *Jesus, sweet Jesus, if you've any decency about you take me now.* I'm now not even thinking about how it would kill my mother if I go before her. What's that all about?

I'm going through too much pain. I'm dying.

Jesus, dear sweet Jesus, this is six hours I've been here in the theatre. There are seven people around me, either pumping blood or moving drips or, it seems to me, just jumping up and down. They are good people and they're all trying to help but I can't take any more.

I just want him to take my body over. I can't take the pain any longer. I've fought all I can. I've nothing left. I've had enough. There's a phone call. I'm sure I hear something like, 'I wouldn't touch him with a bargepole.'

Dear Lord, I cry from inside my body, *help me now.* I don't see his face – Jesus. People say they do. I don't. For me it's a feeling, He's there. I think again about my dear mother, my queen duchess, and about my sisters and brother, and what it will do to her if any of us siblings are to pass away before my mother. She worries about me all the time, always has, and here I am, first on the agenda.

That was 2005. I was not just at death's door. I had opened it and had at least one foot already through it. The medical staff thought I'd shut it behind me! When I went in for the bone marrow transplant, which I needed desperately, I had been told that the survival rate was something like one in fifty. I've gambled on various things in my life, but not generally with such long odds. I wish I'd put a bet on now.

So much has happened since I came through those months of agony and those years of not knowing whether I would be here each following year – so many good things. And then just last year, in 2014, after ten years of being back on the road playing theatres up and down the country, in the States and on the Med, it looked as though it was 'here we go again' when I was diagnosed with cancer once more, this time in my mouth.

But here I am after coming through another time of it.

I've always lived for today and I don't look for sympathy. There are enough in worse positions than me. I was sat next to a chap in hospital when I was having a check-up last year and it appeared that, although I was a few months down the line and doing well, he was just going in for the first time. We got talking and I tried to reassure him that with the geniuses they have in hospitals and with his family all pulling together, he'd sail through it. I've been so lucky. It's been another journey with my James, and he's looked after me all the way through once again.

What I had in 1988 when I was first diagnosed with cancer is called CLL (chronic lymphocytic lymphoma). It's not usually curable and the average life expectancy after having been diagnosed, dependent on when it is found, is five years. There are 2,800 people diagnosed with it every year in the UK. That's just terrible, isn't it? One day, hopefully soon, there will be a cure for all types of this dreadful disease. That's why I try to do my bit to raise funds to help.

I must surely be close to having had the complete set of illnesses and operations related to it all by now. I've had the coming and going of the disease, the life-saving bone-marrow transplant, which so very nearly saw me off and which is the point we've arrived at here, and the double pneumonia that nearly got me once I'd come through the transplant.

Whether it's hearts, brains, lungs, we've all got something wrong with us sometime and we all do get weary, so when I sing 'The Impossible Dream' it's a sentiment that goes all through my show. I sing, and speak, to every single person in the theatre.

Let's get back to the slab. I was given 'last orders' three times. That always gets a laugh at the concerts when I talk about it that way. Most of the fans, those loyal and wonderful people who are more like friends to me and who come to my concerts with such great excitement and love in their eyes, know what I've been through and they have always been a great comfort to me. But I like to show them the funny side of it all. Everyone has had some sort of pain, whether they have suffered themselves or through someone dear to them, and we all need a bit of a laugh along the way to help us feel some relief.

If you're wondering where we are at the moment, it's Manchester Royal Infirmary by the way. Last orders! I had three of them delivered to me by three different priests – Father John, Father Dennis and Father Geoff. All of them wise and good men, they all gave up their time to come and see me, and I'm not saying they got it wrong but if I could have told them at the time I would have said they had no right coming to say to me, 'This is the end.' Strangely enough, when I saw them it just convinced me that I wasn't dying. I was still fighting inside, even though my body had seemed as though I had given up.

I was in hospital for nearly four months before, during and following the bone-marrow transplant procedure, but there's always comedy to be found in everything, you know. I'm laid there in intensive care one day and all I can hear is what sounds like organs playing 'Happy Birthday to You'. It wasn't, I was told, it was just all the machines bleeping, but to me it sounded just like the song. Maybe the drugs I was taking at the time were making me think that way. Then I found out the guy in the next bed had been given my rosary beads. It was all just a mix-up because we had shared a bedside cabinet, but at the time I just thought, *Is nothing sacred?* The wonderful Pat Mancini, who you will hear of later, got them back for me. The other patient survived too, so maybe those beads helped us both.

I was alive and the gifted people of Manchester Royal Infirmary are the reason why I am able to write my story.

CHAPTER THREE

FROM RIFLE TERRACE TO HESSLE ROAD

Joseph Patrick Daniel Longthorne is my full name, and I weighed in at seven and three-quarter pounds on 31 May 1955, at around two o'clock in the morning, at Hedon Road Maternity Hospital in Hull. I was baptised at St Patrick's Catholic Church, Spring Street, in Hull. My mam had nine children all together, but only four of us – Anne, John, Lizzie and I – made it through childhood. Whenever my mother heard 'Happy Birthday to You' it upset her.

My mother, Teresa, and dad, Frederick, are both gone now but I still love them dearly. They were the best. Family is important whoever you are and all of mine mean the world to me. We're from a travelling, Romany background and both my parents were from different forms of travellers. Dad was from the tinkers and fairground side who can fix and make anything, and Mam was from Irish stock. My grandfather had a boxing tent and I seem to have been around boxers all my life. John H. Stracey, that wonderful fighter, is a close personal friend and I also support Luke Campbell from Hull, the Olympic champion.

The Longthornes have their roots in Yorkshire. My great, great grandfather, Joseph Jack, was born in Skipton and moved to Kingston upon Hull to set up as a scrap dealer. My mam's mother, Grannie Annie (Sheridan), was born under a tarpaulin in Walmgate in York. She and my other grandmother, Grannie Lizzie, were both the same age and very close.

We lived at No. 15 Rifle Terrace, just off Walker Street, near the famous Hessle Road in Hull. From what I can gather we (travellers' families) were all moved there, from our trailers, so the terrace was packed full of people I knew. It's no longer there now. Actually, it's been turned into a community centre, which I think is a nice touch because it was very much the centre of our community when I lived there. It was a great terrace. It was always full of hustle and bustle, with horses and carts everywhere, and I was comfortably cocooned there in my own world. There were great characters and our terrace was alive with activity all the time.

Singing is the thing that makes me want to live, and for me that started at a very early age. I can remember listening to my mam singing, and then singing myself before learning to walk. It's just in me, in my genes. Music is what comes out of me. As far as I was concerned, my mam was the best singer I'd ever heard. She called herself a 'Vera Lynn singer'. My dad, as we've already established, could play the piano and I thought he was better than Russ Conway. He played both stride and vamp style.

We've some great singers in the family, but for me singing has always been about entertaining an audience, hearing them applaud and seeing people smile, or even cry, when I sing.

I attended a nursery school called Villa Place, and when we children were supposed to have half an hour's kip in the afternoon I would sing to them all. Miss Tibbs, I think her name was, got me

9

to sing to everyone whilst she sat in her rocking chair. I would sing songs like 'Paper Roses' (a big hit for the Kaye Sisters at the time and later Marie Osmond).

That's where I gather my singing in front of people really started. Very soon, even at that tender age, I was appearing in front of much bigger audiences in the parks around Hull.

I appeared inside a television set before I ever appeared on one properly. At home we had this TV that had been kicked through so it had no screen. I used to practise for my mam by singing behind it with my face where the screen should have been. We always had plenty of television sets because some of the local companies would offer one week's free trial in those days. We had 52 TV sets one year! My grannies used to smash the slot box off the back for bingo.

One of the first songs I can remember singing was 'Sugar in the Morning', which to give its proper title is 'Sugartime', made famous in the UK by Alma Cogan.

I sang it dressed up in braces and a little boiler suit with a safety hat on and a pair of Dealer boots, like a proper little 'troweller' (builder), in a Kingston upon Hull Parks Department talent contest. I was only about four years old, but to me it was the most natural thing in the world. If I'd done it like that today I would probably have been called Bob the Builder.

I won my first competition and got a big, red, plastic, toy racing car and a quid. My sister Anne and I went off and bought fish and chips with it. From then on I was singing wherever I went, but it was Mam who taught me how to go out and be a success. She also told me what would make me different from the rest. Her advice, even at such an early age, was what has stood me in good stead throughout my career.

Mam told me, I remember it clearly to this day, 'We have a lot of singers in the family, Joe, like your Uncle Mick [Sheridan] and your Aunt Violet [Foley] from Leeds, and your singing's more than alright. I know you can sing better than lots of people but you need something else, something to make you stand out. There are a lot of singers going around, Joe, so you need to do more than just sing.'

That's how the impressions came along. My first singing impression was Al Jolson – Asa Joelson, to use his real name, but before that I started out with Steptoe from *Steptoe and Son*. The TV programme was really popular at the time and I found that I could do both characters – Harold and Steptoe himself. I got myself a hat and a muffler from my granny's second-hand shop and that's how my act was born. It was a bit like the children's TV programme *Mr Benn*, with me getting dressed up as different characters. There are still many people today who seem to regard me purely as an impressionist. I still do them and over the years I have added hundreds of 'star guests' to my shows.

Mam was right to advise me to start doing impressions. I don't think I will ever be able to go on stage without someone shouting for me to, 'Do Shirley!' or, 'Do Tom!'

When I was about eight or nine years old I would be singing at funerals – even stood on top of coffins – or performing in some of Hull's great pubs, or both inside and outside fish and chip shops, in front of senior citizens, anywhere just to get an audience and a few bob.

My mam used to tell a story about me going to get our tea from a local fish and chip shop, and that I would go in and sing to earn enough to pay for them. The lady would then put them on the top of the pan to keep them warm while somebody would say, 'Give us another one, Joe.' Then I'd say something like, 'I don't know, I'll have to hurry up,' and if their hands didn't go into their pockets I'd be off home. Singing was already starting to become a business, even then.

I learned all of the songs in my early repertoire from my mam and dad. She sang to me all the time and had the most beautiful, wonderful voice. My mother's absolutely natural technique is where I took my lessons from. She never had a proper singing lesson in her life.

I do find sometimes that I have difficulty in learning songs, especially those where I need to read the lines rather than learn them straight from hearing, because I'm dyslexic. I really have to learn things parrot-fashion. Being dyslexic has caused me one or two problems along the way, but it doesn't seem to have held me back from performing. When I was little the words just seemed to go straight into my head and Mam would help me with them if I appeared to be struggling.

Mam's favourite song at that time was a Bing Crosby number, 'In the Cool, Cool, Cool of the Evening', which went, 'Someone waits for me, if only my eyes could see her. Oh how happy I would be.' I remember that her eyes used to start filling up with tears as she sang it. She also liked my sister Anne singing, 'Put Another Nickel In'.

Sometimes she would send me down to the pub to get my dad to come home – you see where I'm heading with the film idea now. I was only very young, but in those days there wasn't the concern there is now over sending young ones out late at night – and I really *was* young. She'd say, 'Go and get your dad out of the Peever,' – that's Romany speak for the pub.

He was a bit of a lad, my dad, and I was the baby of the family, but I was the only one who could get him out. Once I'd get there – somewhere like The Fisherman's Arms – I'd get on one of the tables and sing. He would just say, 'There's my boy, gnash on charver ['get on boy' in Romany], let's have "Danny Boy", Joe.' So I did and I still get asked to sing it now, although I don't get on the tables anymore – or on any coffins! I've been a bit too close to mine a few times!

Going into the pubs did me no harm. Then Dad would come home with me. The atmosphere in the pubs around Hessle Road and where we lived was something that I have always loved and it's why I still love going back. I'm still a Hull lad at heart and I always will be. But you're probably, by now, wondering what I was like when I was little, other than when I was singing. Well, I was a blond-haired lad and I liked smiling.

I suppose you could have called me a bit accident-prone too. I'm still a bit that way today. I broke my arm falling down the stairs when I was only eighteen months old, and another time I got a bead stuck up my nose! It was a pearly bead and Anne had to take me over to Park Street Children's Infirmary in Hull. I remember her saying, 'Just don't f★★★ing sniff!' Do you know, you can't breathe very well with a bead stuck up your nose? Funny, that.

Apart from the accidents, my early childhood was very happy. Granny Lizzie had the second-hand clothes shop at the corner of our street and I used to love going in and getting dressed up. I'd wear everything – hats, shirts, skirts, trousers, shoes and wigs. There was just so much stuff to play with, to try on and to try out new characters. It was like having my own private props department store. My granny always used to save the best of the clothing for me.

I learned to play the piano when I was young too. My dad taught me. We always had a piano; Dad played and my mam sang. When they played together, everyone in the pub would shut up and listen. They'd then shout at the end, 'Go on, Teresa!' They used to love her singing. She was compared to both Ella Fitzgerald and Patsy Cline quite a lot. She sang all around Hull and up as far as Bridlington on the east coast.

My mam used to work so hard. She would go out to work at the fish house from eight 'til five and come home covered in scales. My sisters looked after me when Mam was at work and

13

they would drop me off somewhere each day, and pick me up. There was a time when I had felt as though I was being sent away for some reason, but I wasn't. I only found that out for definite in writing this, so I've learned something and it has set my mind at rest about what had always troubled me.

It turns out that all that was really happening was that I was getting picked up by what had once been an old ambulance to take me to nursery. In my mind, over the years, I had felt that I'd been sent to a nunnery!

What Lizzie, my younger sister, says is that she and Anne used to take it in turns to pick me up on an afternoon, or see me off from Rifle Terrace every morning. I was always immaculately dressed apparently. Lizzie tells me I can thank my grandma's shop for that.

Lizzie also tells me that my mam had always seen me as a star from the day I was born. She believes that because our mam had lost children and then had me, her life became wrapped around me. I was the youngest and Mam put every bit of effort she could into helping me on my way. When she heard me singing at a very young age, and saw some of herself in me, she always said I had the talent born in me.

But my life wasn't all about singing. I worked hard and I used to go out with my dad on a horse and cart, 'tatting'. We would go round calling and collecting all types of scrap metal. Later, I had a little hand cart that Dad made for me, and as I got a bit older I would go off and do a bit of tatting all around the area, collecting bits of copper and brass. I would go out, come back, unload and off I'd go again. It was our way of life, what we did, and to me it was just a natural thing. No wonder doing Steptoe came naturally to me.

Most of my childhood was very happy, but there were two occasions when my happiness was interrupted. One of those was when my sister Anne was taken away from us for four years; and the other when we moved out from the Hessle Road area, although we moved back pretty quickly.

Anne had been sent to Rampton, the secure psychiatric hospital in Nottingham. She had been involved in violent behaviour. I wasn't told why she had been taken away from me. That's probably because I was only about five years old at the time. She was gone for a long while and, although I was quite young, I remember thinking, 'Where has my Anne gone?' I was so glad when Anne came back that, being young and excited, I actually peed up her back when we were in bed together.

Anne has always been a tremendous sister to me, in fact all four of us – Lizzie, John, Anne and me – are all very close as brothers and sisters.

The move from Rifle Terrace, where I had spent the early years of my childhood, was the worst thing ever for me. I can't put an exact date on when it happened but it was a terrible time. I was just so upset. My world had caved in. We moved out one summer so that redevelopment could take place. All of the travellers' families were shifted out of the terrace. All my extended family was crumbling away. I couldn't even eat because it bothered me so much.

We went to what for us looked like a posh place called Elgar Grove, opposite the Costello playing fields in the Boothferry Road area of Hull. I'm sure it is a fabulous place to live for many people, but it just didn't suit me. Elgar may well have been a great composer, but the place didn't fill me with sweet music and he certainly didn't know how to build houses. It just wasn't where I had come from or where I wanted to be. There were also so many things that, all of a sudden, you were not allowed to do as well.

You couldn't have a budgie or a dog, but we did! I wasn't allowed to play the piano, because the walls through to next door were as thin as you find in Spain when you're on holiday in one of those newly-built hotels. Coming from the great hubbub of horses, carts and great characters, this was definitely not for me. But in the end our move away from the Hessle Road area only lasted three months, thank heavens. I don't mean any disrespect to anyone who lived there then or who lives there now, but it was just such a big culture shock for me.

What put the tin lid on it was when tragedy struck. One of my friends, called Stephen, was drowned. It did my head in. That, on top of everything else, was enough. Dad said, 'That's it. We're getting out of here.'

That's when my mam pulled off her biggest and best deal ever. At that time she worked with a man called Harry Kavanagh, who was the manager at the fish filleting factory. I think he suffered with gout. He knew she wanted to come back to Hessle Road and he fancied living where we had moved. He liked it better there. It was an ideal arrangement. He told my mam, 'Teresa, I've a nice house and yard for you,' and we swapped.

So we ended up with all of the tatters again at Number 39, Woodcock Street, just off Hessle Road. It changed my life. I was alive again! It was a beautiful house and had six garages, a gym and stables, as well as two bathrooms. There was even a Morgan car that had been left in one of the garages. I went back to the rag and bone, and back to the fish and chip shop singing. I was back where I knew I was from. Hessle Road has always been alright for me.

CHAPTER FOUR

JUNIOR SHOWTIME

I was in and out of so many schools in Hull – Boulevard, St Wilfrid's, Westburn Street, Sir Thomas More, Eastfield and I ended up at Sydney Smith. I wouldn't say I was disruptive at all, but I did get chucked out of a few. I was kicked out for scrapping from a couple of them, but I never got a report about me.

I was very erratic and had a temper on me. Hopefully I'm calmer now, but that's probably for others to comment on. It wasn't that I was being bullied and I was never in a bullying gang, we didn't do that kind of thing. All I did was what a lot of kids do at that age. I was bored with lessons. To be honest, I don't know why I went to school at all and there were quite a few times when I wasn't there anyway.

I couldn't read or write properly even when I left school, but it was only once I'd left that I found out I was dyslexic. I can read and write now but I don't really write too much, apart from songs and autographs.

They put me in what they used to call the 'slow class' or sometimes the 'special class'. I really don't like the name 'slow' because of what it implies, and it's unfair being labelled in that way, but that's what it was called. The 'difficulty in learning' class would be a better title for it. Anyway, I didn't mind being in it. In fact, it's surprising just how many of those who were in 'slow classes' have ended up doing really well in life after school.

My own education, where I gave myself my own personal geography lessons, was more to do with travel. Just over the River Humber, years before the Humber Bridge was built, there was a whole new land for me to visit, particularly during the days when I should have been at school.

Back in the 1960s, the River Humber had ferry crossings on the hour from Hull to New Holland in Lincolnshire. Mam took me across on the ferry the first time I ever went, but then I would play truant from school. It was what Hull kids used to call 'twagging'. I'd hop on the Tattersall Castle and off I'd go in my own world.

I always went on my own. I wouldn't recommend it to any children today, but at least there was never any talk of young children getting abducted or mistreated by strangers.

First I'd go to school, get my mark, then I'd walk back out and go straight off to Hull Pier. It felt like I was going to another country, but I was just going across to Lincolnshire. When we landed at New Holland I'd get on the train and go to Barton-on-Humber. I loved it. I'd go and have beans on toast in a café and walk to Thornton Abbey, such a lovely place. So I was getting a bit of history as well.

What did I do it for? Well, like I said, I was bored, but maybe it was also because I thought that places like school were a bit too crowded for me. I just wanted to get away, be on my own. I still like doing that kind of thing today, although I don't do it as often as I really should.

Ravenscar, just along the coast from Scarborough in North Yorkshire, is my favourite place in the whole world. I found this, my perfect place, as a result of twagging as well. For someone who has lived most of his professional life on a stage and in the spotlight, I really enjoy the isolation of Ravenscar. I don't think I'm alone in that either. Many performers like to just get away from it all. We'll come back to Ravenscar later on.

Anyway, back to the ferry across the Humber for the time being. The Tattersall Castle had an upper and lower deck, and the first time I ever twagged I went on it, I had this ice cream. Unfortunately, it fell from my cornet onto someone's head below. I laid low on the top deck for a while that day, and made sure I wasn't caught with an empty cornet in my hand!

I used to get back to New Holland just in time to catch the last ferry back across to Hull. It was always great being on the ferry, especially if it was a beautiful summer's day. When I came back my dad used to ask just where I had been, because by then he knew I hadn't been at school.

Some days I'd just go and get my mark and then go off for a walk around the docks in Hull; then, when it was kicking-out time from school, I'd get back to mingle with the others as they were leaving, especially if my dad was picking me up. But one day I was well and truly found out.

I've just got back from a wonderful day off school and Dad's there in his Bedford truck waiting for me. It's five to four. The bell goes and I'm second out.

'Hi, Dad.'

Who follows me out to Dad? It's my teacher, Mr Gray, and my headmaster, Mr Billingham, in his Singer Vogue car. They ask me how I'm feeling, because I've not been in all day, and the game's up. Dad has a right go at me on the way home!

It wasn't as though I hated school though – and I did have one or two really good teachers. I loved Miss Westaby. She was my favourite and she taught maths. She supported me because I think she knew that my mind was more on singing than anything else. I couldn't do maths at all, but we had a real connection.

The others I admired most were Mr Stott, who taught maths at Sydney Smith School, as well as Mr Woodcock and Mr Underwood, my headmaster at Sydney Smith.

I was incredibly fortunate that at Sydney Smith School we had the greatest jazz pianist in the whole of Hull, and to my mind the whole of the world at the time, Mr Graham Gordon. Lord, he could play jazz! I had more time for him than anyone else and he always had time for me. He was the one teacher who really helped my singing career while I was at school, and I will always be grateful to him for that.

I didn't come out of school with any qualifications as such, no 'O' levels or anything like that, but I did get an A for one piece of work I did in humanities and another in art. I painted a picture of a nun that we had framed at home.

My best mate at school was Kevin Rimmer. I never really took to football, but he was one of the greatest footballers Hull City never had. Kev was a great pal and I remember him coming along with me to a works' children's Christmas party at Armstrong Patents in Beverley, where my mother had moved to from the fish factory.

Football was never for me. I'd start off playing a game with everyone, but as soon as the ball went over a fence they would never see me again. I'd go with it. I just wasn't bothered about that kind of sport. I like boxing, darts and motor racing, but I've never run around after a ball very much.

Kev didn't have the people around him to back him. He should have played for England, never mind Hull City. I remember his dad wasn't exactly the happiest soul in the world. The two sides of our street were like living in different worlds. We lived on one side with this big house with two bathrooms, stables and six garages, and Kev lived on the other. We weren't trying to be flash. That was just the way it was.

My dad would pop a fiver through Kev's letterbox for New Year's Eve as a present for him and then say, 'Happy New Year!' the next day, but Kev's dad would just mumble something back in return.

My first love was Pauline Jubb and we were really good friends. She was a blonde and also a very talented young lady. We spent a lot of time together. She was a singer too and could have been one of the greatest comediennes. I remember we both loved dressing up and once went to my mam's with me dressed in drag. We were like Bonnie and Clyde when we were together.

Pauline was a great girl and we enjoyed each other's company immensely. Our first song we ever sang together was 'Michael Row the Boat Ashore'. We once set up a little hairdressing business in her dad's shed. We were always up to something.

I was always trying to make money. As well as the hairdressing I would also go out tatting, collecting clothes as well as scrap on my cart. I'd then sort the rubbish stuff from the good stuff, wash the clothes I was keeping, dry them out and get them ready for sale the next day. In the winter I ran my own snow team, clearing snow from driveways and the streets, with lads shovelling snow and throwing salt all over. I had three businesses on the go at one time. It's always been in me to try and earn a living.

My father was on the HMS *Espiegle* during WWII. It was a minesweeper and operated in the Mediterranean between Malta and the North African coast. It's often said that you're f***ed if you get put on a mine sweeper, but my dad came through and was decorated for his war effort. He wasn't a big fellah, but he was one of the fittest blokes on the sea.

As much as Mam set me on my way, by suggesting what to do with my act, so too did dad. He would take me to all the pubs and clubs, particularly when I was between the ages of ten and thirteen. He was my agent, my minder, everything, but most of all a wonderful father.

When I first started out I would do just five songs. I used to come on and sing 'I Believe', followed by 'Danny Boy', then two others and finish off with 'My Way'. I loved singers like Hull's own David Whitfield, of course. His hit songs like 'Cara Mia', 'Answer Me' and 'My September Love' were fantastic. He was a great singer. Years later, I played three nights at the Crystal Rooms in Hereford and the sign outside said, 'TONIGHT JOE LONGTHORNE with Special Guest Star David Whitfield.' I'd been given top billing. I asked them to change it around. I told them, 'Look, we both come from Hull and this man is a big star. The billing needs to be the other way around.'

I first met David at the Northwood Country Club in Cottingham, near Hull. He was still a big star. He'd had his own TV show and two Number One hit records. At the time I believe he held the record for the most consecutive nights at the London Palladium as a solo artiste. He topped the bill and there was another wonderful Hull-born act who went on to become nationally famous, Norman Collier. Sadly both are no longer with us.

It was one of the first professional engagements I had after I left the TV show *Junior Showtime*, and the first thing that struck me about David was his humility. I went on to work with him at least six or seven more times and enjoyed them all.

Hull has produced some great singers and bands over the years: Roland Gift (Fine Young Cannibals), The Housemartins, The Beautiful South, Ronnie Hilton – and some great actors too: John Alderton, Barrie Rutter, Brian Rix, Ian Carmichael, Tom Courtenay and Maureen Lipman. To my mind, you can't get a better actress than Maureen. Tom's parents used to live not far from us. I'd love to spend just five minutes with him over a cup of tea, talking about how he made it in acting. He puts so much into every part he plays. He must study his characters well.

These days I study what I sing all the time, and try my best to interpret every lyric with what I feel is the right emotion. In the early days, and indeed for many years, I just went for it without really thinking too much about what I was singing.

I've three advantages now. I'm older, I'm wiser (I hope) and my voice has, very fortunately, stayed with me throughout. No matter what has happened to me along the way, my voice is still there, so I'm really extremely lucky and blessed, despite how unlucky some people might feel I have been. That's why I never ask my fans to feel sad for me. I've had a fantastic career so far. Of course, I hope that it can continue and who knows what's in store, but I would never want anyone to be sad for me over the lymphoma and other things that have happened. I've had a brilliant life and some tremendous highs. Sure, the lows have been pretty damned low though.

In those early years of performing, Dad was always there for me, like I said, and he had his own way of sorting things out when he faced up to people who were messing us about. It was the way things were done at that time.

I remember at one club in Hull, we went along and the club secretary told my dad, 'He does three spots.' My dad said, 'He does two spots. He just goes on twice. That's it.'

The guy gets a bit clever. Dad continues arguing with him at one side while I'm now on stage.

So dad followed him to his office and I went with him. My dad had quite a good vocabulary, as well as being able to handle himself, and tried to explain to the club secretary again.

'If the performer is under the age of fourteen you can't put him on three times. It's not on his licence.' The guy continued arguing with my dad, who had by now had enough of him – so my dad knocked him spark out. Dad's got my wages and I'm back on stage, ready to do 'When You're Smiling', when out comes the guy with claret all over him. The regulars in the club all start attacking my travellers' family and there's fists and furniture flying everywhere. It's mayhem, like something out of a western movie. Another good scene for the film, don't you think?

I saw our Cathy – another of our many family members and a very strong lady, I might add, built like a mountain – pick up a committee member by one arm and use his head like it was a bouncing ball.

Everything's going mad and we're getting back in this Commer van, trying to get the doors shut. My uncle – Sgt. Billy Foley, ex-army – is making sure they can't get to us.

It was all self-defence, let me tell you, not violence, and none of it would have happened if the guy had just listened to what my dad was telling him in the first place. It might seem funny now, like the Clampetts from *The Beverly Hillbillies*, but it was scary at the time. But that wasn't the end of things going on or off at my gigs, not by a long way!

I was still off tatting or knocking all the time, as well as singing on an evening. I had to be back in at half past five to get ready for a club gig if it was local. Lizzie and Mam and Dad would be shouting for me in the street to get in because I'd have to be at the gig for half past six backstage, to see the drummer and the other musicians, which usually consisted of a guitarist and maybe a keyboard player. I'd then come on at about eight o'clock, when everybody had settled. In those days, the clubs were packed by seven o'clock. These were the days when the whole clubland scene throughout the north of England was really buzzing – and in Hull it was a great time to be a performer. There were hundreds of clubs, but if you wanted a seat in any of them you had to get there early.

Dad used to say to my sisters Anne and Lizzie, 'When Joe starts up with "Is This the Way to Amarillo", get up and dance.' That way everybody else got up as well. It always worked. My dad knew exactly what he was doing. I would get around £12-£16 for the night, but if I did an extra couple of songs dad would do a bit of negotiating to get a bit extra for me.

The negotiation sometimes led to a bit more than simply arguing my case as well. All of a sudden, whilst I'm still on stage, the curtains would go flying, arms and legs would be flailing – and the drums would come crashing down. It was Dad having a fight with another club secretary. At least that way the local music stores were always kept busy with instrument repairs!

McLeod-Holden was one of the big theatrical and entertainment agents in the country at the time. Dad told me that Don Holden had asked him to stop doing deals because that was their job. My dad just told him that I was thirteen years old and that if he had to negotiate for me, he would. Dad always had a business brain and made sure I got what I was due.

Right from being four years old and winning that toy car, I had always taken part in talent competitions, either in clubs, pubs or parks. In the early days my sisters would get me ready and make sure I looked good on stage, and it was one of the talent competitions that led to me getting my first big break when I was fourteen.

The big talent competitions in Hull were run by the Kingston upon Hull Parks Department. They were very forward thinking, bringing on the talent and giving Hull people a great opportunity to make their mark in show-business. Hull had a fantastic live entertainment scene at the time, with masses of clubs. In this particular competition the final was held in the City Hall, and although these days I prefer the acoustics in the New Theatre in Hull, I thought it was absolutely amazing.

Whenever a talent show came up I was always put into it. Anne and Lizzie were always busying themselves looking after me, and the City Hall final was the biggest I'd been in yet. In the final there was a country singer called Ian Attrell, who I think was blind if I remember correctly. He was very popular. Muriel Nifton was on the organ, but I found her a bit of a 'beng' ('strict' in Romany). I only wanted her to play 'When You're Smiling' but she was just too bossy for me.

I remember my microphone fell to the floor in the final, so I picked it up. Then I started playing the spoons as accompaniment. I wasn't going to be directed by some fat organist. No disrespect, Muriel, if you are still around, it's just the way I felt as a young lad.

Everyone from my family was there, as well as all of the rest of the travellers' families. Both grannies were there too. The talent on the show was really of a very high standard, including a lady singer who Lizzie thought was going to win. There were all kinds of acts – jugglers, drummers, dancers, comedians – and I won it.

During the rehearsals there had been a lot of photographs taken, but I seemed to get ignored. Maybe the photographers liked the idea of taking pictures of the girls in their nice outfits, and who could blame them? Some of them looked gorgeous. Hull girls have always looked fantastic.

So when it turned out that I'd won, the *Hull Daily Mail* didn't have a picture of me. Dad told them that since they didn't want to know me earlier on, they'd have to come around to do a photo shoot the next day. They did just that and I gave my prize money to my first girlfriend, Pauline. I also bought her a black-and-white, plastic Beatles dress and a plastic wig.

One of my fans, or as I call them my friends, Fiona Burt, kept a press cutting of the report from 3 October 1969, which read:

'Little Joe Has a Big Future – There's a twinkle in his eyes, a song in his heart and a cheery word for everyone he meets. At fourteen years old Joseph Longthorne – "Little Joe" – is a Hull lad we can all be proud of,' writes Pru Clark. 'In a few years time he might be one of the big names in show business. For "Little Joe" – he is 4ft 10in tall – has the determination to get to the top. After winning last month's Hull Parks Department talent competition he appears to have the ability too. "Little Joe" of 39, Woodcock Street, found the world his stage at the age of five. "He used to sing in the street and people took notice of him," said his father, Mr F. Longthorne. For several years he has been the favourite of the fish and chip shops and the wonder of the working men's clubs. "He's a natural born entertainer. Send him out for fish and chips and he sings to the waiting queue," said Mr Longthorne. A local police officer entered Joe in a Withernsea talent contest when he was ten and he came second out of twenty contestants. "Since then he's played in clubs and done charity acts at hospitals," said his father. "He has never had a music teacher," said Mr Longthorne. "He once went to a dancing class and left because he was the only boy. But he will spend about twenty to thirty minutes getting a song right." At the talent contest final last month Joe won £25, which he said he would spend on clothes for his set. For all he's a little lad Joe looks set for a pretty big future.'

So it would appear that what I tell you is verified in the *Hull Daily Mail* back in the day! The City Hall final of the talent competition wasn't about the money though. It's never been about the money for me. What it led to was the landing of my first ever TV appearance. Dad wrote to *Junior Showtime*, which was a big children's show on Yorkshire Television at the time. It was a variety show and appropriately enough it was filmed at the City Varieties Theatre in Leeds, where *The Good Old Days* used to be filmed. Variety was all the rage back in the sixties and seventies.

This was also the time when I first realised that I wasn't just attracted to girls and that I might be bisexual, although that term wasn't really used back then. I'm very comfortable with my bisexuality. Some people who have been around me, but are not family or close friends, have thought they were telling the papers something new when they tried to make money out of me by saying I'm gay.

While we're on the subject, my preference sexually has always been a woman and I've loved, respected and still love all of the ladies I have ever been with, no matter what might have been printed and said elsewhere. Yes, I am bisexual and let me tell you, I still really would know how to love a woman intimately.

James Moran has been my partner for the past seventeen years and I love him dearly. He has been alongside me through some of the most difficult and trying times, but I very much love the ladies too. The best way I can put it is that I sometimes help the ladies out when they're busy!

I have a son too, Ricky, who I also love dearly, and grandchildren. More of Ricky, his family and my grandchildren later, I just needed to introduce all of this now because you were probably wondering when I would, and this is the time when it starts fitting in with my story – although there's a lot more to come before Ricky's birth. So far I'm just 'Little Joe' and I'm not yet at the City Varieties.

It's like a big jigsaw, this, isn't it, trying to put all of your life down on paper? I hope I don't leave anyone out! I've certainly tried to make sure I haven't.

No matter how well I have performed on stage, whether in clubs or theatres, I have never really been that good at auditions. When I went to an audition in Grimsby for Yorkshire Television's

Junior Showtime, I was to meet Jean Pearce, comedian Billy Pearce's mother, and on this occasion all went well. Jean was responsible for all the choreography on the show.

I was just thirteen at the time and I went with my own piano player, David Carter. He was a bit posh, but he was a good lad for me. I played the spoons again and sang 'I Believe' and Jean seemed impressed, but I wanted to make sure. I just said, 'Wait a minute, I can play the spoons as well.' I was desperate for this. I wanted it so much. So I dashed to the kitchen of this church where the auditions were being held.

Jean put on her notes that Jess Yates, the producer, 'must use this boy'. Jess was known as 'the Bishop' and he had a formidable reputation. I warned Jean that while I could sing, I couldn't read or write, but she stuck by me and told the Bishop that she'd got this kid with a good voice, 'a bit cheeky and does his own stuff', but he can't do scripts and things'. Well, Jess was a scripts man, but he decided to give me a chance thanks to Jean, and I was in!

All I knew was that for the first time in my life there could be something really happening for my singing. But at the same time, the idea of a scripted programme frightened me to death. After all, not being able to read and write, you can imagine how I felt. I just thought, *How am I going to fit in?* I could sing anything, but I was worried that I wouldn't be able to conform to what the show was going to need.

Bobby Bennett was the show's presenter and really helped me with learning the scripts, by going through them so I learned parrot fashion. Jean always helped too. I found out later that although Jess really thought a lot of me, he had said he didn't want me anywhere near him when it came to reading scripts. Jean and Bobby were my best mates on the show by a long way.

The show was really popular and gave a lot of performers their first taste of television: Glyn Poole, Bonnie Langford, Mark Curry and Pauline Quirke all appeared, and it even made it into a TV programme that celebrated the best 100 children's shows. That's not bad considering it was just children appearing in it. There's nothing like it today.

My first *Junior Showtime* appearances were a bit of a joke. I'd asked all my friends in Hull to watch the show, but for the first couple of months I was either dressed as a mushroom, lion, Chinaman or rabbit. Mam said all she could see of me was my legs. But I was still enjoying being a part of it. I loved all the make-up and getting dressed up in different outfits. It was like being back in my gran's shop.

The programmes were made over a weekend in Leeds. I would leave Hull after going for a bath on a Friday afternoon at my Auntie Peggy's, who lived in the centre of Hull. Then I would catch the train from Paragon Station to Leeds. There I would meet up with Penelope Keith, who was filming at Yorkshire Television at the time, and we would travel together. The funny thing was that I was there with a case full of scripts I couldn't read, which I'd been given the week before. There was really no point in giving them to me. We would rehearse on Saturday, record on Sunday and come back home Monday morning. While I was in Leeds I would stay at my Aunt Rose's in Crossgates.

I had the scripts with me at home all week, but I couldn't even face looking at them. We had a really good club man in Hull called Ted Cuthbert. He worked for Carmichaels, the posh department store in Hull at the time, and he had sorted Mam out with this perfectly decent case as a present for me. It really was lovely and it looked mightily impressive, but I still couldn't read anything that was inside. Dad also had 'Yorkshire Television' printed onto it. I used to hope they had got something that made life a bit easier for me every week.

Junior Showtime was so important to me because I knew this was the real start to my career. It was what I was made to do, and here I was performing on television at fourteen years old. Many of the others would probably have gone on to 'proper' jobs, but for me this was my life. Thank God for Jean and Bobby, that's all I can say, they helped me through!

It wasn't all just television and learning what to say and do though. I also got into one or two fights with some of the other kids on the show.

I used to go in this room and every kid, I mean every kid apart from me, would know their lines or be learning them. Some of them were really too clever for their own good and so I'd bring them down a peg or two. I'd say to this big lad from Barnsley, 'My mam says you look like Humpty Dumpty.' He'd then say, 'You want to tell thee mother she looks more lark Humpty Dumpty than me.' That's when I'd go 'smack' and lay him out. It was childish I know, but we were kids and it was probably bound to happen when throwing a lot of us in together from different backgrounds all over our wonderful county of Yorkshire.

My first pantomime appearance was in *Cinderella* for Yorkshire Television, just after I'd joined the show. This is how the *Hull Daily Mail* reported it:

'Pantomime TV spot for Little Joe – Hull's youngest showbiz personality, fourteen-year-old "Little Joe" Longthorne is to appear in his first TV pantomime. Little Joe, of 39 Woodcock Street, will sing and dance in the chorus of *Cinderella* to be broadcast on Yorkshire Television on New Year's Eve, after winning a Hull Corporation summer talent contest. Little Joe's greatest ambition was realised when he was given a chance to appear on television. He recently completed twelve recordings for *Junior Showtime* including a Christmas Special, which will be broadcast on Christmas Eve.'

My most successful time on the show during my two years was as soon as I was singing on my own, but I might not have been as successful if it hadn't been for my Uncle Joe (Wilson). You'll find I have so many family members who keep cropping up it's sometimes difficult to keep up. When you're part of the travellers' community, that's the way it goes.

Uncle Joe was a real hard man; we're talking serious tough traveller here. Joe was a dealer from Leeds and felt he could make sure I got to sing the right songs for me, the ones I was already good at. Jess had got me singing stuff like 'I've Got a Lovely Bunch of Coconuts', but Joe said, 'I want him singing "Marta",' which The Bachelors had a hit with. It was a very popular song for me at the time. I'd sung it in all the clubs in Hull and everyone liked me doing it.

Uncle Joe wasn't known for mincing his words. He told Jess, 'He's singing "Marta" or your head's going through that f***ing wall.' I'm not sure whether Jess was swayed by that but it seemed to pay off for me, because he let me sing it and Uncle Joe even gave me a 'flim' (Romany for 'fiver') afterwards. Uncle Joe wasn't around all the time, but it appeared to me that from that moment on Jess gave me a bit more respect. I was no longer a mushroom or a Chinaman. I was now out on the front line.

In the end I was introducing the show with Bobby. Not bad for a lad who couldn't read or write! Jess was a master at writing the openers and closers to programmes, and I just carried on learning everything parrot fashion from Bobby and Jean. I cannot over-express just how much these two wonderful people did for me. I will forever be in their debt because without them I probably wouldn't have lasted longer than a fortnight. And without Uncle Joe I might not have made it to the front line.

When I wasn't performing on the show I would be back in

Hull, either at school, or not at school when I should have been, or out calling and tatting or playing the clubs.

One of my major moments during filming *Junior Showtime* was being asked to get involved in a programme called *George Martin Presents*. I didn't know who George Martin was, but suddenly there's Ringo Starr on the phone to Jess – and Jess wants me to sing 'Octopus's Garden', which Ringo sang on The Beatles' *Abbey Road* album. The Bee Gees were on the show too, along with Lulu, Madeleine Bell, this big orchestra and Pan's People. It was fantastic to be involved with.

Again, the *Hull Daily Mail* reported it all:

'Aged fourteen, Joe is a TV veteran – A TV appearance with Ringo Starr on New Year's Eve was one of the highlights in the career of fourteen-year-old Joe Longthorne of Woodcock Street. "He was very nice to talk to and not at all big-headed," was Joe's comment on Ringo. Joe is rapidly becoming a TV veteran himself. He reckons he has taken part in about fourteen *Junior Showtime*s so far. These are all pre-recorded. "You never know which one will be coming on when you sit down to watch," says Joe. Pint-sized Joe hopes to take up entertaining full time when he leaves Sydney Smith School. His current TV work does not interfere with his school work. "I never miss school to take part in it," he said.'

I was also to appear in a film! But don't get carried away here, it's not what I was talking about earlier or anything like it. I'll let the *Hull Daily Mail* tell you all about it. I'm still waiting for the call from Hollywood!

'Joe (fifteen) in film – One of Hull's up and coming young entertainers, Joe Longthorne, has been busy in recent weeks.

> Along with his numerous clubland appearances Joe has just
> finished a fortnight's filming. He took the main role in a film
> produced by Mr Edward Little, a lecturer at the Hull College
> of Education. He and his half-dozen student helpers decided
> to make a film on the problems of a poor reader with the
> object of providing stimulus for discussion for students
> within the college. *Do You Read Me?* was the title of the film
> and in it "Joe had to play truant," said his father with a laugh
> last week. "He's never played hooky in his life!"'

I don't even ever remember seeing the film! I wonder whatever
happened to it, if it was made at all.

Junior Showtime was great but none of it ever went to my head,
because I just felt as though I knew where I was going from the
beginning. There was a moment when I thought I had hit the big
time by being on the show, but the feeling didn't last too long. I
knew there was a lot more to do before I would ever make it as a
real success in the world of show-business, but it was a great way
to start.

I think you do believe you've got it made when you go back to
school and all your mates say they saw you on telly and you were
great. But I never came home and acted the big shot. I remember
taking all my mates to a place called The Gainsborough in the
centre of Hull, which was a big fish and chip restaurant at the
time. David Whitfield once owned it. And that was the way I
celebrated my success. Any of the money that was earned from
Junior Showtime went straight into the bank, my mam made sure
of that. Jess had told her that I should look after my money.

It was around this time that I started taking notice of other
big-name singers, people who were to have a massive influence
on my style and my future routines on stage. As anyone who
comes to my concerts or has seen me on television will know, Dame

Shirley Bassey has been a huge part of my life. My impression of her on stage is one thing, but it should never be understated just how much I adore her singing style and her stage presence. It's not all about getting a laugh out of performing as Dame Shirley. She is and always has been a fantastic performer. I have always looked up to her and thoroughly admire her work. Now don't get the idea I'm some kind of Dame Shirley 'stalker' here, but you will see just how much I think of her as my story unfolds.

The first LP I ever bought was one of Shirley Bassey's. I just knew then that I wanted to perform and deliver songs as well as she has always done. Dorothy Squires came next to me, then Judy Garland; later I also liked Charles Aznavour and then Sinatra came into my life. That was it. I didn't need any more. I had what I felt was the complete set of wonderful singers. Sure, there have been great ones before and since, but these to me were the best.

I just love performing as Dame Shirley and I feel as though I turn into her for those few minutes each night. It is a wonderful gift to be able to 'do Shirley', as my fans ask me to. There's a tingle goes right through me as I spread out my arms, extend my fingers and make those big eyes.

While I was being awakened to the show-business people I wanted to learn from, my early TV career was about to come to an abrupt end in 1971. I hadn't done anything wrong except become sixteen years old. That was the way it was with *Junior Showtime*. Once you reached sixteen you were off. The good news for me was that at least it meant there were no more scripts!

Let's take a little break from the early days right here. We'll pick it up again soon, when my clubland career started going into fulltime work, when I fell in love several times, when my son Ricky was born and when I nearly landed up in jail. All of that is coming soon, as well as my elopement with a fantastically sexy woman, and my wonderful friendship with a lovely man.

There's such a lot to tell and I'm just hitting my stride, but for now, I don't know about you, but I could do with getting a glass of something or other. Will you join me? Come on then, let's have a little drink.

CHAPTER FIVE

CLUBLAND

Ah, you're back. Did you have a nice drink? Is it still by your side? Whatever you're doing, maybe even reading this on one of those Kindle things, let's get to clubland.

Once again, I was so lucky to have been around at such a marvellous time for singers. Clubland was going through what was probably its best time in the late sixties and early seventies, and every working men's club in the north of England could afford to have acts on because the clubs were always full. If you became a name, someone they wanted to see, then your diary would fill up very quickly.

I had been packing out the clubs all over Hull throughout my teens. It seemed like I played every single one of them at some time or other, and I had still been playing them while I was doing *Junior Showtime*.

My dad and I had a few run-ins together over the years, like fathers and sons do, most notably when I made a mess of his prized possession, his Bedford truck, but he was always there for me. I don't think there can be many in my business whose parents showed as much faith and belief in their ability.

After my two years on the TV show I was back on the road fulltime, and all of a sudden I was now an adult performer playing every night in clubs, earning my living from what I had always felt was where I belonged. This was when the real travelling started. When Joseph Patrick Daniel Longthorne went up and down the North East, back to Hull, to the West Riding and York, and over to Lincolnshire. We were everywhere.

What really changed was that I started going out and singing the songs that they wanted in the clubs. I shifted my emphasis on to more up-tempo and feelgood numbers like 'Beautiful Sunday', but I never left out the ballads. I've always been a big ballad singer. Songs like 'I Believe' and 'Till' (which Ken Dodd had a big hit with). I also loved Matt Monro. I always make a point of singing his songs like 'Portrait of My Love' and of course 'If I Never Sing Another Song'. But back in the seventies I also put in a lot more that fitted with the era we were in. When you listen to my earliest recordings, those I recorded around the mid-seventies, you might also hear a little bit of a nod to other singers around at the time like David Cassidy.

I did anything. I could sing from ballad to rock and from soul to country, but some of the ballads I really wanted to sing at the time I felt were maybe a bit too gay or camp, and they contained feelings I had about a man even though I was with a lovely girl. This was the first time I really started thinking about my sexuality on stage.

There was always a lot of talent on the clubland scene, and of the other singers performing regularly in Hull at the time I remember Gloria Dixon at the Jesmond Club. She really was like Shirley Bassey and a great singer, but it was when I started hitting the North East circuit that I really started finding my feet.

What I found in the North East was that they had the best bands for accompanying singers like me. Back in Hull I'd often turned up and been backed by a drummer and organist. Up in Sunderland, Newcastle and all the other pit towns in the area, you would invariably get a four-piece or five-piece band behind you, and to a singer like me that made all the difference. It always has for me. I'm a live performer and when I have a live band backing me we fly! That's perhaps why the North East remains so special to me today. I have such happy memories of my clubland days up there.

Playing the pubs and clubs was not just my main business by now, it was also my main happiness. I think I have always needed to travel. It's in my bones, it's my heritage, and the North East was a wonderful area for me. It still is today and it's a real joy to go to places like Whitley Bay and South Shields. Some of this country's finest artistes have come from there: The Animals, Alan Price, Sting. The furthest north I played at the time was Ashington Miners Welfare Club, about fifteen miles north of Newcastle.

Many people talk of working men's clubs being difficult places to play, but I didn't find them tough to crack at all. That doesn't mean you didn't get a hard word or two when you first turned up at a club that was new to you, though. You would even get children saying things like, 'Do you like your car, mate? Well, you'd better be f***ing good or it won't be there when you come back later.' I well remember that type of comment from some of the lads outside of clubs like the Downhill, and Redhouse Workman's Club in Rawmarsh Road, Sunderland.

Today, working men's clubs are nothing like they were. It's really sad that there is no longer that feeling that everyone should be in their club on a Saturday night, but that's just the way things go.

Those were the days when we only had three TV channels, no videos, no mobile phones, no satellite TV, no Playstations –

this was Mum and Dad's night out and believe me, people really wanted to be entertained. They had worked all week down a pit or at sea, and if you weren't good enough they would soon let you know. I loved it.

My dad used to talk with the club committees to either tell them or suggest what they should do to promote me, especially if he found that all they had done was scrawl my name in chalk outside. He was always very professional about how I should be promoted and would make sure they had a proper poster up the next time, if they'd gone for the chalk routine, announcing me as 'Joe Longthorne – direct from *Junior Showtime*.' He wouldn't stand any messing, but I guess you already worked that out earlier when the drums came crashing down and all of the club members launched into us.

One of my best friends in the business today is Roy 'Chubby' Brown. Roy comes from Teesside and he played that whole North East circuit too, including the Hull clubs with his band. I have always found that the people of the North East really are special, and those who come to my shows from there are very important to me.

At that time I wouldn't say I was too concerned about my act. I was singing and enjoying it and, of course, I was thinking about which songs to use, but I wasn't thinking about it the way I do today. I was just getting through, finding my way.

I changed my show every week, building up quite a catalogue of songs and impressions. I think it's called bobbing and weaving in boxing terms, but I've always been concerned about presenting a completely different show from one night to the next. If you come to my show today I guarantee the next night it won't be the same.

I was working for entertainment agencies like Bill Fredericks, Stage Space and Ronnie Lundy from Middlesbrough. They were some of the big names in the North East circuit and by now, as well as Dad, I also had my brother-in-law Mick Holliday, Lizzie's husband, taking me to gigs.

Mick used to work his arse off all day delivering coal, then he'd lock up his yard, go home and pick me up to get to somewhere like York for seven o'clock. My suit would be on the back of his lorry, waving about. My sound system would be strapped in at the back too, and we'd make for the Post Office Club or the Viking Hotel. I still have a copy of a contract from the York & Leeds Branch Union of Clubs & Institutes which shows how much I was paid for an evening on Thursday 7 September, 1972, at Huntington WMC. It was £14. There was no mention of 'riders' in those days. You were paid the fee. That was it. The only thing with that copy of the contract is that the name of the artiste on it was 'Joe Longthorpe'. I hope they got the poster right.

Most of my bookings at the time were handled through McLeod Holden. This itinerary for the end of October and going into the beginning of November 1972 gives you an idea of my workload at the time. I was seventeen. It was the year when Slade, T.Rex, David Cassidy, Donny Osmond and Gilbert O'Sullivan all topped the charts:

Friday 20 October:	Dixon's Arms, Woodmansey
Saturday 21 October:	Unity Club, Hull
Sunday 22 October:	York Street WMC, Wakefield
Thursday 26 October:	Teddy's Club, Withernsea
Saturday 28 October:	Wombwell British Legion, nr Barnsley
Sunday 29 October:	Hodgson's Club, Beverley
Monday 30 October:	Upper Healey WMC Club, Sheffield
Wednesday 1 November:	Gatehouse WMC, Clayton, Bradford
Friday 2 November:	Blackburn's Social Club, Brough, Hull

Those were the days when a pint of beer cost just 11p and a pack of twenty cigarettes cost 25p. When you put it like that it seems a long time ago, doesn't it?

Having the right stage equipment had become a priority for me and my first proper microphone was a Calrec, one of the first battery-enhanced microphones on the market. I had also invested in my own sound system. Before that it was often a case of using bingo microphones, and what you sang and how it came out were two completely different things. I bought my system from one of Hull's finest musicians and entertainers. He's still performing today and his name is Johnny Paterson, but he's better known as Johnny Pat with his band The Aces. I recall him letting me have the gear without charging anything on the hire purchase either.

I had also soon learned that the bigger the star you were on the clubland circuit, the less 'spots' you did on a night. So I went down from three to two, and then down to one.

While my entertainment career was moving along nicely, my love life was about to become complicated. Pauline Jubb had been my first love, like I said earlier, and we had been great friends. My next girlfriend was the lovely Janice Brown. We had some good times together and she was a really lovely girl, and is still in my heart today. I had some beautiful girlfriends; Denise Santos was gorgeous too.

It was Susan Moore who was the first girl that made me think I ought to be within a relationship, like my mam and dad. I thought it was right, her and me, but in the end I was wrong. This is really important, this part of my story, because it involves Ricky, my son, who means so much to me. I didn't have any contact with him for a long while, but there have been some better times in more recent years

I thought Susan and I were made for each other. I honestly also believed we were going to have more children. At seventeen I

42

was enjoying what it feels like to make love to a woman. There's a cheeky side of me that wants to tell you all of the intimate things I wanted to do, but let's keep this a family book at least for now.

Susan was beautiful. She was just a year older than me and lived in Cholmley Street, not far from our house. I was always with her. I really respected her. She was the eldest in her family and had brought up the other children as her mum had left them, and her dad was at sea for weeks at a time. Her father, Tom, was a massive Frank Sinatra fan, so we got on really well when he was back. He was also a very hard-working man who spoke a lot of sense.

When Susan said she was pregnant there were three thoughts that came into my head. The first was just how lucky I was that I was to be the father of a son or daughter. I thought, *That's it, I'm straight. Not gay, not bisexual. This is what you do, a bit of singing then come back home to your wonderful wife* – even though Susan and I were never married.

The second thought was, *I really don't know who I am.* I didn't know whether I was gay or straight. Then I knew I was gay. Then I knew I was bisexual. I didn't know what was going on with me. Some of that might have had something to do with drinking two bottles of cider every night. But seriously, at that time I didn't know whether I was Arthur or Martha. It was only years later that I realised I was actually a bit of both!

My third thought, and it probably won't surprise others in my kind of position, was, *What happens to my career now?* But just at that moment none of this seemed to matter, because I was so excited about being a father. Susan was growing bigger and bigger, and I loved coming home and wrapping my arms around her tummy like any man would. It doesn't matter whether you're gay, bisexual or straight, it's still the same feeling.

Ricky was born on 12 November 1973. I was eighteen and in my local pub, Rayners on Hessle Road, at the time. Half an hour after Ricky was born, I was cradling him in my arms. I felt like Champion the Wonder Horse. It was one of the proudest moments of my life, as it is for any parent. Susan and I were still alright at the time, but that was soon all about to change.

I loved Susan, I really did. She was a very sexy young lady. But she didn't see things the way I did. I think she liked the idea of stardom, but she thought that stardom was more like Diana Ross and the Supremes or The Temptations than me. I could see where she was coming from. It's sometimes hard to imagine that someone you know will be able to reach beyond their own area and become far better known.

I really don't think Susan felt I could get much further in the entertainment world than performing in clubs. I don't think she ever thought I had that much talent and all of a sudden, now that we had a son, the issue of show-business was a problem for her. Maybe deep down it had always been a problem for her. I was forever travelling, earning a shilling out of town, but I always knew where I was going.

My dear sister Anne was unsure about her, because she felt she would take me from being an entertainer to being an at-home-all-the-time daddy. I felt it too, but I didn't blame her for it. I think it's only natural for most women to want to get married and have a happy family life. I think that's what Susan really wanted, but I couldn't give her that commitment. I knew it could never be just me, Susan and Ricky. I knew I had to be back on the road, doing what I do best.

When I parted from Susan it wasn't anything to do with falling out with her, or not loving Ricky. I told Susan – and I hope she remembers it this way, because even if these are not the exact words it's how I'd like to think I said it – 'It's not that I don't love you. I do love you, but I'm not IN love with you.'

I was headstrong. I was probably thinking more of myself and my career, but I also like to think that I'm a good man. We've all got our faults and I know I've got mine, so I'll never come out and say somebody else was wholly wrong. Things aren't that simple. Susan was a woman who needed her man to be with her more than I was ever going to be, that's all. Of course, I had all sorts of other things going on in my head too, but that's all it really came down to. We weren't meant for each other after all. We still keep in touch.

Sometimes there are things that just happen, and lovers who just come into your life when you least expect them. For me that was a young man. I can't name him because it just wouldn't be right, even now.

How it happened was like this. I was with Susan, living with her in her dad's house, when I met this young man in a local pub. *Bang!* That was it. I fell in love with him instantly. The trouble is that I do fall in love that way and with both sexes. I couldn't hide the fact that I was in love with someone else, and anyway I think Susan knew straightaway. Women do, don't they? It's female intuition.

I still loved Susan, that didn't change, but I had also fallen in love with this young man who I ended up spending two years with. We were just two blokes who got on well together.

I had still hoped to look after Ricky financially and be with him whenever I could, but I had moved out of Susan's house where we had been living together, so that wasn't easy. Ricky was a beautiful baby boy with blond hair like me, and I was still feeling good about being a father. I've always felt good about that. I've never once wished Susan and I hadn't had Ricky.

Did I feel bad about what was going on? I actually felt quite relieved. At least Susan knew that we weren't going to make it as a couple, because we'd been living under quite a bit of tension. We were getting further and further apart as time went on. My life was with him – or so I thought at the time.

So was I gay or was I bisexual? I still didn't know for definite. Yes, of course I had feelings, but knowing exactly who you are and what you are is sometimes very confusing. It certainly confuses others!

There was never a big announcement anywhere. I didn't advertise anything. That's because I think I always knew I was bisexual rather than purely gay. It wasn't as though I hadn't been around girls while I was up in the North East, and I certainly wasn't oblivious to the ladies, as many readers of this book may testify.

Fortunately, I've always been a fairly good-looking guy and I've made wonderful love to a number of beautiful women, including a contestant from the Miss Isle of Man contest at one time.

You hear of people losing their minds over working out who they are and trying to understand their sexuality, but none of what happened did anything to my head. I still knew I was a singer and entertainer first and foremost. That was always there over everything else.

In brief terms, the move from Susan's house went a bit like this (although I'm sorry if I've got any of it wrong if you're reading this, Susan):

After Ricky was born I felt that Susan was blanking me. Within six weeks I was on tour back up in Sunderland and the North East, and both Susan and Ricky were with me. The truth is that Susan never wanted to tour, and when we came back I just knew it was time to move out. I ended up living with two lesbians in a flat, as well as my new partner.

My partner (no names, like I said) very rarely came to my gigs because he wasn't a gig type of person. He was a college boy and liked fast cars. I had a big, gold Ford Zephyr at the time, which my mam had bought for me, and it went like a bomb. We had two fantastic years of being great mates. It was wonderful but then it just frittered out in its own way.

I can't even give his first name because someone in Hull would be bound to work out who he was and, like I said, that's not fair. I hope he's still around though.

But that's just the start of the heartaches, break-ups and love affairs! I'm only just getting underway here, and thinking back to my past loves from Pauline Jubb onwards is giving me a very pleasant feeling! That's because, truthfully, everyone I have ever fallen in love with I am still in love with in some way today.

It wasn't all about falling in love though; some of it was pure, unadulterated lust, as you're about to find out next! We'll keep the book right though. I'm not about to turn it into something smutty.

Let's stick with the love life a while longer. Like I said, when Susan and I parted I had two fantastic years, but they weren't all just with the young man who cannot be named. I was also seeing Sandra!

What can I say? I was young, virile and Sandra wanted me, and wanted me a lot! She knows she did. Her husband, John, didn't seem particularly bothered by it. They ran a pub in Hull. Sandra was f***ing gorgeous, extremely sensual, had really firm breasts and boy, could she make love! We had some fantastic love-making and neither of us could stop. It is one of the best drugs you can ever have when it is like that. Sandra was my sexual dream woman.

Have you ever made love in the daisies? I have and it's not too uncomfortable. What is more uncomfortable, though, is when half of your family and friends turn up whilst you're doing it! This has to go down as one of my most embarrassing moments, although I've had a few! TV programmes like *Shameless* are nothing compared to some of the things that have happened in my life!

I used to go diving in the ponds at Brandesburton, which is a little village going towards Bridlington from Hull. I would go there when I was younger, with one of the greatest boxers Hull (and England) ever had, Ricky Beaumont – and no, it wasn't him I was with in the daisies! I was with Sandra.

It was a beautiful summer's day in July. We went out for the day to talk about our future together. We used to go round to her mother's place while she was out and enjoy ourselves. I'd pick her up from the pub and we'd go straight there. Anyway, this particular day was lovely, brilliant sunshine, everything was right with the world.

Sandra was an absolutely fantastically sexy lady. She was both beautiful and stunning, and she certainly confirmed a lot for me about my manhood. Susan had already confirmed that earlier, of course, but Sandra was at me every minute and we had such a good time.

Anyway, back to Brandesburton! It was a beautiful July day. One thing led to another and we were doing what comes naturally! It certainly did to both of us, at any rate. We were making love in the daisies when, all of a sudden, a bit like the Battle of the Little Big Horn (no pun intended), the 'injuns' came over the hill and surrounded Custer on his last stand (again, no pun intended).

The injuns, in our case, were none other than half my family popping up from over the hill. I couldn't believe it. There we were with loads of travellers looking at me and Sandra in all our glory!

Amongst them was 'Knockie' Windass. His son, Willie, is now married to my beautiful niece, Theresa. There are times when you'd prefer it not to be the small world everybody says it is. This was definitely one of those. All of the travellers were saying things like, 'Now then charver, how's it keeping?' Honestly, how can you allow for things like that happening?

You're probably thinking now that I was cheating by being with two people at the same time. I guess I was in one way, but as I said, my relationship with the young man wasn't the same.

Then another man entered my life when I was twenty. He was

my sound and lighting engineer. We never had a sexual relationship at all. It was purely business and real companionship. We were to be best mates for years. For personal reasons I've kept his name out of this book, but he was with me on the road for seventeen years and is now married to one of my nieces. They have a lovely family too.

We formed a bond and became great friends, constantly in and out of tricky situations, sharing the laughs, and at times the despair, that comes with the entertainment game. Throughout our time together I could never once fault him over our friendship.

It was outside the Cholmley Club that I first met up with him. Susan lived directly opposite. He was talking about the acoustics.

'That didn't sound too good in there,' he said. I came out with the reply so quickly: 'Tell you what, you do it for me then.' And that was that. I didn't muck about in those days, and if he was giving his opinion and reckoned he could do better, then I was up for it.

We were great working together. He made sure I was okay wherever we went and we were a team. I probably love this man more than most of the people I have ever loved, simply because of the man he is and the times we had together. We spent so much of our lives travelling all around the world over the next seventeen years that he probably knows me better than most will ever do.

Now, back to Sandra…

While she and I had gone to Brandesburton to discuss our future, we actually went much further than that in the end, and I'm not talking about what happened in the daisies! You see, at this point, around 1974–75, I'd only ever travelled as far as places like Sunderland, Leeds, Barnsley, York, Lincoln and New Holland. Then suddenly everything pointed to Jersey.

You'd better get ready, because if you think things have been getting pretty hot at times up until now, they're about to pale into insignificance against some of the stories that took place over there! But we haven't got there just yet. There's still *Lock, Stock and Two Smoking Barrels* to tell you about.

First, I've got to introduce you to a new character in this book, someone I've not mentioned up until now. His name is Mr B or at least it is here, for legal reasons. He was one of the finest singers I have ever heard and let me tell you, when you had Joe Longthorne and Mr B together you really did have some night! It was him who really taught me how to sing. By that I mean he taught me the technique of classy singing, how to use the tools of my trade properly. He was very smart and had a great voice.

Somehow, Sandra had got me an invite to go out to Jersey to meet a man called Jim Lamey, who owned five hotels. He also owned all the tugs on the Mersey and he was on the board of the Variety Club of Great Britain. It was all part of Sandra's master plan for us to elope, but first I had to meet Jim. Sandra had said she'd make things work for us. She was also managing my affairs by this time too.

Mr B was sick of the woman that was effectively his mother-in-law. He wasn't married but his partner's mother was doing his head in. He'd had enough. We knew it wasn't the right time of year to go to Jersey because it was now November and out of season for bookings, but Mr B and I thought it might give us a chance to go around auditioning for Jim's hotels.

At that time, you couldn't get summer season bookings in the UK if you were just a clubland act. They wanted big names on the posters, people who had been on TV, and Jersey offered an opportunity for those prepared to go there.

I'd been happy going around and around the clubs for the past four years since *Junior Showtime* had ended for me, but you can only do the same clubs so many times. It was time for a change, to go somewhere different.

Before we left and before we get to *Lock, Stock and Two Smoking Barrels*, I had gone into a recording studio for the first time. The first session had been in 1974, with two more in 1975. Fairview Studios in Willerby, on the western edge of Hull, was one of the few recording studios outside of London that was fully equipped. It is still going strong today, run by Keith Herd who recorded me back then.

Keith had played the clubs himself in the sixties and seventies, but had started earning a really good reputation for his recording of clubland artists, as well as recording some of the best UK singers. At around the same time as I was recording my first tracks, he had Ronnie Hilton recording a single and country singer Tammy Cline with her Southern Comfort Band. The Housemartins, The Beautiful South, Joe Cocker, rock band Def Leppard and Barbra Dickson have all recorded there too.

The main thing I liked about the studio at Fairview was the atmosphere. Being a fellow musician and singer himself, Keith always looked after every act as if it was his own. The demos we made were well worth it but had never been released up until a few years ago. Dane Morrell was the drummer and there was a big lad called Danny who was on the organ; I think his parents had The Brickmaker's Arms down Walton Street.

Peter Green played guitar and Steve Powell played keyboards. They all played in a variety of other bands in the sixties and seventies. Peter played in The Telstars, The Sunsets, Hammer and Tomorrow's Topic. Dane was one of the finest drummers I have ever worked with. We used to go to his house and he wouldn't have your typical drummers' favourite tracks on the stereo, he'd have Sammy Davis, Frank, Dizzy Gillespie and Judy Garland. Steve Powell wrote and arranged some of the songs we recorded, such as 'Can't Get Enough'.

My first ever recording was a song called 'My Life Is Just Like a Symphony', which was written by a local man called Gary Nicholson.

Keith was so conscientious with his record keeping that, a few years ago, he sent me the tracks I recorded. My first session in 1974 saw me record two demos: 'The Way We Were', which both Barbra Streisand and later Gladys Knight had hits with, and 'My Life Is Just Like a Symphony'. The second session brought about four songs: 'Hurt', which I have sung many times over the years, the Timi Yuro classic 'Crying in the Rain', which Keith tells me came from a demo by a chap called Vince Everitt in the North East, a song called 'You You You', also written by Gary Nicholson (not the Alvin Stardust song of the same name), and a fully worked-up version of 'My Life Is Just Like a Symphony'.

I have recently spoken with Gary for the first time in years. He is still writing songs, still lives in Hull, and when we chatted he told me one of his songs was just about to be used in a promotion on American television. Good lad, still doing well. When I heard 'My Life Is Just Like a Symphony' again for the first time in years, it struck me just what a brilliant song it would be for someone like Joe McElderry.

My final session with Keith was on 4 November, 1975. It must have been just before we were heading for the plane to Jersey. It included my version of Gilbert O'Sullivan's Number One, 'Get Down', and on reflection sounds to me like we did it a bit fast; plus the song I've already mentioned called 'Can't Get Enough', which wasn't the hit by rock group Bad Company released around the same time. This one actually has a bit of a Wham!/George Michael feel to it. The other track was 'Until It's Time For You To Go', which was written by Buffy St Marie and recorded by both Willie Nelson and Elvis.

Keith recalls that I also helped out with financing a recording by a local duo, Ruth and the Rudens, who sang 'Crazy' and 'Good Love's Gonna Go Bad'. Keith also remembers a row of 'scary' ladies who just sat and stared whilst I was recording. I think that must have been my mam, Lizzie and Anne. 'Scary'? It was the beautiful ladies of the family. 'Formidable' may have been a better way to describe them, Keith, ha ha.

Mr B and I were about to go to Jersey, so it's likely I was using them as demos for future gigs on the island and elsewhere, although I can't fully recall. It was good to hear them again though after all this time.

Are you ready now for *Lock, Stock and Two Smoking Barrels*? You are? Here we go. We are heading for Mr B time!

I had a bright orange Granada Ghia with the Everflex top and I was looking like a big-time Charlie. I picked up Mr B, who said the one thing he wanted to do before he left was a little bit of business. Well, I didn't think any more of it, I just thought he was joking and that we had to go round before we set off. Little did I know just how much he meant by this until a few minutes later. Mr B got me into a lot of trouble in Jersey but maybe I should have known he was a bit dodgy, based on what took place next before we'd even left Hull.

We're on the Orchard Park Estate in Hull. Everything is going fine, we're chatting away about Jersey and it's good-natured stuff when suddenly... and legally I can't tell you what happened next, except for the fact that I'm driving the 'screeve' (Romany for 'car') and I'm saying something like, 'Do me a favour.' I sound like the late Mike Reid from when he was in *EastEnders*, or Bob Hoskins in any film he's ever been in. There may have been a lethal weapon involved, that's all I can say.

'Just drive around the block,' he says. I'm now thinking more about getting to Leeds Bradford Airport as soon as humanly possible, as well as hopefully living for at least a short while longer, since I now have what appears to be a man with a vendetta alongside me. Then, as we go around the block, I can't believe what's happening. He's only forgotten to wind the window down for what he's about to do and our car window is shattered. There's glass everywhere, lights going on everywhere… Jersey here we come!

I'd never really been anywhere overseas until I went to Jersey. The nearest I'd been to going abroad had been sailing on the Tattersall Castle ferry across the Humber. The only thing I seem to recall about Jersey from my childhood was that I think my Aunt June was married there.

When I got on the plane for my first ever flight, all I was thinking about was whether we were going to stay up in the air. I was frightened to death. I seem to remember it was a Viscount, a turboprop, which had four propellers. I've flown a lot since then and I like jets, but I always make a point of getting into something that has at least two engines. You'll see why later.

We caught an early morning flight and it was f★★★ing freezing when we got there. It was late autumn and a few years until *Bergerac* became the most famous name on the island. They started filming it in 1981.

If Sunderland and Hull had been the clubland version of a school education, Jersey was about to be my cabaret version of a college education. It also brought me into contact with some of my greatest pals in the business for the first time – and, just to complicate matters further, it was also to be the place where I met yet another new love! But before we go there, let's set the record straight about an issue that has kept coming up over the years. Then we'll start on Jersey.

CHAPTER SIX

MY SON RICKY

About Ricky.
    There have been a lot of groundless rumours going around for a long, long time, questioning whether I am Ricky's father or not. I have always believed I am his dad. Susan and I certainly made love many times. I was there when he was born, I loved Susan and we had some wonderful moments. But there are always rumours and when they come back each time you find yourself asking those same questions, again and again.

What I can say is that whether I am Ricky's real father or not, I have always taken my responsibilities very seriously. I call him my son and he has had everything he could ever want, even if for a number of years he didn't want to see me or get to know me. I've helped him along the way. I gave him his first trials bike as a present when he was twelve years old. I followed him in my yellow Roller as he rode it through the woods.

I suppose there are always going to be doubters as long as rumours persist and unless we get to doing one of those tests, which I refuse to do, I suppose we'll never find out for certain, biologically speaking.

My point is what good would a test do now? Isn't it better that he's my son, rather than opening up a can of worms if he isn't? I think it's the right thing and I know I've always loved him right from the start, when I cradled him in my arms at the maternity hospital. No one wants to give anyone any unnecessary heartache surely? I know I don't.

Susan and I did split up for a short while and it could have been around the time of conception, that's the honest truth – and that's why there is some conjecture over Ricky's parentage.

There was a time when Ricky sold a story to a national news-paper about the doubt and the rumours. I was disappointed. I thought he'd let me and Susan down. I never mentioned a word to any newspaper or any form of media. This is the most I have ever said publicly about it. In fact this is as far as I have gone at any time in talking about it, because this is how I really feel and I want it to be clear.

Ricky was very forward about why he went to the papers, which I think was champion really. He told me, 'Dad, I just needed the money.' He was going through some tough times and he saw it as easy money. Like I said, I was disappointed, but Ricky knows he has always been and always will be a big part of my life. He's got a beautiful family, and Dominic and Megan are lovely, adorable grandchildren. As I keep saying, no matter what has happened to me along the way, I'm actually a very lucky man.

There, that's it. You've got it straight from me now. It's quite therapeutic writing your own life story, you know. Let's try some more. Let's fly, pack up, let's fly away… to Jersey!

CHAPTER SEVEN

JERSEY

Rupert the Bear, Pancho Villa, a massive fake lottery win, living in a shed for months, detectives running all over the place – these were just some of the acts and bizarre moments I experienced on the beautiful, wonderful island of Jersey. Although I didn't know it at the time, this was to be pretty much my second home for the next five years.

Jersey was where I really learned my craft, because up until then I had been performing but not watching how others performed. On Jersey I got to see some very talented entertainers, people who have gone on to do big things in the business like my dear friends Cannon and Ball. Bobby Ball has produced my summer shows in Blackpool and he regularly pops round for a cuppa and a chat. His sons, the Harper Brothers, are an impressive double act in their own right and were part of my show a few years ago.

It was also while I was in Jersey that I tried out for the TV talent show *New Faces*, failing miserably I might add. As I told you, I'm no good at auditions; and then there was the one that gave me my first real break as a professional singer and entertainer on TV, *Search for a Star*. Get ready and get yourself another drink. Jersey was full of moments and lots of action. You're going to enjoy quite a bit of this.

When Mr B and I had first arrived in Jersey we headed straight for the Woodlands Hotel. It was one of Jim Lamey's string of holiday establishments. Jim has since passed away but I'll tell you this: the top three men I have most respected in my life are my dad, he's number one; my brother-in-law, Abdul, who we haven't got to yet, but he's on the way; and Jim. If you hear me mention them several times in my life story I make no apologies for doing so. All three were and still are so important to me, even though all three are no longer with us. They all made such an indelible impression on my life and I really wouldn't be anything like I am today without them. I thank the Lord for the time I had with them and I can feel the tears welling up in my eyes as I speak about them in this way, even now.

Jim Lamey was one of the finest, most wonderful, likeable and courteous men I have ever met. I'm sure anyone who had the pleasure of his acquaintance would say the same. Jim was always immaculately dressed wherever he went and never once treated me less than wonderfully well. I remember getting up and singing for about 150 of his people, so it wasn't an audition where you're singing to just one or two, and I was okay with that.

Jim seemed to take a shine to me straightaway and said he would use me in his hotels. But he didn't just leave it there, he also put me on to Maurice Segal who ran the Modern Hotels Group, a huge chain. Maurice was also hugely instrumental in the building of the great Fort Regent complex, Jersey's largest and most fantastic conference and leisure centre at Mount Bingham in St Helier. It was originally the site of a Napoleonic fortress, which is why it is named that way. The views from there are tremendous. I played

Fort Regent regularly throughout my time on Jersey, often with Rupert the Bear who was fond of his drink. More of him soon.

At first though, because it was out of season I just seemed to be singing to Germans all the time. It was coming up towards Christmas and Jim had put me on at the Woodlands. Mr B was with me as well and we put on some show! But he then went off to be in a band, one of the show bands like The Barron Knights or Black Abbots, something like that.

Once I'd got the hotel bookings I went back over to Hull to tell Sandra that I'd landed a job or two in Jersey, and that her contacts had come good. I told her that I'd got the summer season sorted out through Jim to play at Maurice Segal's hotels.

Sandra and I had talked about eloping before I'd left for Jersey that first time with Mr B. At least that's what we were meant to talk about at Brandesburton that day, when we had been interrupted by half the travelling clan! Sandra was ready to come with me. It was she who had told me it was time I left Hull and that I needed to move to get anywhere in the business. She just said, 'I'm coming with you.'

What happened next was not quite what I'd expected though, and it caused quite a bit of bad blood with not just John, Sandra's husband, but also another man, who just happened to be in the local constabulary back home.

This wasn't the best laid-out plan in the world looking back at it, but Sandra really was a very sensual woman, like I said earlier, and well, when I'd got that kind of attention from someone like her what was I to do? I'm only flesh and blood.

I left Hull to go to Jersey for the second time. This time it wasn't dramatic in the sense of shotgun fire as we left, but it might as well have been for the impact it made back home.

You see, I didn't go with just one beautiful, gorgeous, incredibly sexy woman but two! Sandra had brought her friend, another sexy lady, and we all eloped together. You couldn't make it up could you?

The big problem with it all was that her friend just happened to be married to this top-dick detective! I know it doesn't sound like the brightest career move I've ever made but I was just living for the moment. To me, the fact that two lovely girls came with me wasn't a problem. It wasn't as though I wanted both of them. It was Sandra who I wanted, and she wanted me, and we wanted each other constantly!

Having returned to Jersey, Sandra, the top-dick detective's wife and me booked into the Woodlands, one of Jim's hotels. At first everything was okay, but back home in Hull, perhaps not surprisingly given the circumstances – his wife having run off with an entertainer – John was not a happy man. I'd been told he'd gone barmy.

Also, it turned out nobody had told the cop where his wife had gone, so after a couple of weeks both girls went back to Hull. Sandra went back to check out what John had done and to sort the pub out. She was due to come back over to Jersey once that had been done. The wife of the copper went back and I never heard from her again.

Sandra did come back, but by that time I'd met Rita.

Rita was Jim Lamey's daughter and my next true love. We're now into the early part of 1976. It's not the summer season yet, which I'm looking forward to. I'm playing at the Woodlands Hotel. Rita came down the staircase. I was singing Morris Albert's 'Feelings', that was really big at the time. I was playing the piano in the reception area. Rita and I got eye-to-eye very quickly and we really hit it off together. She was a wonderful, warm and compelling woman.

When I met Rita it was to be the start of a relationship that would last well over twenty years, the longest I've ever had with a woman. Rita was with me through all of my TV years and ran my fan club too. She ran it majestically, but there was so much more to her than that. She believed in me. She talked with me properly. It felt so good. I felt so very comfortable with her.

'Feelings' was also my first ever single release. It was backed with 'This Ol' Heart of Mine' and 'The Way We Were', and it was released while I was on Jersey in 1977. It went out on the Arny's Shack Records label. I had recorded it at Tony Arnold's garage studio in Blandford near Bournemouth, and it was distributed by Pye Records. (I am grateful to Christine Whitnall who spends much of her valuable time updating our Facebook site and website, as well as helping out at home in Blackpool, for that first single release information.)

But let's get back to Rita. Talent, whatever talent you have, is always a hook for bringing people closer to you, and I don't just mean my talent. Rita was a very talented and very knowledgeable lady, and I loved her dearly. I'm still in love with her now. If I say I loved her brain, don't get the idea I didn't love her sexually as well, because I did. We had an extremely intense and passionate relationship. I think she knows I still love her, I certainly hope she does. Rita, if you're reading this, I really do mean every word. You continue to be a part of my life even now.

Rita was and still is a wonderful woman and she wasn't after anything from me. Susan had wanted a family man. Sandra had wanted raging sex. Others had wanted me just because I was a singer. None of those are bad reasons at all, but it was good to have a girlfriend who was interested in me as a person, someone who wanted to get to know me properly for who I was and who I am.

Rita wanted me for being me and she wanted to help me in any way she could. Rita had what I have always loved in a woman – intelligence, regard and lovemaking, of course. She also taught me how to be as eloquent as I could be. I had a lovely time with Rita in the 1980s, and throughout most of the 1990s too. I will love her until the day I die. She made me feel like a man, a complete man.

Both Rita and her father, Jim, were so significant in my career progression that I can never thank them enough. You'll hear that line a few times in this book too. One thing I have learned along the way is it is always important to thank those who help you. I'm not one of those who believe success is down to me.

Like I said earlier, this is not meant to be a 'me-me-me' book, even though I know it's my autobiography. So many people have touched my life for the better. Forget about those who have touched it for the worse, they're not important. The people who have helped me along the way deserve the very best from me. They are the ones who it is important that I mention.

I know some people might think that the only reason I got on with Rita was because she was a multimillionaire's daughter, but it wasn't like that at all. She had charm, intelligence, and I found her exciting. We didn't just jump into bed together. We courted. We laughed together and we enjoyed each other's company.

Rita spoke nine languages and had been educated at the Sorbonne. Me? I was just a lad who didn't understand reading or writing in English very much, let alone all the other languages. Her head, her body and her brain turned me on completely.

I had to go back to Hull before the summer season started in Jersey because I needed to honour a few verbal agreements to play there. Over the past forty years I have had to cancel shows from time to time for a variety of reasons, mostly down to my health situation, but wherever I have been able, I have always tried my best to fulfil what is on the schedule. That's why I also went back to Hull from time to time during my Jersey years.

Sandra went back as well, this time for good.

We had finished. She had things that needed sorting out back at home. I don't know what she's doing now, but I think she still lives in Hull. She will still be a stunner, of that I have no doubt. She was certainly all woman! The last I heard, she had split up from John.

Sandra was more than just a vivacious and sensual woman though. It was thanks to her that I got to Jersey, and it was her approach to Jim that set the ball rolling for me further afield than the clubland circuit of Yorkshire and the North East, so I've a lot to be grateful for. So again, if you're reading this, Sandra, I do hope it gives you the same tingle thinking about those times, all those years ago. It's such a long while now, isn't it? But I still think good thoughts about when we were making love.

Sandra put me into what turned out to be the right place at the right time. The only thing she might not have counted on was my relationship with Rita.

In show-business the press is always interested in stories about entertainers, particularly if they involve sex. I don't know whether Sandra went to the newspapers about me or if they approached her, so it would be wrong to jump to conclusions, but a story was published. What I can tell you is that, far from being annoyed with what had been printed, I was more than happy with the way Sandra's story came out in the press. In fact it wasn't bad for my reputation at all. She was telling everyone I was like a stallion. There really is some truth in any type of publicity working for you. Who knows? Maybe Sandra was still managing and promoting me with that story. It certainly worked out that way.

My sound and lighting man hadn't come over with me at the start. I had asked him to fly out with me when I first went to Jersey with Mr B, but he'd said no. When I'd got the bookings I contacted him again, telling him I needed him. Good sound and lighting men are hard to find, but I needed a good mate too, someone I could rely on during the performances. All I said was that Jim had got me the shows, and that if he wanted to come over I'd meet him on the tarmac at the airport the following day. I left it up to him. The tickets were there.

He came and he ended up being not only my light and sound man, but also the perfect friend and an all-round good mate. His friendship and our working relationship have always meant so much to me. I think of him every day and of the scrapes we got into. Together we made it from me being a clubland act to hosting our own TV shows. He was with me every step of the way throughout that time.

He had such a good ear. I know that's what you'd probably expect from someone whose job was to make sure that the sound was right, but he really did know what was what. I once asked him how he did it, how he always got it right, and he said, 'I just listen.' He did everything. He put the equipment up, roadied and was the one person I could always talk to before and after the gigs. He would always tell me straight about anything. We used to travel all over Jersey, doing shows at different hotels on the island.

It's time for another name in my story.

Paddy was my road manager. I think he now looks after a theatre in Tunbridge Wells. He drove us everywhere in his Volkswagen van. There would be my sound and lights man, the organist, the drummer, dancers called Rusty and Nova, and me. We were doing three shows a day on the island to audiences of French, German and British people. We would do about two hours at each hotel. It certainly wasn't the glamorous lifestyle that people might think, but Jersey really did give me a fantastic showbiz education. I found out the difference between performing in clubs, hotels and theatres, the skills needed for each and how different audiences reacted. I made costume changes in more kitchens than Gordon Ramsay has ever sworn in.

I learned about audiences, especially audiences that were a little bit more on the posh side. For those I was singing more as after-dinner entertainment and finding out what they liked. They wanted to laugh, not just listen to a singer, so my comedy routines became bigger. They wanted more of a Las Vegas feel to their holidays, so I gave them that too. I also found that certain songs and parts of the act were now becoming more permanent. My Shirley Bassey stayed as it has always done to this day. I can't imagine a time when I won't be asked for it, but I was expanding my routine all the time with even more singers.

One of the changes that I eventually made to the act was that I had originally dragged up for the female singing impressions with wigs, dresses, the lot. I had then moved on to purely using wigs. By the time I'd finished on Jersey, I wasn't doing Shirley other than as an impression with no props at all.

That's the way it's always been since then. Tom Jones stayed in the act as he has always done, as well as Frank Sinatra and Willie Nelson. 'For Once in My Life', the Sinatra version of the Stevie Wonder song, was in there too, but I was adding other hit songs of that time as well. It wasn't all about the big ballad singers.

I also learned a little more about how entertainers were treated by people who weren't as gentlemanly as Mr Jim Lamey. We're talking accommodation here.

My first impression of where we were to be put up in Jersey didn't seem at all bad, but I was quickly to find out just how wrong a first impression can be!

Dick Wray was the 'guvnor' of the island's entertainment scene and I was on £100 a week with him. He had a lot of property in Jersey and owned the Opera House. He had venues throughout the island. Working for him was Dave Marshall, who picked us up from the airport and took us to where Dick had arranged for us to stay. The idea was that it would be cheaper than staying in one of the hotels.

It all felt good to start with. Dave picked us up in this big white Jag. He took us to this big house and we both thought that it would suit us fine. We thought we'd fallen on our feet. What we didn't know was that he was going to walk us right through the big house, take us out of the big backdoor and then tell us about our humble lodgings.

Actually, the word 'digs' is used to describe where performers stay when on tour. Never would it be a more accurate word than now – we were to live in a shed! So these 'digs' even included the spades.

'That's yours,' he pointed at this hut for us both. We couldn't believe it. We just looked at each other in amazement. So I was on £100 a week for Dick Wray and we got £16 knocked off the rent for cutting the garden and clearing the trash. I know I come from a travellers' background, but a shed? It wasn't my idea of accommodation. The thing is, we couldn't afford to lay out £38 a week to continue staying at Holden Hotel in St Saviour's, where we had been previously.

So here I am, supposedly the star of the show with a wonderful little band and some beautiful girl dancers, and I'm living in a shed in the backyard of a beautiful Victorian house in Beach Road, alongside a row of dustbins and expected to do the f★★★ing gardening.

Fortunately, 1976 was the hottest year on record and we had a fantastic summer. We stayed in the shed for about a year and then a Portuguese man called Clem Freer took me on. We then moved into far better accommodation, and I worked for Clem and his wife Ann at a place called El Rancho. That doesn't mean Clem's accommodation was brilliant. One night when I was on the toilet, I saw a rat walk between my feet and it was quickly followed by a whole army of them. Sound and light man, Rita and I were all stopping in this place with three great dancers called Charade, but this was no charade. The rats were for real.

I was performing at El Rancho in 1977 when Elvis died. I had never really sung Elvis songs as impressions. I had just sung them as me, songs like 'The Wonder of You' and 'Always on My Mind'. Today, I sometimes sing 'American Trilogy' with my collar hitched up out of respect to the great man, and one of my own personal favourites, 'Mary in the Morning', which has become a favourite with many of my fans.

Before we left our accommodation at the shed, we had a bit of fun at Dave Marshall's expense. We doctored the aerial for his television in the big house we had walked through, before showing us where we were to stay, so we kept changing the channels he was watching. That messed with his head a bit. We saw him getting madder and madder inside the house as he tried to watch one programme, only to find seconds later that his television had switched channels!

The best moments came when he would be watching a football match. We would try to make sure that if it looked like there might be a goal, he would suddenly be watching something like *Panorama*. One day just before we left, a guy came to fix it for him and told him someone had sabotaged it. I think it cost him quite a bit to have it fixed. I don't believe in people just getting away with things and he had been a bit of a naughty lad to us, but we did him in the end.

Dave Marshall really upset me when he told me that, with our travelling show, I would top the bill one week and then someone else would top it the next week. It was just a way of giving everyone top billing and making sure the show looked different every week, but I wasn't having it. There was Pancho, the girls, Welsh comedian Bryn Phillips and me touring around the island.

'Pancho b★★★★★d Villa above me on the billing?' is what I said. All Dave would say was that the others had to top the bill sometime. I said 'Do they?'

When I'd been appearing in Hull just before going over to Jersey, I'd got up to about £15-£20 a night and I'd played every night there was available. I was working harder than ever for probably the same amount of money in the end, but to me it wasn't about the money. Sure, I've enjoyed the money I've had along the way, but that's not what thrills me. It really isn't. The audience, my fans, they are what give me the thrill. Just walking out onto that stage every night and hearing the applause, then delivering the best performance I'm capable of. That's the adrenalin rush I get.

Before I gave up with the costumes I used to get dressed up as Cleo Laine, Dorothy Squires, Barbra Streisand and Shirley, as well as plenty of other famous singers, including Demis Roussos. I looked fabulous, or at least I thought I did, but there was one time when Rita and I saw a poster of me that made me look like a docker trying to be a drag queen. When we saw it we immediately went all around the island and ripped down every poster. That was the start of me getting rid of the dressing up, the dragging up. I knew by now that I didn't need it. But before I got rid of the props and the dresses there was to be an incident that helped my decision quite a bit.

I think it's time to introduce Rupert and Pancho properly here…

Rupert the Bear liked his drink a little too much in my opinion. I still don't know who he really was to this day, but he was dressed like the character and his act always started with him singing, *'I'm Ru-u-pert, Rupert the Bear, everyone knows my name.'* During one performance at the Fort Regent, just before he was to go on he stank of brandy. It wasn't the first time I'd seen him in that state, but on this occasion he was far worse than normal and in a pretty bad way. He could hardly stand.

I was just about to say, 'Roope, you can't go on like that,' when he lost his balance completely and fell the whole length of the stairs. Rupert became a bit of a fall guy after that. He even got in the way one night when I was in a bit of a temper about something, and ended up falling down the full length again. Maybe it was part of his act in the end.

Whilst Rupert may have been fond of the tipple, Pancho Villa was an absolute imposter! He always overran, which is criminal in the entertainment world when you're in the early part of the show – and he sang too, because he thought he was an all-rounder. He wasn't. That was criminal as well. He was a comic and actually a pretty good one, but singer? No way. He also pinched my material. We all do that a bit. We hear something somewhere and then incorporate it if we think it fits for us and we can do it. But he wouldn't toe the line at all, and what really topped it for me one night was when I was waiting for Pancho to come offstage.

He's overrun yet again, something I've never done when there are other acts that have yet to come on. It just messes up everyone's timing. If an act overruns it is really stealing the time off another performer.

I know my act isn't going to work now. I'm dressed up in the full kit as Demis Roussos and I need the smoke machine to blast out fog as I sing 'Happy to be on an Island in the Sun'. It's supposed to be all about welcoming the audience to Jersey. But his act has gone well so he's chosen to stay on, which isn't fair to your fellow professionals, like I said. He's nicked my time. And the fog machine has now blurted out liquid onto the stage, which fog machines used to do. It's something to do with the time between when it was plugged in and the time of me going on stage. Things are starting to gang up against me and I'm already thinking, *Panch, I'm going to kill you for this*.

I go on stage, full Demis Roussos outfit, flowing robe, wig, the lot. My feet go one way, my arms another, the wig flies off, I split the outfit and I go down, arse over tit. The audience are laughing, but not the way I'd intended, and I know I've got to go back and sing sentimental stuff like 'Danny Boy' and finish as Shirley yet, when all I want to do is get hold of Pancho and wring his f***ing neck!

We were at the Lido de France in St Helier. There are probably still people around who remember it. I'm sure many of them will think it was hilarious, and probably one or two who think it was all part of the act. But it wasn't. I'm not some kind of slapstick, knock-me-down-and-I-get-up-again kind of performer.

The producer had told me before the show that he wanted me in drag for Bassey, with twenty minutes at the end to appear as myself. But when I went down, I remembered there was a thing in the programme that said, 'This show could be changed at any time.' It's a thing that all production companies put in, just so that people can't claim their money back by saying that what they have seen was not as it appeared in the programme.

I used that line myself and changed my show, right there and then. I changed the whole show, the props and costumes were thrown out and I went on as me. I still did the impressions but without the props, apart from one or two incidental ones like caps and wigs, and I went on to win the Best Top of the Bill award in Jersey that year, so it was the right decision.

That didn't alter what Pancho had done to me though, and after the show I had some seriously unfinished business. I finished the act, went straight to Pancho's dressing room and knocked him clean out. *Bash!* My sound and light man was as mad as I was about what had happened too. It had screwed up all of his lighting arrangements. We both took care of Pancho that night and he never ran over his time again.

I'd been doing drag in the first couple of years on Jersey in 1975 and 1976. It was camp and I enjoyed doing it, but I also felt in retrospect that maybe it showed me trying to hide away from who I was. In the end I just realised that I could impersonate everyone without the need for props, apart from the little ones I use occasionally today. A hat for Steptoe sometimes, but the rest of the time I either just move my hair a bit, for Ken Dodd, my sleeves, for Barry Manilow, my collar, for Elvis, and slip my jacket off my shoulders for Shirley.

Maybe Pancho did me a favour in a roundabout kind of way, but he's one person I'm determined not to give any credit to. It still irritates me now that I'm thinking about it again. I have pride in what I do on stage, but that night he just made me look stupid. I rescued the act of course, and the night was still a success, but no thanks to Pancho. So wherever you are, Pancho, I hope you are not overrunning today.

There were some tremendous acts appearing in Jersey during the time I was there. It was an era when a lot of the talent that was to appear on television in the coming years all seemed to be on this one wonderful island. One of those great performers was Dustin Gee, who came from York originally and was a fabulously talented man. He worked with Russ Abbott for many years and formed a great TV partnership with Les Dennis.

Dustin died tragically early of a heart attack, when he was just forty-three, in 1986. He was a brilliant impersonator and he dragged up too. I remember when Cannon and Ball first came over and Dustin was top of the bill at the time. There was some pressure from the agents and managers to get Dustin out. I don't quite know why, because Cannon and Ball were just an up-and-coming act and Dustin was already established.

Around that time, from what I can recall, Dustin's boyfriend jumped through a window. Dustin went mad, and then I believe that the cops found some marijuana in Dustin's dressing room. That was it for Dustin. His time on Jersey was over and he was banished from the island.

Cannon and Ball were top of the bill at Behan's the next day. They deserved it because this was their time. They were on the brink of making it really big and to be fair, they were murdering him on stage. It was real dog-eat-dog billing at that time and the competition was great, because all of the headlining acts were quality performers.

One of the best and funniest acts on the Jersey scene at the time was The Grumbleweeds. I would go and see them and learned from their stagecraft. They were a great show group. Graham Walker sadly passed away recently, but until then he and Robin Colvill were still going strong. Maurice Lee appeared with me on tour about five years ago but Carl and Albert gave up a while ago. Tony Jo, who I know very well in Blackpool these days, was with them at one time too.

Yes, I was a script-nicker as well. I took a few lines from The Grumbleweeds. They were a great set of lads. I went go-karting with them sometimes.

Are you ready for the return of Mr B? Well, here he is.

Mr B was still around. With his voice he could never be ignored – and he really was one of those larger than life characters. I hadn't seen him for a while, but with Mr B you never knew what would happen next. One day, while we were still living in the shed, he turned up in this big flash Merc. He was excited and pretty pleased with himself. We had always got on well together.

'I want you. Get in the car!'

I got in. He was on such good form. You couldn't not do what he said when he was like this. 'I've only won the f***ing lot, haven't I? I've won the pools!' At first I couldn't believe it. 'You've what? Well, good luck to you.' He said, 'I'll get you some new kit, some new clothes. Come on.'

Mr B then took me to the most expensive shop he could find in St Helier and bought me three amazingly expensive outfits. Shoes, shirts, trousers, ties, he didn't skimp at all, and we bought the lot. I asked him why he was doing it for me and he just said he'd won it and wanted to share it. What's more, he reckoned I deserved it, probably for bringing him to Jersey in the first place. He took me back to the shed and off he went, happy as Larry.

Next thing I know is that I'm back home in the shed. There's a knock on the door. It's Detective Sergeant Charles Quinn. Well, it was too early for it to be Jim Bergerac, wasn't it? He wasn't invented then and by the time he was, my Jersey experience was over.

I quickly found out that Mr B's 'pools win' wasn't as it had appeared. Don't ask me how he got the money or why he then came along and bought me what he did. I'll never know. It was still good of him to look after me, but with the police coming around he had also put me under a lot of unnecessary pressure.

Charlie Quinn, who I went on to become really good friends with, gave me a hard time at the start. He looked in my wardrobe and saw all the brand new clothing: Boss stuff, shoes and shirts. He knew I didn't have the money for all that kind of gear. He'd seen my shows with his wife and I knew she really liked me. I told him, 'Sergeant Quinn, as sure as I am standing right in front of you now, I do not know anything. I'm just a singer. I'm busy singing, performing. All I can tell you is what he told me, that he'd won the pools.' Like I said, Charlie liked me and he told me he wouldn't take the clothes in as evidence, so all the stuff Mr B had got me stayed with me. Maybe Mr B was a modern-day Robin Hood looking after the modern-day minstrel like me.

The last time I heard from Mr B was over twenty years ago, when I was playing eight weeks of cabaret in London. He phoned me, out of the blue, said he was calling from Stockport. He wasn't doing too well. I said that from what I had gathered he had upset a few people back in Jersey, and he hadn't done me too much good with the police – even though I had a new wardrobe out of it. He apologised – and put the phone down. Within a minute there was a knock on the door and in walked the man himself. I said that I thought he had told me he was in Stockport. He just said he had to be very careful wherever he said he was. I'm certain there were people after him, but knowing him it could have been anybody – even his mother-in-law. I've never seen him again. He was a great singer. What a waste of talent.

There were some even stranger characters on the island. One was Ian Parker, heir to the famous Parker pens fortune. I worked for him for a while in one of his hotels – the Hotel De France. I always thought he was quite eccentric for someone who was hosting entertainment in a hotel. It didn't matter which act was on in his venue, he used to say everything was too loud. One night I went on stage only to find he'd cut all the microphone cables!

My five years on Jersey weren't continuous, I didn't just stay there throughout that time. We would be on the island for six months, then we would come back for me to play the clubs in places like Hull, Sunderland, Sheffield and Barnsley. My sister Anne would come over to Jersey quite frequently and so would Mam, but Dad never came. He wouldn't fly. I saw him every time I was back in Hull.

I will always be grateful for what Jersey gave me. It transformed me from being purely a clubland entertainer to a much more rounded performer. I had seen different acts, fabulous singers and comedians, and I had learned much more about my own performance. I had also learned so much from Rita, as well as having a wonderful time with her.

The people on the island didn't want me to leave. They invited me to take up residency there, which was very flattering. Apart from cabaret singer Stuart Gillies and actor John Nettles, there are few others who can say that. But the time had come for me to make a choice. Did I stay on Jersey or did I go elsewhere? I chose to go. It would be a decision that would eventually see me team up with one of the biggest family entertainment acts around, and hook up with the manager and promoter who looked after me better than any other.

But those other characters didn't come along just yet. There were a few years to go before all of that started. First, there was the little matter of a TV programme that would launch my broadcasting career and lead on to so many good things.

You see, Sandra really did set me on my way, because if I hadn't gone to Jersey I would never have had a man called David Bell come to see me. David was a TV producer. He was working on the TV programme *Search for a Star* at the time. I had already failed two auditions for the popular ITV show *New Faces* while on the island, plus one for another programme called *Starburst*. Add those to several auditions with Hughie Green for *Opportunity Knocks*, which I had tried out for back home as a teenager, and you can see why I wasn't particularly taken with auditioning. All I wanted was for people to come and see me in concert, doing what I did every day and every night. Funnily enough, that's exactly the way it happened with David.

But let's hold it right there.

After all, following all that activity on Jersey, you're probably not quite ready for when the breaks started going *bang, bang, bang!* So let's take another time out in the story. It's about time you recharged your glass, isn't it?

You know, I don't look at them myself but I understand a regular feature on the various websites and Facebook sites about me is which songs are people's favourites. I thought that here would be the perfect place to tell you about some of the songs I sing, why I sing them and what they mean to me.

CHAPTER EIGHT

MY PERSONAL FAVOURITES

'Mary in the Morning' has been a part of my show for many years now. I cry when I listen to Elvis doing it. There are two Elvis versions and I particularly like the one where he cries when he's singing it. He has a big towel around his neck and it was recorded in his house.

I don't know how many people notice, but I sing it slightly differently every time. I love it. It's such a passionate song. When I sing, *'I want to kiss her face so softly,'* I'm actually thinking I want to kiss her on every part of her body, whoever she is I'm thinking about. And I am talking female here, let there be no doubt at all. The emotion Elvis gives to the song comes out far, far greater than anything I have ever heard or seen. I feel the emotion too when I sing it. I think that's why my fans always want me to do it.

'When You're Smiling' is such an obvious choice for me because it sums up everything about entertainment. It's a song I've sung from very young and it is one that everyone knows and enjoys. It was also first made famous by Asa Joelson (I prefer using his real name rather than Al Jolson).

'Smile' fits into a similar vein. But what I would like to know is how could Charlie Chaplin be so gifted? He wrote such a beautiful song like that, as well as being the world's greatest clown. He could do no wrong at all in my eyes. You know just how good a song is when so many artists have covered it over the years: Nat King Cole, Frank Sinatra, Diana Ross and Hull's own David Whitfield, to name but four, and I put it on my studio album *You & Me*. It's a beautiful song and the lyrics are particularly poignant for anyone who is ever going through any heartache.

'Cycles' is one of my all-time favourite songs by Frank Sinatra and was written by Rod McKuen. Sinatra sang it on his *Cycles* album, released in 1968, and I finally got round to recording it on *You & Me*, released in 2008. It was my first all-new studio CD for nearly ten years. This was a real challenge for me and my interpretation is once again fuelled very much by what has happened to me. Even when the chips were down, I've still had something to give.

There have been lots of 'live' CDs over the years and lots of compilations, constantly going into my back catalogue of hundreds of songs, but it has been a real pleasure to be back in the studio in recent years.

'You & Me' was written by one of the men who I consider to be amongst the best songwriters in the world, Peter Allen. He's written some fantastic songs and I love everything about that one.

The David Gates song 'If' is another favourite, and my good friend and fellow performer Andy Mudd gave it a very special, tender and yet powerful arrangement that was featured in my shows for several years.

'Let Me Try Again' is yet another of those songs where I can put so much feeling into it, because of what I have experienced over the years.

One of the things Chris Evans has said he likes about my act is the big finishes I have always done. I appeared on his Friday-night TV show *TGIF* on Channel 4, and all I did was finish a few songs with my band. The audience loved it. This leads me on to the next two in this list that could probably go on forever, as I love all the songs I sing.

'Somewhere' from *West Side Story* is an all-time favourite. In a number of my shows, I used to come on and the first song would be the final part of 'Somewhere'. It still gets a great reaction from the audience when I do it now.

I couldn't go through this chapter without mentioning this next number: 'If I Never Sing Another Song' has become another of those songs that those who come along to see me constantly request. Of course, Dame Shirley recorded it and the wonderful Don Black wrote it originally for Matt Monro. But when I sing those terrific lines it's almost as though Don wrote it especially for me.

'The Impossible Dream' is absolutely wonderful and another that is a really great number to close the show. Once again the lyrics are so powerful.

A few years ago I added 'I Started a Joke' and 'The Morning of My Life', which have become favourites of mine. They are both Bee Gees songs from the sixties and it was my great, great pleasure to be able to sing them for Robin and Barry's special Variety Club Silver Heart award.

I know my loyal and very loving fans have their own favourites: 'As If We Never Said Goodbye' from *Sunset Boulevard*; 'As I Love You'; 'If I Loved You' from *Carousel*; 'Hurt'; 'Danny Boy'; 'My Mother's Eyes'; 'I Wanna Be Where You Are'; 'I Will Drink the Wine'. I'm sure I've missed quite a few more, but these are just some of the ones I hear being called out during a concert. I love singing them all.

Right, where had we got to? We've had our little intermission. Is that glass fully charged? Come on now, you're lagging behind. Now it's time for the real breaks. The ones that saw me become whatever it is I became!

CHAPTER NINE

SEARCH FOR A STAR

Actually, we're not quite off Jersey just yet, because my first big break, as I mentioned a short while ago, was to start happening while we were still on the island.

David Bell was a lovely Scotsman who helped my career enormously, and not just by scouting me for the talent show *Search for a Star*. We went on to work together a good deal on further TV programmes over the years.

David had worked on Scottish Television. He had worked as producer for many of Stanley Baxter's great shows and had come down to work for London Weekend Television with two other producers. Their flagship production was to be the talent show *Search for a Star*.

By this time, in late 1979 to the early part of 1980, I was coming to the end of my time on Jersey and had been signed up to play summer seasons at Pontins holiday camps throughout the UK.

I had got a bit fed up of failing auditions. I felt that producers and TV programme makers would get a better idea of what I did, and the potential I had, by simply sitting down and watching one of my shows. I'm sure there are many other performers who feel the same, but I just knew that once they'd done that they would know what I was really capable of giving them.

I'd failed four Hughie Green (*Opportunity Knocks*) auditions when I was in my teens. Dad and I used to follow his Rolls Royce, just making sure I was seen. There was one time when I actually heard him say, 'Not you again!' We gave up in the end.

Probably the best audition I ever did was the one that David Bell saw – and it wasn't even an audition at all! That's also the reason why it went so well. As I've said before, I don't do auditions, I do performances. I need an audience in front of me, real people where I can see their smiling faces.

Nearly everyone else had to go to London to try out for the show. There wasn't a Jersey audition so far as I know, and it certainly wasn't anything along the lines of *X Factor* auditions, where they have thousands of people turning up. In those days artists were handpicked from clubland and basically anywhere where people performed.

David had come over especially to see me. He'd heard about how well I was doing. He particularly wanted me because I was different – a singer impressionist. There have never been too many of us in that line. David Copperfield, who had his own TV show with Tracey Ullman and Lenny Henry, was pretty good, but after that you would struggle to name more than one or two. So I was different, just as my mam had always said. I had something that made me stand out from the rest – and by now I had served quite a bit of my apprenticeship in the clubs of Hull, Sheffield, Lincoln, Sunderland, Newcastle, York and Barnsley. I had proved myself on the cabaret circuit of Jersey, and was about to do the further hard graft of getting around all the Pontins resorts. I was still only twenty-four when I met David for the first time but I was ready. He came over to see me at El Rancho.

I remember David telling me, 'We don't usually do this sort of thing you know, coming out to see acts. Normally we get those who we are interested in to come to Waterloo. You know I shouldn't really be here. But we've heard a little bit about you.'

If he'd got me to go over to London, to Waterloo, maybe I would never have got on the show, but he had come over without me knowing. He saw me in action, the right way, and he signed me up for the show the same night. It was a done deal, I was about to be back on the box for the first time since *Junior Showtime*!

London Weekend Television did three series of *Search for a Star*. The first was started at the end of 1979 and went into 1980. The second was near to the end of 1980, with the third and final series – the one I was in – starting just before Christmas in 1980 and finishing with the final, on 31 January 1981.

I didn't appear on the show until 1981, so by the time I was back on TV for the first time since my *Junior Showtime* days, ten years previously, I was off the island and touring all over the UK.

It really was a fine talent show, and it launched the careers of several entertainers who went on to do wonderful things in the business. Many of them are still around, like me, today. I think that's because David knew what he was doing with the show. He knew he wanted good acts from day one, and he also had the fantastic Alan Ainsworth and his orchestra, who were just brilliant.

Lenny Windsor – a great comedian who went on to write scripts for Benny Hill – won the final. He regularly plays the cruise ships today and is a sought-after speaker at corporate events right across the UK. I read somewhere that he was touring with The Temptations a year or two back.

Paul Rafferty was also in the final, I think he sang 'Guilty' with Annie Noel, who I understand is still singing jazz with her own Annie Noel Swingtet in Torbay.

Quite a few from the northern clubland scene were on the

shows too. I was up against Bobby Knutt, a very popular comic who went on to appear on TV's *Emmerdale*, in my first round on 10 January 1981. Tammy Cline, the lovely country music singer from my home city of Hull, who was recording at Fairview Studios at the same time as me, appeared in the same series too. She went on to do really well over in Nashville, playing at the Grand Ol' Opry, and had a successful radio career.

Comedian Jimmy Cricket had reached the previous final, and some of the others who took part included Wayne Dobson, a fabulous magician who was later to become a regular on my own TV show, and the really popular Irish singer Rose Marie. There were also some strange sounding acts, probably none more so than Gutbucket & Camelfoot, a folk-music duo.

I've done my research on this, you know, because I honestly couldn't remember all those off the top of my head. Looking back there was also Gordon Haskell, who went on to have a massive hit with 'How Wonderful You Are' from his album *Harry's Bar* in 2001. He took part in one of the early rounds in my year.

Scriptwriters would work with you on new scripts, or they would help hone your existing material. There was clever direction. The wardrobe department couldn't do enough for you. Suits, dresses, whatever costumes you wanted you got. There was no way you could fail if you had the right act and mine was there just at the right time. All of those nights on Jersey, all of those nights up and down Yorkshire and the North East, had given me such experience that I felt ready for anything. One of the main differences between then and today's *X Factor* was that everyone involved was a working entertainer. We were all involved in show-business, so it was already our profession.

I won through the early round and David was privately telling me, 'Joe, you've won it here. It's in the bag.' But that didn't prove quite right. The voting in the final was different to the early rounds, as it was a 'live' show. The others were all pre-recorded. It was conducted a bit like a Eurovision type of thing where votes were cast by areas. There were only five areas in all – London, Leeds, Glasgow, Cardiff and Belfast. Where I came unstuck was with the Irish vote after being hotly tipped to win, and not just by David and his team but also the national press. Everyone, it seemed, loved my Shirley. For many it was the first time they would ever have seen me do it, and I'd worked on it even further.

David had been fantastic about the way I did her and, having watched me in Jersey, he had pointed out things that nobody else had ever noticed. It is David's comments that helped me take my impression of her to a new level. I cannot possibly tell you all that he told me. It's what you call a trade secret. He certainly taught me how to do her properly though. He said to me, with his arms outstretched and fingers spread, in his wonderful, camp Scottish accent, 'Joe, darling, this is how you should play Shirley.'

I came third in the final. Apparently the Irish vote had said they didn't give any points to people who weren't using their own voices. They thought the voices I was doing were mimed. I suppose I should have accepted it as a compliment to what I was doing, but I have to say I didn't feel that way at the time. David's comments had led me to believing that I really was going to win.

Next day, the Irish version of the story was all over the newspapers, and even though I hadn't mimed in any way there was still a big hoo-ha about it all. I really didn't mind by then, there's nothing you can do about it after the event. I knew I'd done okay.

But once again, bad news hadn't done me any harm and it was about to lead me on to my next big break. Things were starting to happen – although they didn't really pick up until after we had seen off a few vans. Read on!

CHAPTER TEN

HOLIDAY CAMPS

While we were together, both in Hull and on Jersey, Sandra had done anything she could to make me better known. She was always onto Radio 1 and the TV companies about me, and one time she got Don Jones, who you'll hear more of very soon, to come and see me in a talent show at Tiffany's nightclub in Hull. She also introduced me to Harold Shampan, who was a children's writer. Harold then introduced me to record producer Dick James, who asked me to sing 'If You Look for the Lord'. He told me he didn't want me to sing it like Tom Jones, and that if I could do it he'd record me. Unfortunately, it didn't happen; however, the contact with Don did lead me to recording my first LP, *Only Once*, as well as my first two singles.

Search for a Star hadn't started for me at that time and I was managed by a man called Keith Johns, who lived in Bournemouth. He used to have the Round House Hotel, which had earned a great reputation and was quite famous on the south coast. Keith was to be my manager for a while before Don Jones took me on. But it was actually Don who met us when we first arrived in town.

We turned up in Bournemouth, from Hull, with nothing, just the clothes we stood up in. As you will constantly hear me say in this book, I'm really not good with money and it has never been what I'm about. Of course, I like to look good and I know that things cost money, but I guess I'm just not cut out to look after myself in that way.

That's where James does such a good job with me today, and it's also how I have managed to get back on my feet since the nervous breakdown, the bankruptcy and the bone-marrow transplant, as well as many other unfortunate events.

So what can you do when you've turned up somewhere with nothing, apart from what you're wearing at the time, and you really do have no money? Well, we blagged it, didn't we? Yes, we did. We had our story ready. My sound and lighting man and I were by now a highly competent double act on tour, and we knew the kind of act that was needed on this occasion. We said something along the lines of, 'You'll never guess what's happened, Don. On the way we stopped to get some petrol and someone's taken all of our clothes out of the car.'

I had a Mercedes at the time, but don't get any ideas about it being flash. It was an old Merc and had only cost us £200. Anyway, back to our little scam. I know it was a pretty feeble excuse looking back, and I don't know whether Don ever believed us or not, but he was more than helpful. He took to us and was kind enough to take us into Bournemouth, where he made sure we got some clothes from the famous Four Seasons shop. Don was a gentleman.

I loved Bournemouth, and I still do. It is a very attractive town, has a wonderful university and the place did me proud. I met up with some very talented musicians and entertainers there. One act, The Lyndrics, which consisted of Eric and his daughter

Lynne, were a scream. They were illusionists of the old-fashioned variety. They did all the magic tricks with pigeons and doves everywhere. Eric would put Lynne in the box and saw her in half. You know how it used to be. They were great fun and really well known in the area.

The Majestic Hotel in Bournemouth was the home of a great jazz club. There were quite a few others at the time, but the Majestic was the top one. I loved it in there. Whenever I wasn't performing I'd go and see who was on. I'd perform in all the jazz clubs and hotels in the area. The only thing about jazz, with me, is that I can't just listen to a piano solo forever.

Bournemouth was also where I bought my first house. You know, I've only ever been to see a bank manager twice in my life and the first time was while I was in this lovely town, because I was about to buy my first property, so I went into Williams & Glynn's. I've had times when bankers and other moneymen have come to visit me, although not quite for such happy reasons!

Incidentally, by now you're probably starting to wonder when the first thoughts of cancer, or lymphoma, CLL, or whatever, started kicking in. Well, it wasn't just yet but we're at least now in the right decade.

At this point none of that was on the horizon. I haven't yet found out about cancer, leukaemia, haven't yet gone bust or broken down, although it is likely that I had CLL all of this time without ever knowing. These are still the early years, the times when I was finding my way, learning my craft and learning more about who I was.

Up to now there has been drama, there's been humour, there have been fights, there's even been a certain amount of success – but we're getting closer to all of those real highs and lows.

And I haven't even introduced you properly to Abdul yet either. Well, he's on his way! Time for a little more drama!

Our first accommodation in Bournemouth was above a Chinese restaurant in Lansdowne Road. It was at least a step up from a shed in a backyard on Jersey.

We played all of the hotels and clubs of Bournemouth and the surrounding area. Looking back, we had a fabulous time playing there, apart from when a girl was murdered upstairs in one of the flats where we were staying!

The first place I worked after I'd signed up with Don Jones' organisation was Keith Johns' Round House Hotel. As well as jazz they also used to have cabaret there. Neil Martin, who had won *Opportunity Knocks* in the seventies, was also there regularly. He was one of Keith's acts.

But now we're heading for Pontins while still living in Bournemouth, and two years of almost constant travel throughout the UK that include some of the funniest moments in my life. It's also now time I introduced you to Abdul.

Abdul 'Shahid' Shaibi's picture hangs above my mantelpiece in the lounge at home in Blackpool. He's with me now even though he passed away years ago. This man meant so much to me. He taught me so much about family, respect, honour, all of the good things you can ever imagine. He knew I was bisexual and he knew that didn't really fit in with his religion, but he never once crossed me about it. He was an absolute gem, a man you could always look up to.

He married my sister Anne. He looked after her better than any man could ever have done. They met in Attercliffe, Sheffield where Abdul ran a little café called Arab House. Anne had been having a few disagreements with my dad at home, and Abdul's one concern was that she went back to see Mam and Dad, to make things right. He believed in families being together and in families sorting out their problems. Family was always the most important thing to him, as it is to me.

Abdul had come over to Jersey a few times. He loved it and he went everywhere with me. He was such a steadying influence on me and he was always onto me, when the bigger money started coming in, telling me that some of the people around me were only ever interested in my money. He was only about 5ft tall but he was the biggest, most warm-hearted and wisest man I have ever met. He also had a wickedly funny sense of humour too.

When we were working the Pontins holiday centres he was with me all the time. There was the sound and lighting man, Abdul and me. Rita was never out of the picture either, but she preferred to stay at home, whether that was in Bournemouth or attending to some of the business interests of her father on Jersey.

I also now had a musical director for the first time, Nick Potter. He had ginger hair, a bit like an afro style, and wore a purple catsuit on stage. He now lives in Australia. Nick was my first ever touring band. A one-man band, yes, but a touring musician nonetheless. In the van as we toured the length and breadth of the country, there would be the sound and lighting man, Abdul, Nick, three girl dancers and me. Abdul did all the cooking, and everything about his cooking was so clean. You certainly didn't touch anything whilst he was on it.

We were doing something like eighteen shows a week for Pontins for what amounted to next to nothing! All those people who queue up for the TV talent shows of today, and who just want readymade success selling millions of CDs, should see what it's really all about. I don't begrudge anyone anything though, so I'm not having a pop. I got my chance through a talent show as well. But for people like me, this was the way we learned our business.

Now, about Abdul's wicked sense of humour, are you ready? Prepare yourself for a laugh here.

We also had a magician on tour with us at one time, so you can now add him to the passengers in the van. His name was

Mike Danatta and I believe he went on to run a sex shop in Bournemouth. You can just imagine how that would go down today if he was still playing the holiday resorts, can't you? Anyway, as part of his act he had some doves and a chicken called Friendly. Are you starting to get the idea? Ha ha.

At that time the food at Pontins left a lot to be desired. It was way before Burger King and McDonald's took over everywhere, and things like scampi-in-a-basket, garlic bread and chicken Kiev were the 'new' foods.

Muslims are quite careful about what they eat because of their religion. As I've mentioned the magician's act, I guess you're already a bit ahead of me here, aren't you?

Mike's on stage with his act. The doves are coming out – one, two, three. The rest of the act is going well. Everything's going to plan. Then Mike comes to the wings of the stage.

'Where's the chicken? Where's Friendly?'

He's panicking a bit, you could see the sweat just coming up in beads on his forehead. 'Did you feed Friendly?' Abdul would feed him each night. That way he would be ready the way Mike wanted him.

But Abdul had been hungry that night and the meal we'd eaten earlier had been, you've guessed it… chicken! Abdul looked him in the eye and with a big grin, he said, 'Friendly, love? Friendly in your f★★★ing stomach, love.' We had all eaten Friendly. And the magician had helped eat his own act! Mike turned yellow at that moment.

We were going round and round the UK like a Ferris wheel, playing all these gigs. It was no wonder things got a little heated sometimes, including the vans. In ten weeks we had eighteen Transits that had failed us. Inside the van with the sound and light man, me, Abdul, Nick, the dancers and a magician (now minus his chicken!), things occasionally boiled over. One of the arguments saw us dispensing with one of the girls – and no, Abdul didn't eat her.

The argument was all about why Abdul should be in the front of the van instead of her. So I said, 'All you've got to do is get out if you don't like it.' I'd had enough of her. She was getting on everyone's nerves at the time. We were on the Dorchester-Bournemouth bypass and she was all dressed up in her show gear. She looked like something out of a Danny La Rue show. She took me at my word and got out. I don't think she expected us to drive off, but that's exactly what we did. Well, she was stroppy at the time.

There was also one Pontins holiday park where they charged a little bit more. It was Barton Hall in South Devon. Each time we played there I couldn't help but think, *They pay extra for this!* It was no different in my eyes to anywhere else we were going. I got myself into such a laughing fit over it. But I didn't get tired of Pontins as such, the people we played for on their holidays were lovely and many of my fans today remember seeing me at the different resorts.

The travelling was tiring, especially with the sheer number of gigs and mileage we were getting through. To say nothing of the vans we were going through as well! I had the energy, that wasn't a problem, it's just that after a while I didn't feel as though I was getting anywhere.

I suppose I could have taken up other jobs, like being an entertainments manager for one of the camps, as some do to be able to stay in one place, but I knew that it wasn't for me. I never saw myself as a bluecoat or redcoat. That kind of thing might have been fine for others and a number of top entertainers have done that, but I always saw myself as an artiste, a singer, entertainer – nothing else.

Everyone in the entertainment world accepts that travelling is your life when you are a performer, and I love going to all of the places and seeing all those lovely people who come along. I've never been one of those who feel that the whole world revolves around just one city, but the time was coming for me to spend some time in the city where everyone tells you it is important to make your mark in the UK – London.

But before we leave the south coast, I have to tell you about another landmark in my life. During my time in lovely Bournemouth I spent several days at Arny's Shack, making my first ever LP release. As I mentioned earlier, my first recordings were at Keith Herd's Fairview Studios in Hull. I had subsequently recorded the single 'Feelings' at Tony Arnold's studio, which came out in 1977, but I hadn't recorded an album until 1980–81, when I put together *Only Once* on a record label called Roxon. It featured one of my own compositions, which I co-wrote with my musical director at that time, Chris Summerfield: 'To Live Without You'. The LP also included several well-known songs of the time, 'Fame', 'You to Me Are Everything' and 'Ain't No Stopping Us Now'. It was also the first ever recording of my impressions and included Elvis, Barry Manilow, John Lennon, David Bowie, Stevie Wonder and Neil Diamond.

This is what I wrote as my sleeve notes to *Only Once*:

'A big hello to all my friends! I hope that you had a great evening [because the LP was sold after the show] and that you enjoyed the show! We thought that it would be a good idea to record something to enable you to take a little bit of the show home with you – and we came up with this, my debut LP. I thoroughly hope that you will enjoy listening to it as much as I enjoyed recording it.

'There's a bit of something here for everyone, from up-tempo numbers like "Fame" to my version of that great old standard "What Do You Want to Make those Eyes at Me

For?" (Emile Ford and the Checkmates) – and I think that "Only Once" should get a mention too, because that's one of my great personal favourites!

'At this point I would like to take the opportunity of thanking my faithful "team", the unsung heroes who travel everywhere with me. My personal musical director, Chris Summerfield, who is to be found behind me onstage, enthusiastically directing the musicians, plays keyboards with superb proficiency, and is also a very talented songwriter. He co-wrote with me "To Live Without You".

'Something that people tend not to notice, unless it is bad, is the sound and lighting in venues. The man who sets the mood onstage for me is my good friend the sound and light engineer [I did use his real name in the notes].

'And last but not least, a big thank you to my manager, Ron Page [who had taken me on by then] who handles all show production and pulls everything together, taking the worries away, leaving me to my singing!

'What more can I say, except to leave you with all my good wishes, and to hope that I see you all again soon!

'Love, Joe.'

I have always made a point of thanking my fellow musicians, because it is their playing that allows me to perform the way I do. It's not often the sound and lighting gets much of a mention, but once again it is an essential part of any show.

There is one other man I should thank too. Tony Arnold's studio was the first to specialise in an echo sound, which I understand is today called a 'stereo stack-tracking Ampex sound'. His engineers, Bob Pearce and Les Payne, did a great job for me. I had some excellent musicians with me on that recording too. As well as Chris Summerfield, we also had Chris Rae on guitar.

Tony Arnold's studio saw many of the great names in popular music pass through it over the years, people like Van Morrison, Eurythmics, and Dave Dee, Dozy, Beaky, Mick & Tich.

Ron Page's wife, Traci, wrote some very nice notes on the sleeve too.

> 'To quote a very famous song, *"You've either got or you haven't got style,"* and after watching a Joe Longthorne concert there can be no doubt about it, the man has an abundance of style. His exciting and powerful voice, coupled with his dynamic personality, has added sparkle to the world of British showbiz. The professional and exacting qualities of his style of showmanship have gained him many admirers from all walks of life, and have earned him the supreme and coveted title of "The Entertainers' Entertainer".'

I always liked Traci! I'm sure I must have thanked you at the time, Traci, but if I didn't then please accept my thanks now.

There was another release from Arnie's Shack too, what used to be called an EP, with the song 'Lido de France' – written by myself and Summerfield especially for Jersey – Abba's 'Thank You for the Music' and my own 'Joe's Song' on the A side; and a collection of impressions on the B side including 'Misty', 'It's Not Unusual', 'Till', 'Forever and Ever', 'The Wonder of You' and 'My Way'.

It was a few years later, in 1986, that I recorded my next LP, called *The Singer*, on Great Britain Records. As you can see by the sleeve notes, my management had by now changed over to Ron Page. Let me tell you how that came about. I wasn't fed up with Bournemouth, it's a great town. That's still where we were living during the two years I spent touring the Pontins sites up and down the country, and we had moved into the first ever property in my name – 138 Herbert Avenue, Upper Parkstone.

One of the good friends I had made at that time was John H. Stracey, one of our fantastic, British-born, world boxing champions. He knew that I needed to move on professionally, and proved a useful man to have on your side when you needed to convince someone about what you wanted to do! Ron Page believed I had potential to do well in the clubs around London.

Don Jones and a lady called Bridie Reid, who worked together as entertainment agents and booked all the acts for Pontins, wouldn't sign me off from my contract with the holiday resorts, so I couldn't capitalise on my new fame from appearing on *Search for a Star*.

This was to be my first-ever ending of a contract, giving notice. All I wanted was to be nearer the real action in the entertainment world and I'd had several approaches following my TV appearances. I didn't want to miss out on it. But Don wouldn't let me go.

However, one day he wouldn't let me go, the next day he did. Cue John H. Stracey! I don't know fully what was said, but John told me later that he had rung Don and told him that he was stopping me from going where I wanted to go. He also told me there was no violence involved. Anyhow, the next day I was under contract to Ron Page. So that's how it happened and how the second LP came about.

It was time to leave Bournemouth, the doves, the stroppy dancers and the magician's new chicken! We moved to Maidenhead. Ron wanted me closer to London and I went on to play many times in his really great club, The Silver Skillett. It was a very popular venue and he booked everyone from Lonnie Donegan to Bernard Manning to play there. When we first moved from the coast, we lived with Ron and his wonderful wife Traci before getting our own property.

I had also been introduced to a man called Malcolm Vinecor, who looked after me for a while as I moved over from Don to

Ron. Malcolm was to be around for a few years yet, and lived near to Jimmy Tarbuck. He was also chairman of Crystal Palace FC and ran the Priory clinic, the rehab centre.

You would be silly if you didn't like Maidenhead, it's beautiful and the Thames Valley area is gorgeous. I was very happy and felt very lucky to be there. Myself, Rita and the sound and lighting man, as well as Abdul most of the time, lived in Maidenhead through quite a bit of the eighties, at 14 Cranbrook Drive. I had some very happy times there and, career-wise, it became another real step up for me, with the biggest live dates of my career about to come my way. And I was ready for them.

Instead of playing holiday camps – and no disrespect intended to those – I was now playing the big, well-known clubs like The String of Pearls in Wembley, where I played regularly. I remember the time when I was booked to play at the legendary Talk of the Town in London. This is where all – and I mean all – of the world-famous cabaret acts had played: Frank Sinatra, Sammy Davis Jr., Eartha Kitt, Stevie Wonder, Dusty Springfield, The Carpenters and, of course, Dame Shirley. She recorded a tremendous live album there in 1970.

I was actually the last headline artiste to play the Talk of the Town, which closed in 1982. Peter Stringfellow took it over. Funny thing is that it's now back as a cabaret venue, as well as a major casino, under its original name of The Hippodrome. I've played it recently and am due to play there again this year.

I played The Talk of the Town for a month, which was a real kick in the teeth to the reviewer on the *Evening Standard* in London. He had said something along the lines of, *'Who's this bleached-blond guy from up north who has come to close our beloved Talk of the Town? Why him? Why not someone like Sammy Davis?'* Well, I got up there and gave him Sammy Davis and all the rest of the Rat Pack. We had four great weeks and the shows were all sell-outs. So much for the *Evening Standard*'s reviewer!

Here's a funny story. My family also did a bit of business when the place closed down. My Uncle Joe – the same Uncle Joe that turned the trick for me with Jess Yates on *Junior Showtime* – bought all the curtains, and by the time we had left for the after-show party he had also taken all the tables! Not sure he'd agreed a deal on them, but they went – *bosh!*

I remember seeing Roger Whitaker at The Talk of the Town; I have always loved his songs like 'Durham Town'. The Bachelors were one of my mam's favourites and they appeared there too, so I already had a fondness for the venue before I played there.

This wasn't my first time in London. I had played the big city during the seventies too, when I had come off Jersey to do a show or two, but now, by being in and around London, basing myself close to the city and performing regularly in front of a lot of influential people, I was beginning to earn a reputation amongst the TV people who were based there.

What *Search for a Star* had done was to put me in front of millions of people, and it had proved to be the launching pad for a decade of being 'on the box' in a number of entertainment shows, including my own series. Ron Page knew that would happen and that was why he was so keen to sign me. Can't fault him there.

My first recordings for mainstream record labels were still a distance away, but television was knocking even if *Opportunity Knocks* hadn't knocked.

I appeared on another TV show called *The Big Top Variety Show* with Michael Barrymore, in 1981, and was well on my way to fame… and a fortune that came and went.

But first let's go to Scarborough, that beautiful jewel on the Yorkshire coast. I love Scarborough. I think every kid growing up in Yorkshire loves Scarborough. There's something about it that's still great today.

And no, you're not getting a break this time. Maybe after Scarborough!

CHAPTER ELEVEN

SCARBOROUGH AND RAVENSCAR

Tony Hardman and Mike Hughes get their first mention here. Tony is an agent and had seen me over on Jersey where I once appeared with Des O'Connor. I make fun of Des when I'm on stage, but truthfully he is one of the nicest guys in the business.

Tony was always really good for me, apart from introducing me to 'Stanley Kubrick'. I'll tell you more of him and that slightly embarrassing tale later.

Mike Hughes was the best manager and agent I ever had up until James. I've had some really good ones. Jean Parkes, who I'll come to later, was another. But Mike was a seriously great operator and was always so sincere. It was him who put me on for my first summer season in Scarborough, and it was Mike who was also the man who negotiated for my TV series.

But first let's talk about Scarborough. It's now 1982 and this is to be my first time with a full live orchestra. Meeting the band was a big thing for me. I went into the orchestra pit with Maurice Merry and his Merry Men. They played as Gene Pitney's UK band when he came over, so you can imagine how I felt. I was there in the pit with all these great musicians. I was now twenty-seven and had my own orchestra for a season. To me it was like being told you could have all the sweets from the shop!

I was up at the Floral Hall in Scarborough with The Krankies. They were the number one family entertainment act at the time. They were doing shows like *Crackerjack* on the BBC and appearing in Royal Variety shows. They're still going strong now, and what I really like about them is that they have kept their act as a family show, they haven't given in to smutty talk or sold out commercially.

I loved Jeanette and Ian (The Krankies), but soon there were to be changes to the billing. I was supposed to come on after Stu 'Crush a Grape' Francis had opened the show. He was then to come back on after me.

Now I'm not talking daft here, but I knew that within twenty minutes of being there I was going to be top of the bill! Maybe I couldn't be top on the posters at that time, because they were already up, but for the first time in my life I was on stage with a wonderful orchestra backing me.

It's exciting and I can't stop smiling. I'm a singer – Stu, Jeanette and Ian are comedians. This band is mine – all mine. It felt so good. This is what all those years in Hull, Sunderland and Jersey had been about. I am still smiling about it now as I write. Mine, all mine.

The TV stardom was great later on, but there is nothing to compare with playing live with your own band. There is nothing I get a kick out of more.

When you give Joe Longthorne an orchestra, all you have to do is stand back because you've already lit the blue touchpaper. I had Maurice Merry on keyboards, Alan Savage on drums, one of the best in the business, but I could go through everyone in the band and give you the same reaction. These fellahs were quality players and I was going to use every one of them to the full.

I don't think anyone properly realised just what would happen if you put an orchestra behind me – probably not even my own family, who always had belief in me anyway – but they all soon found out. I was going on in the first half of the show and the audience would be on its feet. They just couldn't get enough – and neither could I – but I never once did what Pancho had done to me. I came off on time, every time. And every single performance I stormed it, thanks to Maurice and his Merry Men. I can't say it enough, musicians are everything to me.

In a short while I had ripped up the first set of the show. I didn't care what anyone else thought, I just knew that was the way to go. I told Mike Hughes that Stu wasn't coming back on again after me. Why would any promoter want to do that to a show once you had the audience on its feet, giving a standing ovation? No disrespect at all, but Stu would have to do more than crush a grape to get that kind of reaction. The first half had to finish with me.

Jim Davidson once said that he would only ever go on before me, not afterwards. He knows the power I have in my voice and the way an audience reacts to it. Jim has always known what I've been capable of, and the special relationship I have with those who come to my shows.

Back to Scarborough. I think Jeanette and Ian started getting worried at the point when Stu was being dropped from his second spot, but they never mentioned anything and they were always very friendly.

I know I was a bit ruthless at times, but I just knew this was how things were meant to be from then on. I just love having a big band behind me and this one was simply top dollar. I have immense respect for all those who have played alongside me over the years, because I know that their contribution to what I am singing is also why the audience applauds so much. It's a team effort on stage, not all me-me-me. Now where have you heard that before?

I'm not being big headed here, just perhaps a little excited, but if you give a singer like me an orchestra the show is going to be big. The songs are just going to be fantastic, and everyone is going to go home happy that they have had a fabulous time.

My good friend Bobby Ball, who produced my summer season show for me a few years ago, said to me recently, 'You know where me and Tommy went wrong, Joe? We got rid of the band.' I told him that wasn't it at all. They are two of our greatest comics, an absolutely brilliant duo, and have no real need for a band. But for me, as a singer, a band is everything. I also like my audience to see where the money goes when they are buying the tickets.

Mike took a calculated gamble on me with that first summer season. After all, I was untried in the big theatre venues at the time. I had played The Talk of the Town; I had played resorts, clubs and hotels, but nothing as big as that first season. There was no guarantee that I would be successful throughout the run, but I knew once I was there, and even before I was there, that it was right for me. I will forever be grateful to Mike.

Like a lot of people who come from Hull, I have always loved Scarborough, the town, its people and the beach. Mam and Dad didn't have a lot of spare money to take us to many places when we were young, but we would go there on the train like a lot of families did from all over the county. Actually, Dad wouldn't quite make it to Scarborough. He would 'come over all funny', he would say to Mam, and end up back in the peever (pub) in Hull.

I remember Mam on the beach, her lovely big legs and a warm jug of tea! We usually ended the day singing back home at pubs like The Beresford or The White Lion.

Scarborough is wonderful, but now I want to introduce you to my favourite place in the world. It's just a little further up the coast.

Like I said earlier, when I used to play truant from school I didn't just go to New Holland and into Lincolnshire. I would also come up to Scarborough and that's how I found Ravenscar.

It's a tiny village by the cliffs looking out to the North Sea, and has been called 'The Town That Never Was'. If you ever go there you will see why. It's four miles off the main coast road from Scarborough to Whitby. It is so isolated and I have always been at peace there.

The first time I found out just how much I loved Ravenscar was when I was about thirteen years old. As soon as I saw it I knew there was a connection, that it was my type of place. I fell in love with it. It's the peace, the absolute tranquillity of it all. As a kid I can remember thinking, *I really love you*. You see, I fall in love with places in the same way I fall in love with people, and I never forget any of them. I then had to walk the four miles back to the main road to get a bus back into Scarborough, and then the train back to Hull – and home before Dad realised I'd done it again.

George III stayed at Raven Hall, which is now the Raven Hall Hotel. There was also once a railway line that ran from Scarborough to Ravenscar, but that had been closed down in 1965.

I lived for a while in the old stationmaster's house, staying in it while I was doing a twelve-week summer season in Scarborough. I used to love going across to Raven Hall. One of the houses in Ravenscar (and there aren't many) was owned by a man called Otto and his wife, who looked after children who had difficulty in learning, which is close to my heart for obvious reasons. I regularly used to go across and chat with them while I was there, and I still long to go back there whenever I can. I've been all around the world – Australia, the States, Thailand, right across Europe, Hong Kong, on cruises through Scandinavia and the Eastern Bloc – but there still isn't a single place that compares to Ravenscar. It is a real hidden gem. The view from Ravenscar to Robin Hood's Bay is fantastic.

Okay, let's go. There's plenty more to tell, but if you're ever looking for somewhere that's a bit different to anywhere you've been before, try the Raven Hall Hotel in Ravenscar.

CHAPTER TWELVE

TELEVISION AND THE STATES

The eighties and early nineties saw me combine regular live gigs with plenty of TV work, releasing albums, touring the States and winning my first Variety Club award. It was also the era that saw me with two Rollers and four Bentleys, a massive house with seven acres of land and its own swimming pool. But life isn't measured that way. I know it's far more precious than that, as I was to find out right at the start of my TV career.

It was a great time, as you might expect, but truly today I am just as happy as I have ever been. When you can have all of that, lose it all and be at death's door along the way, yet still entertain people, you realise what's important.

I loved it when I was earning really big money from TV contracts, of course I did, as anyone would, but it's not the be all and end all.

Did I ever lose the plot? What do you think? How can a man who has suffered a nervous breakdown say he hasn't lost the plot? How can a man who has been bankrupt say he hasn't lost the plot?

How can a man who has taken drugs quite extensively over the years say he hasn't lost the plot? And although I'm not after the sympathy vote here, how can a man go through what I have and not lose the plot?

Yes, I have lost the plot along the way, several times.

But before all those negative things came along, first let's just take a look at the good things that were happening.

By 1982, I hadn't just appeared on *Search for a Star* and performed for a month at The Talk of the Town; I had also appeared in Scarborough for the first time in a summer season – and I had made my debut at the Palladium.

The following year I was to pick up the Variety Club's award as Most Promising Newcomer. I nearly had an embarrassing moment as, at the last minute, I realised I'd forgotten my suit. Fortunately, The Grumbleweeds were there and I borrowed one of theirs!

I also appeared on a TV special gala evening and was on the top-rated game show on TV at the time, Ted Rogers' *3-2-1*, which was filmed at Yorkshire Television, bringing me back full circle to where I started on TV with *Junior Showtime*.

A few years ago I bumped into a man who was an extra at YTV at the time I appeared on *3-2-1*. He mentioned that I was one of the few 'stars' who would pass the time of day with him and his fellow extras. That's just what I do. I enjoy talking with people whoever they are. Hopefully, that has come across wherever I have been.

In 1983 I appeared on two TV programmes – one was *Live from Her Majesty's*, which I was to appear on several times over the years to come, but the other was more important for me because it was the first time I'd ever had my own TV show. It was part of a series on Channel 4 called *The Entertainers* – and mine was called, appropriately enough, 'The Joe Longthorne Show'. It was a one-off and I wasn't to get my own TV series for another five years, but it was a start. It appeared on screen 13 October 1983.

David Bell had been instrumental in getting me the programme, but he didn't produce it and I wish he had. The producer had previously done *Opportunity Knocks*. Funny how life works out!

Four years later I had my next stab at a show, this time on ITV on 26 August, 1987. David Bell managed to get me another break, and *Joe Longthorne Entertains* featured my good friends in the business Kate Robbins, who was a great impressionist and had a hit single with 'More than in Love', and Wayne Dobson, the magician who I still feel had the best sleight of hand ever in this country. The show was meant to be a pilot for a series and it must have done okay, because the following year I had my first ever six-week series with Wayne as my resident guest. Mike Hughes was pulling the strings in the background.

There were plenty of other shows too. I appeared on the late Marti Caine's series that was very popular at the time, and I was by now a regular on *Live at the Palladium* and *Live from Her Majesty's*. David Bell had looked after me by getting me on TV, while I had Mike Hughes negotiating all the TV and stage deals.

Unfortunately, looking back, I managed to hit a few self-destruct buttons as I went along. Maybe if David and Mike had been around all the time then some of the things that happened might not have. Mike always liked to lay out a five-year plan for the people he managed, but I never wanted one. It just wasn't me. I know that tours have to be booked in advance and that TV programmes are planned well forward, but five years! I don't look at life that way. Maybe if I had then Mike would have stayed with me.

Back in 1985, for a short while I very nearly didn't have anything other than a possible jail sentence to look forward to. This was before I landed my first TV series and just prior to my latest adventure – the States.

Following my initial successes on TV shows and around the country, I had been signed up to play in America. I was to perform in some fantastic theatres and meet some great people. But just before I signed up to go over to the States I had been back home in Hull, and it nearly cost me my US dates. I just happened to be in the wrong place at the wrong time, but it did create a lot of problems for me.

What had happened was a pretty extreme fight in a pub, which led to one of my nephews being viciously attacked. Its aftermath saw me and others up on a charge of affray. It had all been due to go to court, but I had to fly out to the States. These were to be my very first US gigs and I was looking forward to them, but I knew I had this case hanging over me.

The court case came up while we were in Philadelphia, which meant we had to fly back so that I could appear at Beverley Crown Court, a lovely historic market town just north of Hull. I made up some phoney excuse, as we weren't about to tell those who had booked us why we were coming back. The idea was to get back to the States by Wednesday, having been in court on the Monday, otherwise the Stateside deal was off!

I was all set to represent myself in court when my barrister stopped me, saying, 'You have your stage, Mr Longthorne, this is mine.' He did a good job. All I wanted to do was get back across to open in Philadelphia, as we had just finished a Chicago run. The affray charge was dropped to a lesser charge of carrying an offensive weapon, and we settled for that. The judge ordered me to pay a £2,000 fine and I was so relieved that I could go straight back that I said, 'Can I pay you now, your honour?'

Within an hour of the court case closing, we were back on our way to Heathrow Airport. To this day, until the publication of this book, very few people have known too much about it and it's still probably best left that way.

Ron Page had done everything to get me over to the States. He had made contact with a man called Al Anthony, who had produced the famous *Superstars* shows in the US, and an Italian called Tony De Santos.

It had always been my biggest dream to play in Vegas and, although this wasn't that, it was at least a step in the right direction. I didn't see it as my big break in the US. It was all about getting experience.

I was scheduled to play at the Drury Lane Theatre in Chicago for five weeks, and they had already sold 2,000 tickets by the time I got there. I went down so well that I ended up playing for five months before Shelley Winters took over. It was here that I started rubbing shoulders with some of the greats in the business. I had lunch with Tony Bennett and Sammy Davis Jr.'s manager.

Tony De Santos was great with us. He told us there was a car in his garage that we could use while we were there. When we opened up the garage it wasn't just a car, it was only a Rolls Royce Corniche! I can still remember his face as our jaws dropped. I also remember it was f***ing freezing at the time, something like minus 25 degrees with the wind chill, and white over with snow.

There was some problem with the side window but we managed to fix it easily. Tony showed us the bank and the fire station next. Why? Because he owned them both.

'There's your bank account and there's your fire engines and there's your car,' he said to us. He looked after us splendidly throughout our year in the US.

Philadelphia, our next venue following my courtroom appearance, went even better than Chicago. I was appearing in two shows a day at the Encore Theatre. I was also invited onto Jerry Lewis's *Telethon*. It was such a great experience. Something new was happening every day. It has to be one of the favourite times in my life.

Before we went out to the US, we had to get some backing tracks recorded because there would be no band with us. I prefer everything live, like most performers, that way your energy can help all of the musicians and you can feed off theirs too. Obviously, backing tracks are useful for rehearsing, but on this occasion it was something that just had to be done.

When we returned to the UK in 1986, after twelve months of being away, the regular guest spots on TV shows started again. I was back on screen with *Jimmy Tarbuck & Friends* almost immediately, and I also appeared on *Live from Her Majesty's* and *Live at the Palladium*. Jimmy was compère on both shows too.

This was also the year when The Joe Longthorne Friendship Club started, with Rita at its helm, and my second LP, *The Singer*, was released. Many of the songs on it later appeared on *The Joe Longthorne Songbook* album that did so well and ended up going platinum.

By this time we had moved to Northern Heights in Bourne End, Buckinghamshire. Dennis Waterman, who made his name in *Minder* with George Cole, lived in Bourne End too. Ours was a lovely house, but we weren't to stay there too long before moving to the biggest house I ever had.

The catalyst for that move came when I landed a regular support slot on *The Les Dennis Laughter Show*, which I was to appear on for four series. Mike Hughes was once again the man who sorted it out for me. He conducted all the negotiations. That's also the time when I started spending some serious money. I was starting to live the celebrity life and I used to go to the recordings in my beautiful yellow banana of a Rolls Royce.

Although I like them, as anyone would, possessions have never meant that much to me that I got too carried away with them. And if you believe that you will believe anything!

I remember pulling into my driveway one day. There it is, worth twenty-eight large ones and sat on my driveway. I'm admiring it when seconds later, my housekeeper, Jean, is backing into it, crunching it and causing thousands of pounds worth of damage. I wasn't that bothered though. Things like that don't matter so long as nobody is hurt.

Not true. I went absolutely f***ing barmy. No sooner had it arrived than we were carting it back to the garage!

The Les Dennis Laughter Show didn't just give me more money, it also gave me an opportunity to perform on television every week. I was very lucky that Mike Hughes had got me the contract and conducted all the negotiations, but he wasn't content with just that, he was already working fast on the next part of my career, my own TV series. I might not have wanted a five-year plan, but he had already planned it out for me.

Wherever I was needed I joined in with Les's sketches, but I wasn't involved with too many of them. I would have liked to have been included in more of them, even though I still wouldn't have been very good with the scripts.

I had an ambition to act. These days though, I'd love to just play myself in *Benidorm*. Now that's a programme – and written by a Hull lad, Derren Litten.

Another *Live at the Palladium* followed in 1987, as well as regular appearances with Des on his *Des O'Connor Tonight* show. Whitney Houston and Dionne Warwick were on the shows when I appeared, and I sang 'We Are the World' with Dionne.

At the same time as all this TV action, I was also in the summer season on the North Pier, in Blackpool. Little did I know then that, just a dozen years later, this town was to become my home. In fact, the North Pier itself was to become a temporary home as well, but that's not for a while yet and involves a few more funny tales.

The most important event of 1987 to me, though, was not a TV appearance or the summer season, but the opportunity I had to honour one of the greatest entertainers our country has ever seen. One of my all-time favourite singers, Matt Monro, passed away on

7 February 1985. As I mentioned in the 'favourite songs' chapter, I still sing the songs he made famous even today, such as 'Portrait of My Love' and 'Born Free'. 'If I Never Sing Another Song' went on to become one of my most famous songs, and was recorded by him in 1977.

Matt died of liver cancer in his fifties, but strangely, for some reason, his life wasn't celebrated on screen in the way that other singers or entertainers have been over the years. When you see how some performers are honoured after they have passed on, it is nothing short of criminal the way Matt was ignored by television. Matt's daughter, Michelle, was hurt and angry that her father had been ignored by the television companies and decided she wanted to host her own tribute to him.

Michelle did everything. She organised the whole evening at Grosvenor House in London, Sunday 22 February – the room, the invitations, the menus, the toastmaster, the raising of funds for cancer research – and she was going to top the whole thing off with a 100-strong choir singing a medley of Matt's songs 'acapulco' – ha ha, that's close enough for me – with video footage of the great man himself. But she was short of one thing.

This is how Michelle thanked me afterwards, with a story which now appears on my website. It makes me feel so humble every time I read it – and also so pleased that I was able to help:

'… But still I didn't have a star name, and then my white knight came along, Joe Longthorne, who was at the height of his career, had won every accolade, had his own television series and was at the top of his game. Joe rang me out of the blue.

'He offered to be my escort at the top table for the evening and absolutely tore the room apart with his cabaret performance. He not only offered his services for free but also was there because he genuinely admired my father. Not once did he throw a "wobbler" because he wasn't closing the show, which is what every star would normally expect. He just asked what he could contribute and accepted his fate humbly. That is the mark of a true star.

'Joe usually does a tribute in his stage shows to Dad, which is a great honour in itself. He always talks highly of my father and his voice, but in fact Joe has the most amazing voice and a range that very few singers can compete with.

'Joe is a very unassuming, gentle man. He did me and my family a great service that night and contributed in making the evening a resounding success. He has overcome adversity himself over the years and although he has won fights against his illness, he hasn't won the war.

'I have only met Joe a handful of times and each time he has been more gracious than the last. Although I do not know him really well, he will always have a very special place in my heart. There are not many people who can make me see reason when I don't want to, but the one thing he did for me that evening, when he stepped on that stage at the Grosvenor House Hotel, was that he took away my anger at the world. He made me realise that you don't need corporations and television companies to acknowledge what a great talent the world has lost. You just need people – people who love and admire the legend that is Matt Monro – and the amazing legacy he left behind.'

That's so nice isn't it? Thank you again Michelle, but really it was the least I could do in the circumstances. I still love Matt's music very much today. He provided the world with a fantastic catalogue of wonderful numbers and is still sadly missed. In many ways, he was never appreciated as much as some other singers in this country. Recently, the TV producers have set the record straight and finally Matt has received the programmes his voice deserved.

Looking back, I was somewhat luckier than Matt television-wise, and in 1988 the roof blew off my career. Everything was underway. I was now appearing in not one but two regular series – *The Les Dennis Laughter Show* on BBC1, as well as my own series on ITV. It was the start of a massive time for me, the time when I really was in my heyday. It was a time when young girls wrote to me and everybody seemed to have time to devote to me. It was a time when everyone I saw swore they knew me. I think there's a song that goes a little bit like that, isn't there?

Now before this all becomes too much of a list of TV programmes I have appeared in or hosted, let's go to Turpin's. You've not heard of Turpin's yet? Well, this is your time to find out. It's time to see how far I had come – and also how far I had to fall!

You may need a glass of something soon. Off you go. Get charged up and let's get on with this next bit.

CHAPTER THIRTEEN

TURPIN'S

So what is this 'fame' thing all about? To me it means a good laugh, good times and good prospects. I had all of those back in the 1980s and early 1990s.

Let me tell you what life is like being a celebrity from my side. These are not complaints, just facts. I know I have had things that many will never have. I understand all that, but what does it all mean?

Firstly, in my case it means that when you're young you never really live anywhere for very long. By that I mean that you don't live somewhere that you can call home all the time, because you're touring or recording. I know there are some who would say, *'Well you're a traveller, Joe, you should be used to it.'* They're wrong. There are many times when all I ever want is quiet, peace, tranquillity.

Sometimes a big house can give you that, if you can afford it, and I thought I could. One of my problems back then was that I thought I could afford anything.

I had gone from £6 a week on *Junior Showtime* to £18 a night in Hull and Sunderland, followed by an increase to £25 a night if my dad had done the deal, in whichever fashion he chose! I'd played Jersey and Pontins for £100 a week. Now all of a sudden I'd had a few goes at television and the money was much bigger. For a lad who has come from Rifle Terrace in Hull, I suppose I was always going to be in danger of a fall!

I guess it's all about going out and getting what you thought you could never have – and it did get out of hand. As James tells me today, I know nothing about money. I don't have the first idea of the value of money and if it's there I just spend it, or give it to others who say they need it to buy things they want. I never, ever knew how much I had. I just thought that since I was earning a lot of money at the time, I could say 'yes' to just about anything.

I would go out for a pint of milk and come back having bought another Bentley! I bought a car for my niece. There were always people around me who needed feeding, and I didn't begrudge one bit of it, ever.

This was only 1988. I wasn't hitting the bottle any more than I had always done since I was sixteen, and yes, I was doing cocaine and generally enjoying the celebrity lifestyle. Rita was with me and so was my sound and light man from Hull. Abdul was there, Anne came down to stay many times, but none of them were taking drugs. Everyone came to visit and quite a few stayed awhile. What was I saying about getting a little peace?

Maybe I would have been better just buying a place at Ravenscar, but that wasn't how my life was going at the time. I was flying, and in more ways than one.

The big contract that Mike arranged for me to take on my own TV series had made me feel as though I could buy anything, and at that time, when I wanted something I would buy it; after all, I was doing well. That's all I knew.

I fell in love with a house by the side of the River Thames in

Maidenhead. It was right next to where another celebrity lived at the time. I won't name him here, as he has been in the newspapers quite a bit in recent times. Sheila Fergusson of The Three Degrees lived close by too.

I was out in the big yellow banana, my bright yellow Rolls Royce, with my two Rottweilers. Typical of me at the time, I had only gone out to walk the dogs and I came back having bought a mansion! Or so I thought.

Let me take you through it as it happened.

I am stood on the bank of the river opposite this house and the agent is putting up the 'For Sale' notice. By the time he has put the notice up, I'm calling him from the other side of the river. 'Look at the opposite bank,' I said. 'That's me with the big yellow banana on wheels. I'm buying that house. I'm putting the deposit in your bank account tomorrow and I'm having it.'

They say money can buy anything, but in my case money couldn't buy that house – at least not my money. I did get to look at it on the inside though. The table inside it must have been worth a fortune! It was like the table you would have expected King Arthur and his knights to sit around. It had a fabulous indoor swimming pool, moorings on the river. I just had to have it, but unfortunately, from what I can gather, someone from Arab royalty wanted it for their family.

I had been determined to get it, but the agents kept telling me I was being gazumped. The house was originally priced around £380,000 – this was 1988, remember – then it went up by £20,000, then up to £430,000. And this was all happening when house prices were crashing everywhere else.

The agents also told me of the disadvantages of having a house that backed onto the Thames, especially if you were a celebrity: 'When you sit in the garden, people will go by on the river and they'll all be watching you and pointing at you in your garden. So it's best you don't go there, Mr Longthorne.' That was their advice. It's not what you'd expect an agent to say.

I wasn't to be put off that easily. I had fallen in love with the house and I still desperately wanted it. I went back into the agents' office. They really were lovely people. What was going on wasn't their fault, but by now I was getting quite demonstrative.

'I'm having that house,' I told them in no uncertain terms. There may have been a few expletives thrown in at this point, I grant you. All of the people who were in the branch started walking out and you could hear customers tutting as they went. Can you imagine that? It's a bit like a sketch all of its own, something out of *Mr Bean*. So the branch is now empty apart from the manager and me. That was when I found out that I was never going to live there.

He told me, 'Joe, you can't have it. It's just not going to happen.'

The sheik, or whoever he was, planned to buy it and knock it down to build something even bigger. I'll say no more about it, other than I was looked after for all of my inconvenience.

After I'd finally realised the deal was never going to happen, no matter how much more I offered, I moved into Turpin's, so called because, allegedly, Dick Turpin had once stayed where this house had been built. I tell you, if he'd had a house like this he'd never have bothered with his main job.

Turpin's was my palace. It had everything I could ever have wanted and it cost about £480,000. It will probably be worth around £8m today. It had a 500yd frontage, a swimming pool, sauna, snooker room, recording studio (built by my brother-in-law Mick), stables and plenty of grass in its seven acres of land for what was to become my very own smallholding, including lots of animals.

All of the bedrooms had their own en-suite facilities. So much for peace and tranquillity; everyone came but, of course, I wouldn't have wanted it any other way. The thing I learned, though, is that none of it is clever. Like I said earlier, life's not all about what you've got possessions-wise.

When I needed to go abroad to tour, everyone would come in and house-sit for me. I have such a wonderful, adaptable family who are all so different and who all look after me today. Who better to look after your home for you?

The daft thing is that every time I would come back, there had been something different done to the house. One time I came back and the kitchen had been painted in corporation green. Corporation green, I ask you! It was horrible – and I remember the fridge was always full of stuff I never ate as well!

Anyway, enough of that for now, let's get back to the fun times we had at Turpin's, rather than my grumpy old man routine I just slipped into there.

It's important for me to tell you that I wasn't ever trying to be flash. Well, maybe just a little. I know that Turpin's sounds a lot bigger than just something comfortable when you read what I had back then, but all I can say is it felt good at the time.

One of my favourite parts of the house was the beautiful recording studio that my brother-in-law Mick – Lizzie's husband, the one who used to take me to the gigs – built for me.

There's a saying that once a songwriter gets his own studio it f★★★s him up, and that was true for me. While I had always sung other people's songs, I had also written my own material as well. Once you're in a studio you're constantly fiddling with everything to make a recording better, or so you think, rather than writing new material. Every time there was a new bit of recording equipment on the market I'd buy it. Whether it was three grand here, four grand there, it didn't matter. Being full of cocaine didn't really help, I guess, but I still loved it. Who wouldn't? His own studio is what every singer wants. There can't be many more perfect things than that, can

117

there? There was also a constant flow of fabulous musicians in the house as a result.

Turpin's also gave me time to look after my own animals too. I have always loved animals and at one time we had pigs, chickens, goats, horses and the Rottweilers. My brother John was always at Turpin's and he would go to the local supermarket, where he had a deal going with the manager to buy the leftover foods to feed the livestock.

There was nothing better than walking around with my dogs. I had my two Rottweilers, Bill and Ben, at twelve stone each you could hardly call them the Flowerpot Men! Then there was my Yorkshire terrier called Sparky, my Labrador Henry and Kizzie, my Jack Russell. All my other animals had names as well. You see this was my peace, my solitude, walking in my very own bit of land. It was to be my real solace when I was at home; even if the house was full, I still had the land.

It must have seemed slightly eccentric to some of the locals when John used to go off in a Bentley just to get the bales of hay for the horses. He'd get them bunged in the back. Seems a bit mad, doesn't it, using a beautiful car for that? But it's not, that's just how we all are in my wonderful family. We just get on and do things. We don't worry about whether we're in a big, expensive car or a Bedford truck, to us it's just a way of going from place to place.

If you have animals, you have to spend time with them and make sure they are cared for when you're away; so before I'd leave for a tour, I would always tell whoever was stopping to make sure the chickens were locked up of an evening. Unfortunately, there was one time when whoever was responsible hadn't remembered, because all the chickens had gone by the time I got back. Maybe it was the revenge of the magician from Pontins! Either that or they had all seen an early copy of the film *Chicken Run*!

I have more happy memories than I have bad ones of my time

at Turpin's, but there was one black day that will always stick in my memory. It was one of the most distressing times in my life, to say nothing of my Aunt Rosie's. It still affects me when I think about it today.

Me, my mam, Aunt Peg and Aunt Rose had been for a wonderful day out at Windsor Zoo. We had videoed the whole day and everyone was in high spirits. It had been gorgeously sunny and really, things couldn't have been better. We had come home ready to watch the video, feeling full of the joys of spring. It felt like the world really was a great place.

Then the phone rang.

It was a call to tell us that one of my cousins from Leeds had been killed. We watched my Aunt Rose drop like a stone. After such a wonderful day at the zoo, and so much laughter, the day ended in tears. It had suddenly become the worst moment ever in my life. I cannot explain in any more detail how I felt that evening. I cry just thinking about what happened to my dear cousin. I have never experienced anything like it in my life, or the change in mood that day. And I've been through some dramatic times since.

I can sense we need a break here. There's so much more to come, but after something like that maybe it's best if we lighten the proceedings up a bit. Come on now, I can see that your glass needs a refill. Stick with me here; hang on in. We're about to have a bit of fun as I tell you about some of my favourites.

CHAPTER FOURTEEN

FAVOURITES

We haven't even got to the first time I ever knew I had cancer yet, and I'm still a long way from being declared bankrupt. It's still 1988 and my TV work has been growing steadily, but I'm about to ride even higher on that wave of fame. But first, what and who do I really like? Here's an interesting and diverse list for you:

THE HUNCHBACK OF NOTRE DAME
RUFUS WAINWRIGHT
FRANK SINATRA
BORIS JOHNSON
TAKING CARE OF BUSINESS

Now I'll explain…

My favourite film of all time is the epic version of *THE HUNCHBACK OF NOTRE DAME*. Charles Laughton came from Scarborough and he was one of the greatest actors the world has ever seen. He was brilliant in this very moving film. It just shows you can have all the special effects in the world but there is no substitute for real talent.

RUFUS WAINWRIGHT is a brilliant young man, and his song 'Dinner at Eight' from his *Want One* CD is really powerful. He is a great singer-songwriter, and he has such a unique vocal style. His re-recording of the whole of Judy Garland's 1961 *Live at Carnegie Hall* show was an amazing feat and it is a true masterpiece.

FRANK SINATRA – do I need to say anything more? He was one of the greatest exponents of singing a lyric in his own way, his own style. I learned so much from the way he performed. We play his album *Live at the Sands* in Vegas regularly back at home. Mr Sinatra was a real man's man who stuck by his principles too, and looked after his people. I hope people feel the same way about me.

These names are not in any particular order, so please don't think I'm putting Mr Sinatra below Rufus Wainwright in the pecking order.

BORIS JOHNSON will probably come as a bit of a surprise to some, but I do take an interest in politics. I have always listened to Radio 4. I am very concerned about how the world is today and the future for young people. Boris is a breath of fresh air because I think he takes politics away from the norm. He breaks boundaries between Conservative, Labour and everything else.

TAKING CARE OF BUSINESS was the live album that saw Diana Ross and the Supremes join forces with The Temptations in 1968 on a TV special. It's always been a favourite of mine and includes the song 'The Impossible Dream'.

Right! That's your very short break! I could have given you more of my favourites but let's get back to the story.

121

CHAPTER FIFTEEN

MY OWN TV SHOW – THE START

So I'm at Turpin's. The family's here and the breaks have kept on coming. There don't seem to be any clouds on the horizon. How wrong was that? The cloud that was to come would be the darkest there could be. But it didn't concern me, or any of us, at the time. I think we were all just enjoying the moment.

1988 was a massive year. My own TV series, *The Joe Longthorne Show*, saw us with twelve million viewers, as many as *The X Factor* gets today! I was also still appearing with Les Dennis on his *Laughter Show* and there were even more TV appearances on other shows.

For the *Laughter Show* programmes we used to write six minutes of the show every week, but it wasn't like writing a script. What we did was decide what six minutes of music I would be singing. One week we would concentrate on country music, another week Latin, and so on. We used to go in every Monday to organise what we were going to do.

Mike Hughes had even more good news for me. It was all happening now. He was putting me on with Roy Walker for the

1988 summer season at the Futurist Theatre in Scarborough. That's the one right on the seafront on the South Bay. It had a capacity of over 2000 seats and would be full back in the days when clubland was big and club goers would holiday on the coast. Sadly, it is now close to being demolished.

But back then it was one of the top places to play, not just in Yorkshire but in the UK, and Roy was a household name with his *Catchphrase* programme being one of ITV's top-rated shows.

'I'm going to put Roy Walker with you,' Mike said. 'And Dana, but you're going to top the bill. You're not going to play the clubs anymore.'

Layton Institute Club in Blackpool was my last main club gig around that time, and during those years to come. I did it because I'd already had it booked and, as usual, I wasn't going to let anyone down.

Mike was always very straight with me. He always told it like it was. He has made millionaires out of several very talented people and even one or two who are not so talented. He is a very direct man too.

His first question about the house when he visited Turpin's for the first time was, 'Do you like it?' I said yes and his next question was, 'Yes, but is it paid for?'

I said, 'No, but isn't it lovely? We'll pay for it down the line.'

That answer probably told him all he needed to know, and was what he perhaps expected anyway. I wasn't bothered whether it was paid for. I'm sure he knew that, but he also probably knew then that it would never be paid for.

In my head I thought I was earning enough at the time to pay for anything, so I never thought about the money. I thought that's what you paid accountants to sort out.

I'm a performer, I'm more concerned about what goes on when I hit the stage rather than getting involved with finances.

That's where I am very lucky today. James looks after all of that. He keeps me on the straight and narrow, but all I had back then was an accountant.

As I said, Mike always had his five-year plan for each artiste. He had them for Freddie Starr, Roy Walker, Les Dennis and Russ Abbott – and most of his acts were successful. He tended to stick more with comedians than singers and, like I've already said, I don't do five-year plans.

There was one time when Mike and I had a big argument, and it was after that when he said that he didn't want to manage me anymore.

I was on £64,000 a programme for my TV series, plus what I was on with Les's programme, plus everything else that was going on. Mike had sorted all of that for me. The first of my mainstream release UK albums on Telstar was out. An EMI contract was on its way a few years later. Things were going through the roof. I seemed to be in demand everywhere. No wonder I felt like I could buy anything.

Mike said that although he would no longer manage me, he would continue to negotiate all my TV contracts, and he earned me hundreds of thousands of pounds over a number of years. They really don't come any better than Mike in the business. He made me a household name through those TV show negotiations.

But if you are a performer and you are successful, it means that you attract a number of people who might not be as straight with you as Mike was. That's what Abdul was trying to tell me at the time and I have to say that Abdul was right – as he was most of the time.

I'm not a 'money man', as you know by now, and I was about to start finding out what life is like when you suddenly seem as though you have such a lot.

We'll get one thing straight from the start here. Nobody ever stole anything from me, or at least not that I'm aware of. Nobody could ever be found guilty of ripping me off along the way. You know why? The reason is that I should have looked after what was happening better than I did. I'm not saying I should have suddenly become a figures man. I just should have looked after the money better myself. I should have got someone in I really believed in. It's always easier looking back after the event, isn't it? But that's what I should have done, so I won't name names because I cannot prove things.

What I really do feel though is that, without swearing, there are some who probably took more than their fair f★★★ing share! Oh, I did swear after all. Well with good reason, I think you will find. But there was far worse to come than overinflated bills and people with lesser principles than Mike.

My first ever TV series was about to hit the screens in September 1988 when the wheels came off! My world stopped. You might need a stiff drink and to grab your Kleenex for the next chapter!

CHAPTER SIXTEEN

CANCER

'I'm going to do the best for you that I can.'

They are the words I see in his eyes. He hasn't spoken them, but I know what his eyes are saying to me. I am sat in front of Dr Anthony Childs in his house in Leeds. The year is still 1988, but it could be 2088, or even 3088 so far as I'm concerned. I have nearly completed my summer season with Dana and Roy Walker in Scarborough.

I am one step away from the biggest TV event of my life – my first ever TV series. There is a 32-piece orchestra waiting to back me in Nottingham.

Nigel Lythgoe, later to become Nasty Nigel in the *Pop Idol* TV shows and then a worldwide TV star in his own right, is my producer and director. My first album for Telstar, *The Joe Longthorne Songbook*, is set to hit the charts for Christmas.

The whole of my future, my bright and shiny future, is ahead of me. But is it? Or am I about to die tomorrow? These are just some of the thoughts that go through your head when you are faced with what I found out.

CANCER

I had been losing weight. I thought it was great at the time. At thirty-three years old you want to look good, particularly when you're on stage. You don't want the audience staring at you thinking, *He's getting on a bit, isn't he?* At least not at that age! It's not a thought that enters your mind when you're in your teens or twenties, but when you're in your thirties that's different. When you're just past the next big one, sixty, as I am now, it is not quite as important as it was then, but this was a big time for me so I wasn't concerned about my loss of weight at first. It was Dana who noticed that I was losing probably more weight than I should have been.

The next thing that happened was that I started getting a stiff neck. I thought I'd got it because I'd been driving back from Scarborough to Ravenscar after the show with the window not going down properly. I just thought it was a muscle thing and thought nothing more about it, but my loss of weight accelerated. I lost getting on for two stones. I had never been fat, but I was now starting to look more like Stan Laurel.

Darryl James, who was my PA at the time and was a sweet guy, told me I had to get myself checked out. He knew there was something wrong, something that needed sorting out. So I went for a blood test and saw Doctor Baxter in Scarborough. As soon as I saw him I asked him whether I'd got AIDS. That's what everyone was talking about at the time. He didn't beat around the bush and told me I had to go to see a specialist in Leeds as soon as I could.

His actual words were that if I didn't go I would be in a 'wooden overcoat' by Christmas. It was some shock, I can tell you, and I felt as though I had to scrape myself off the floor!

I still had three weeks to go of our eight-week run at Scarborough and I was just a few weeks away from my TV series.

It was the worst kind of feeling I'd ever had. I was depressed. Was it AIDS or cancer? The next thought was daft, I know, but I thought, *If it's cancer it's alright, I can cope with that, but I don't think I*

127

can if it's AIDS. That's how frightened I was at the time. I carried on with the show for a few more weeks before I finally decided something had to be done.

Darryl took me to Leeds where I met Dr Childs at his home in Roundhay Park. His home was so peaceful. He had a big fat grandfather clock ticking in the hallway. I could see wellington boots out in the porch area. There wasn't a TV to be heard. I had to wait half an hour for him. We went through to his study. That's when his eyes told me how serious this was. Then he told me for real:

'I'm going to stay up all night to look through what we think we've got here. First I'll have to take you for a biopsy. We have to get you in as soon as we can.'

The following day I was under his knife.

I only ever thought I was definitely going to die when I saw the brown soap in the bath! I had to take one before my operation. The bath water was six inches deep with cold, tepid water. It was Dickensian. I honestly felt that, at that moment, Oliver Twist had a better life.

I thought, *Brown soap, tepid water, I'm used to far better than this. I know I'm National Health but this is f***ing serious.* All I felt was that I would be dying in the next six months. I thought about my mam and my sisters and John. I didn't want to go before my mam, because of what it would do to her, losing another of her children. My world was literally turning upside down just at the time when I should have been on top of it, and the results were confirmed by the end of the summer season. I had cancer.

My mam, who's not usually very outgoing, sang me the song 'Good Luck, Good Health and God Bless You'. It meant so much to me.

As I mentioned at the start of this book, what I have is called CLL – Chronic Lymphocytic Lymphoma – it's a particular strain of leukaemia or blood cancer, a lymphoma. So now I knew.

Soon everyone knew. I was still in Scarborough when my story hit the headlines. There it was emblazoned over *The Sun* and *News of the World*: 'Star dying of AIDS!'

But there's always a funny side to everything, you know – even cancer!

Whilst I was in the Brotherton wing of Leeds General Infirmary for the biopsy, my family were still there for me but they were also proving a bit of a handful, it seemed.

My nephew Keith has toured with me ever since he was fifteen. He has played a major part in looking after me over the past thirty years as my minder, my driver, my one-time manager and as simply a great man. I was one of the first people to hold him in my arms after he was born. He, his brother Derek and Keeley, my niece, were in a big camper van parked outside the hospital. They were all there for me.

It just so happened that the camper van was opposite the nurses' quarter.

There I am, half-dead in hospital, and the ward sister asks me whether I can go and see some people in the car park and tell them to quieten down. They were watching the nurses all the time. You couldn't make this up, could you? It was only youthful behaviour and they were looking out for me, as we travellers do. In their mind I was the first thing, that's what I like to think, although Keith and Derek were probably having a few testosterone-charged moments too. I wouldn't begrudge them that. It certainly helped me to get some perspective on life and have a laugh, even in my predicament.

Cancer is such a powerful yet meek word, because you can beat it. Not everyone can, I know, but you can have a go. I've been having a go ever since and there have been lots of times when I've had to get myself back up again after another setback. I guess it's what life's all about. I've even thought I've beaten it sometimes and found it has come back.

CHAPTER SEVENTEEN

LIVING WITH IT

By now, the professionals at Leeds General Infirmary had found out what it was that I was suffering from and my treatment started. CLL is a disease of remission and relapse. That means it keeps coming back. When you're in remission there is no sign of it. When you're in relapse, it's back. When it comes back you have more treatment. It's a nightmare. You never know whether you've beaten it or not.

I was immediately put on to a drug called Chlorambucil, which a lot of people will know is the first thing they put you on. It's a tablet you can take which is reputed to have very few side effects.

Dr Childs told me, 'Look Joe, nothing's going to happen tomorrow. The cancer isn't going to march up on you.' He also told me that I would need to be in hospital for quite a while, and not to go to work.

I was out within the week and I went straight back to performing. You see, it's all I know.

I had everything still to live for. My own TV series, my first nationally released album on a major label, more TV appearances scheduled – there was no way I was missing out on anything. I felt great now as I looked in the mirror. At least I now knew what I had, and there were things in place to help me. And I had Dr Childs on my side. I knew, looking into his eyes, that he wasn't going to let me go.

This was also the time when my charity work really started. I had always done charity gigs but this was when I started some serious big-bucks work for others. I have continued raising money ever since. There must be some way we can find to beat these awful diseases in the end.

The thing with CLL is that you don't feel like you've got anything sometimes, then other days it's the worst thing ever. People who haven't got it cannot possibly understand what it is like to live with that constant fear that, every time it comes back, you might be given only months to live.

Cancer was the last thing I expected when everything else in my career had been going so well. I had felt invincible and suddenly, out of the blue, I felt so helpless. I had two choices – to give in or to fight. I chose the latter. I did what every other performer has done before me, I dusted myself down and I got on with the show.

CHAPTER EIGHTEEN

MY OWN TV
SHOW – THE SERIES

Throughout my first series of *The Joe Longthorne Show*, I was undergoing chemotherapy and I've had 'chemo' many times since. But despite having the treatment, this was still a fantastic time for me. You see, I was probably luckier than most again, because if I hadn't had the programme coming up I may have been very depressed.

What actually happened was that it was a great success and it made me into a real household name. I won't deny that it was also a very trying time though, because of what I was going through.

Where I was very fortunate was to have Nigel Lythgoe as producer and director. He gave me great direction. Terry Wogan had his own show on the BBC at the same time as mine was going out; he was interviewing people like Madonna and yet we were pulling in more viewers. On the show I had the lovely Lisa Maxwell, and of course my favourite illusionist, Wayne Dobson, who deservedly also ended up getting his own TV series.

I'll admit I wasn't the easiest guy to accept direction, as Nigel will tell you. I've never moved too much on stage. It's usually a case of just give me the microphone and I will entertain you, but there was far more to it than that at Central TV studios, where we recorded all three series.

I remember feeling that having my own programme was actually quite frightening at first. It's always nice to be on someone else's show and get off after you've done your six minutes, but here I was with the whole programme to myself, plus my guests.

The set they used at Central was radically different to any other TV show at the time. It featured me coming into the show from out of a tunnel, with the band all around me, playing in the wings on a circular-style set. It was filmed using an all-around camera. We had a thirty-two-piece orchestra and all the musicians came up from London for every show. Every one of them was excellent and we had five musical directors within it. That's how good these players were. The core of them were the 'A' team – Alan Ainsworth's at the Palladium – and I was also exceptionally fortunate to have them tour with me.

We were on at 8.30pm on a Saturday night, the primetime viewing slot. I was singing as myself and doing impressions every week. In the first ever show from the series I did Barry Manilow, Elton John, Stevie Wonder and Al Jolson. In the last show of the six-week run, I impersonated most of the singers who took part in the famine relief recording of Michael Jackson and Lionel Richie's 'We Are the World'.

The TV show should have been the absolute high point in my career as a singer, and I'm sure to many who had followed me up until then it was, but it was also a tremendously tiring and trying time for me. I'm not trying to make it sound like anything it wasn't. Of course I was happy with the show. Who wouldn't be? Primetime TV, *The Joe Longthorne Show*! It's surely what every performer wants isn't it, a programme of their own?

Life at Turpin's was great, my new album was about to be released – but the cancer was making life difficult in a lot of ways. I had to make regular visits to hospital for chemo.

When you have a thirty-two-piece band ready to record a show and they're costing the production company £70,000 a day, that can cause quite few headaches. As a result of having chemotherapy, rehearsals and my live shows were getting cancelled. All the programmes ended up being made, but not without a lot of hassle for the programme makers along the way.

I knew that there were some who were starting to say, 'Don't touch Joe,' or, 'Joe's a no-show,' and for me that also included the Michael Parkinson show.

I had been booked to appear on *Parkinson*. Mr Parkinson had even asked for me to be on, or so I believe. Like a lot of people, I always thought Parky's interviews were the best, but I just couldn't make it when I was supposed to be on and I never got the chance again. I really wasn't very well. Maybe Mr Parkinson never got to hear anything more than an apology that I couldn't get there. All I know was that the opportunity to appear on his show didn't come up again.

Strange how things work out, but when I sang at Don Black's seventieth birthday show in 2008, which was broadcast on BBC Radio 2, Michael Parkinson was introducing all the acts. I sang to close the first half of the show and Mr Parkinson just said, 'There is no way we can follow that, so, ladies and gentlemen, that is the end of the first half.' He also said to me, 'Long time, no see.' That was the closest I have ever come to being interviewed by him.

During the series, which ran in 1988, 1989 and 1991, along with a one-hour special in 1990, I also sang some of my own songs. It was great to be able to perform them on TV, but after a short while Tony Wolfe, the executive director, said he didn't want them. He wanted me to sing the songs that people knew, and do the impressions that the viewers wanted. He didn't see me as a singer-songwriter and I can understand that. That's not the reason I had been given the show. We were in a primetime slot and people wanted to hear what they already felt familiar with. I had been fortunate, I suppose, that I had the opportunity to at least try some of them out on a TV audience before Tony's decision.

I never really wanted to come out of a tunnel onto a stage. I was never really a dancer either, although if you watch any of the old programmes back then you will see that I could move – a bit. I have always been the man with the microphone. I can sing all that needs to be sung just like that. Just put one camera on me and I will interpret the song that will make you cry or smile. For me it's not about a lot of jumping about. It's all about giving me the microphone, the orchestra and the audience. I can do the rest – either as me or whoever you want.

We made some really good TV shows. Nigel Lythgoe certainly made them colourful and fun, and we never dropped below 11 million viewers throughout the run over the four years.

One of the really great things about making TV programmes is that they are opportunities for buying new clothes. I have always enjoyed clothes, right from trying on all of my granny's second-hand stuff from her shop, and when we were preparing for each series we would go off to Oxford Street. But I wasn't one of those who always wanted to get dressed up in different costumes every five minutes. I just wanted nice stuff, Armani, Boss, that kind of thing.

Of all my TV programmes, I particularly enjoyed the one-hour special in 1990. I didn't do a series that year. I think you can do so much more with a longer slot. When you're putting together a half-hour show for ITV, you've only really got twelve and a half minutes for each half, either side of the commercial break. There's no real chance to build much momentum into the programme. The special, which was broadcast on 25 April 1990, featured Grace Kennedy, who had just had a disco hit with 'Take It or Leave It', and I was really happy with the programme. It gave everything more room to breathe.

I really loved the recording of every one of my TV programmes and would dearly love to be back recording a show like they do now, such as *An Audience with...* We could really do something with that, and all of my friends in the business – including everyone from Barbara Windsor, Robbie Williams, Barry Gibb, Jimmy White, Ronnie Wood, Chris Evans, Jeffrey Archer, Engelbert Humperdinck, Phil 'The Power'Taylor, Liz Dawn and many more of them – would be great to have there. I'd definitely have Chubby Brown there too, although I don't think they would let him do a turn.

The Joe Longthorne Songbook was released for the Christmas market in December 1988, and reached number sixteen. It stayed on the Top Forty for twelve weeks, which is still my longest lasting album in the charts. It featured some of the songs I still sing today – 'To All the Girls I've Loved Before', 'Hurt', 'Danny Boy' and 'When Your Old Wedding Ring Was New' – and I was backed by some of the best in the business: Dave Arch on grand piano and keyboards; Brett Morgan and Mike Morris on drums; Chris Rae and Lewis Osborne on guitar; Trevor Barry on bass. These guys had all played in the thirty-two-piece band with me on the TV show. I have nothing against the musicians in the Midlands, where we filmed the show, but these fellahs who came up from London were the ones for me. They never played a single note out of place in any of my TV shows.

Two more Telstar releases came out the following year, with *Especially For You* released in July 1989, at the start of my second TV series. It spent ten weeks on the charts and reached number twenty-two. *The Joe Longthorne Christmas Album* followed later that year. They both went gold for me.

My last TV series, in 1991, featured Kelly Monteith and the

late Marti Caine. Unfortunately, dear Marti wasn't as lucky as I have turned out to be. She had lymphatic cancer and died in 1995. Here I am, still going strong over twenty-five years after having been diagnosed with it, and Marti has been gone for twenty years. Marti was a fabulously talented lady. I can't believe she's been gone that long.

I suppose the years of 1988-1991 could be seen as my TV years, but I was still playing live throughout that time too, and there were several really big shows that meant so much to me. Through my Friendship Club I held my first ever charity gala show to raise funds for the Leeds General Infirmary in 1989. It had suddenly become so important to me, and I have maintained the fundraising ever since.

The biggest show in my TV career came in 1989, when I appeared on the Royal Variety Performance at the Palladium. Even my mam was impressed! Her Royal Highness the Queen attended with the Duke of Edinburgh. I was on the bill with Tina Turner, Freddie Starr, Michael Ball, Jerry Lewis, David Essex and the cast of *Coronation Street*. There I was, just a cabaret act from Hull. You see, I've never forgotten my roots

CHAPTER NINETEEN

SYDNEY OPERA HOUSE

Even though I was waging a personal and constant battle with cancer in the early nineties, I was still riding on the crest of a wave. The TV shows were hits, the albums, while not being massive chart hits, were selling very well and eventually they went either gold or platinum, each making over 300,000 sales.

If I had been bothered about the money, I would be telling you now that I had lots of it and just how much I had, but truthfully I never really knew what I had. All I knew was that I was earning big fees wherever I went.

You might think that I was silly really, but I think we've already established that I'm not a money person, haven't we?

What I really needed around me was the team, the people I have around me today – James, Keith, John, John Boy, Mike and Christine, with Geraldine running the Friendship Club. But just at the time I needed it, the main people who had looked after me and guided me along the way were either going or gone.

I know a lot of people who have made it in show-business

will probably agree with me here that the bigger a celebrity you become, the more you seem to become surrounded by people who may only be looking to you as income for themselves. It is at times like these when you need people around you who you can confide in and are willing to help. Abdul, who was always a steadying influence, had always warned me about what would happen along the way.

Although my sound and lighting man, who had been with me since those clubland days, hadn't left just yet and Rita was still there too, they were both to move out of my life by the year 2000. The sound and light man was to leave in the early nineties, Rita later. I still miss all three of them – Abdul, Rita and him – very much indeed. They would always tell me what they felt, without any thought of money at all.

Mike Hughes had given up as my manager by now, and his business partner Tony Cartwright had taken his place. Tony was to land some good stuff for me, but looking back I think I would have preferred Mike to still be around.

Anyhow, with all of the media exposure I was getting and the money that was coming in, there still didn't seem to be too much of a problem. Within four years my career had spiralled, and it still didn't look too bad for a few years yet, but what I hadn't realised was that the seeds had been sown for my financial downfall. Of course, I didn't see it at the time. I'm a singer, an entertainer. I didn't have a crystal ball, contrary to what you might think about my Romany heritage.

I didn't know that in the coming years I was about to lose some of the good people I had known, loved and respected, people who had been with me every step of the way. I also didn't know that some of the people who were to be around me instead would not look after me as I had been looked after so far. I was to find out the hard way.

Much as I would like to, I cannot name all the names here for legal reasons, but they know who they are – the people who I believe took more than their fair share. They know they did. Cars were bought in my name and given to wives and girlfriends of those working for me; my 'signature' was being written on so many cheques, but not by me. I even saw what I was told later was £10,000 in 'walk-up' money (the cash generated on the night of a performance, rather than the advance ticket sales) on the bed of someone who was working with me at the time! There were far more stories like this, but because everything seemed to be going so well I let things pass.

The thing is that with all the money I was supposed to have earned from the TV contracts, the album sales and touring, I still didn't know how much I had. Little did I know that most of it I would never see, or be able to spend, because of the size of the bills coming in all the time. I really didn't know what was coming!

We'll come back to all that later, because right now we're heading for Australia. We're hopping about a bit here, but we're now in 1991 and we have come to New Zealand first and then on to Australia on the good ship *Canberra*.

By now my fame, from appearing on the Royal Variety Show a year and a half before and my TV shows, had obviously spread to Australia because I was signing autographs as we were getting off the ship. It was my first time down under and I've been back many times since.

We had managed to get an appearance on *The Ray Martin Show*, which at the time was Australia's biggest daytime TV show. My appearance, so I was told, had brought about the largest ever phone-in from viewers. They were so excited about it that they invited me back the next day. I ended up appearing on the programme four times that week. I've had a love affair with Australian audiences ever since.

The first time I ever saw the Sydney Opera House I knew I had to sing there. Call it another notch on a singer's bedpost if you like, but to me it was just somewhere I had to play. Ronnie Corbett and a lot of other big names from the UK were touring over there at the time. Everyone wanted to play this beautiful place.

When we visited the Opera House, I didn't have any of my own management or booking agents with me. I simply went to see the manager and asked how much it was to book it. I was told that it would cost AU$6,000, so I said, 'Here's £3,000 as a deposit. I'll be performing here one year from today.'

Apparently it caused quite a stir at the time. They were planning on having the Bolshoi Ballet and I'd gazumped them. I was told afterwards that there was all sorts of fuss going on, with people saying, 'Who's booked him in? Who's promoting it?' They made all kinds of objections but there was nothing they could do.

So we booked the Sydney Opera House, just by walking in and asking. That kind of thing just doesn't happen, does it? It will probably never happen again either, but we did it!

I had taken a big chance on booking it and now, for one night, the Opera House was mine. It was a bit like going up to the owner of the big wheel at a funfair and saying we'll book the lot for fifty quid!

The following year we went there and sold out all 2,600 seats. I took my band across with me and we tore the place apart. It was a gamble worth every penny.

But even then I had another little problem that needing sorting out. I was still battling cancer, but this time it was my hearing that needed surgery. This is how *The Sun* reported it while I was in Australia:

'I'm finished as mimic if ear op fails, by Joe' – Exclusive from Amanda Cable in Sydney, Australia. 'Comic singer Joe

Longthorne last night admitted that his showbiz career will be ruined unless surgeons are third time lucky in finding a cure for painful deafness in his left ear. Two operations to save his hearing have already failed. Joe, thirty-five, who nearly died two years ago from a rare blood cancer said: "My livelihood relies on listening to other singers and copying them to perfection. If I can't hear them properly or rely on my own impressions my career will be finished. I've always been slightly deaf in my left ear but the cancer made things worse. While I was weak a tiny hole in my eardrum grew bigger. By January this year I was totally deaf in that ear. The only sound I could hear was air rushing in as I breathed."

The top mimic who impersonates eighty-eight stars began slurring his speech, the first sign of deafness. Friends accused him of being drunk or snubbing them in public. Joe, whose one-man show is a hit at the Sydney Opera House, had surgery just before his sell-out summer season in Torquay. In a two-hour operation surgeons covered the hole in his eardrum with a minute graft. They ordered Joe to rest for a month – but he refused to disappoint his fans and went on stage. But his newly repaired eardrum ruptured during an impression of Luciano Pavarotti on his opening night. "I felt an agonising pain in my ear. The graft had ripped apart." An emergency operation repaired his shattered ear. But now the doctors say only a third operation will work. Joe said: "The deafness makes me afraid. I dread radio interviews because I can't hear the questions. I guess at the answers and pray that I'm not making a fool of myself."'

I'll tell you more about my ear later, but first a small, rather sad note, as I lost the man who had been with me through it all, from Hull to Jersey, travelling the UK, the States, TV, cancer.

My sound and lighting man and I were to finally part company in 1992, after seventeen years. I tried to get him to stay a number of times. We had done so much together, but the time had come for him to move on. He was always like family to me, but now he is family for real because he married my niece and together they have a lovely family of their own.

But 1992 was also to bring about the most bizarre approach I have ever had. You might not believe all I tell you, but this next bit is as unbelievable yet as true as they come! Stiff drink for me at this point please, nurse!

CHAPTER TWENTY

STANLEY KUBRICK

Summer season in 1992 saw me performing in both Paignton and Bournemouth. I was back on the south coast appearing with Roy Walker, Wayne Sleep and The Nolans. It was another big show and we were doing really well.

Now there are many famous names that have come to my shows over the years – stars of stage and screen, TV and film, sportspeople, politicians, famous people from London mobs, so I didn't think there was any real surprise in learning that another famous name had been to my show at Bournemouth International Centre, another lovely place to perform.

Stanley Kubrick, I had been told, not only liked my show, he also believed I would be ideal for movies. Of course, when you're already an established performer with TV credits to your name you do get approaches from time to time, so I was happy to meet him and talk about what we might do together.

Tony Hardman introduced Stanley Kubrick to me through

that wonderful actress Dora Bryan. This man was one of the most successful moviemakers of all time – he'd made *2001: A Space Odyssey*, *A Clockwork Orange*, *Spartacus*, *Full Metal Jacket*, and he was to go on to make *Eyes Wide Shut*. I'd just finished my TV series run. I was available.

So why was this American film director watching me in Bournemouth? Of course, there was no reason why he shouldn't.

Well, researching after the event, it turns out that Mr Kubrick lived in the UK for forty years, until he died in 1999. All I knew was that I had a film director, one of the most famous in the world, telling me that he could do great things with my career. I had to be interested. Who wouldn't be?

Only he wasn't Stanley Kubrick at all!

I didn't know at the time, but the real Kubrick was a bit of a recluse. So who was the man I had not only met, but whom I had also laid on one of my cars to ferry him about, and who I had ended up arranging hotel accommodation for? I'd also bought him clothes too. He conned me by saying things like he just didn't have any cash with him, and could I help out?

It turned out he was a very clever man called Alan Conway who ended up as an alcoholic, but who *The Guardian* dubbed 'the Counterfeit Kubrick'.

He would act as though he was on the phone with stars like Tom Cruise when he was in company with me. He persuaded not just me but several other influential people – some of them sports stars and one even a film critic in the US – that he was the man himself. I understand from a press report around the same time that Julie Walters was deceived too, but I'm not sure whether she had the same approach as me.

I went for a meal with him at a Chinese restaurant in London, which is where we found out that he wasn't who he said he was. I'd taken my lawyer, Russell Roberts from the solicitors Sheridan's, with me, and Zeb White, my tour manager by then, came too. Russell looked after me well.

When it came to the end of the meal I said that I would pay the bill but the Counterfeit Kubrick said he would pay. He paid by credit card. As we left the restaurant, Russell went back to ask whether he could have a look at the bill. What he saw on the credit card receipt was the name Alan Conway, so that's when we knew something was wrong.

Russell then contacted Warner Brothers and they confirmed that Mr Kubrick had not been in the vicinity of Bournemouth during the time I had been visited. So I'd been conned.

We received confirmation of this whilst we were on the train back to the south coast. It was like something out of an Agatha Christie story, which was quite appropriate because that summer season we happened to be stopping in the Agatha Christie suite in the hotel. Once we knew his real identity, the people around me took their own action. This didn't involve my solicitors, by the way. We chucked Counterfeit Kubrick into the sea at Paignton!

CHAPTER TWENTY-ONE

THIS IS YOUR LIFE

Tonight I'm going to a concert
To see a very special man.
He's tall, he's blond and handsome.
Joe Longthorne is his name.

I'm getting in a right old tizz
Deciding what to wear.
What dress? What jewellery? What shoes? What bag?
And, oh my God, my hair!
Now does my bag match the shoes?
Does the perfume smell too strong?
Oh my God, look at the time.
The taxi won't be long.

I gather things together
To put into my bag,
My keys, my purse and of course the ticket,
Then get into the cab.

Soon enough we're at the theatre.
The driver gets his fare.
I go into the "Ladies"
To readjust my hair.

I dash into the concert hall
And settle in my seat
To sit and enjoy, and swoon at Joe,
The guy I'd love to meet!
Maggie Prickett of Rushden, 'I'm Going to a
Joe Longthorne Concert'

Firstly, before we move on, thank you Maggie for such a lovely poem!

In 1993, there were still so many good things going on in my life. My first ever show in the Royal Albert Hall, on Sunday, 22 November 1992, had been a marvellous experience. It was yet another high point in my career. I received an excellent write-up in *The Stage*:

ROYAL ALBERT HALL – Joe Longthorne 'It is now over twenty-one years since Joe Longthorne first appeared on television as a fourteen-year-old in *Junior Showtime*. Since then he has made remarkable progress to become one of the world's greatest vocal impressionists and built up a tremendous following that includes a 3,000-strong fan club, many of whom – mainly female – were at this concert in force armed with flowers, balloons and even a banner inscribed "Hello Joe, Simply the Best." Joe Longthorne certainly believes in giving value for money. Opening with "Somewhere", it was an hour and three quarters later before he finally left the stage, his arms filled with flowers and the audience on their feet after his sensational Elvis Presley finish. All his big show stoppers were there: Tom Jones' "It's Not Unusual"; Neil Diamond's "Sweet Caroline"; Sammy Davis Jr.'s "What Kind of Fool Am I?"; Bassey; Sinatra; a moving tribute to the late Matt Monro; even Des O'Connor; and half the cast of *Coronation Street*; he also played piano for Jerry Lee Lewis' "Great Balls of Fire". Longthorne not only has an incredibly large number of impressions to draw on – they seem to include nearly every major star of show-business – but his main strength is the uncanny, consistent accuracy with which they are all performed. The musical backing, under the direction of pianist Ernie Dunstall was superb.'

Thank you to Michael Dynan, who wrote such a glowing report. There was a relative newcomer appearing as support act for me that night that you might just have heard about. His name? Bradley Walsh. I wonder where he ever ended up?

I was later to release both an album and a video of the show. It was amongst the first of many live albums, videos, CDs and DVDs that have been released since, and the CD was the first ever mainstream release to feature me doing my impressions of other singers.

I toured Australia for a third time. We were selling out everywhere and, despite the fact that I was still suffering through the cancer, my world hadn't come crashing down at all – not yet anyhow.

My fans have a lot to do with keeping my spirits up, whenever I have looked like flagging. They have always helped me through, whether by coming to the concerts or sending me letters.

I was also to spend one third of 1993 in the town that has since become my home. Our sixteen-week run at Blackpool's Opera House broke all box-office records and I'm told remains the biggest earning show that has ever played there. The takings were

£1.7 million. It was a fantastic run and I enjoyed every moment – apart from what I found out once it was over. I topped the bill and Little and Large appeared with me. It was a fantastic show.

At the end of a run like that you might have anticipated that I'd at least get around half of the overall monies after the theatre and the band had been paid, but all I ended up with was just £16,000 from a run that had grossed £1.7 million.

It was about now that I was starting to get the idea that things weren't working out on the money front. I asked a lot of people where all of the money had gone, but nobody could tell me.

I'd even been presented with a special award on stage from First Leisure to mark the box office receipts record, and yet this was all I had to my name at the end of it all. Where had it all gone?

The show had been tremendous and everyone had loved it. Some of my fans had been several times and I was feeling great. Any of those TV bosses who by now thought I might not complete another TV series, because of my fight against cancer, should have come to see me.

I'm told that was their main reason for not giving me another series, or even another one-off one hour special. And yet I was at my absolute peak at that time.

I find even an empty theatre fabulous. When you're in there on your own, you can just feel the spirits of those greats who have played there before you. It's magical. It's my home. Later in the year, my name was added to the Winter Gardens Roll of Honour of headline acts, which had also included Dana, Marti Webb and Paul Nicholas.

The core team around me at the time now included Tony Cartwright as my manager, Zeb White, my tour manager and sound and lighting man, and Darryl James on PR, along with the family, as always. My nephews John Boy, Keith and Derek, and my niece Keeley, were all around.

So how did I not end up with much at the end of the run?

Well, I suppose it was partly because I had people for this, people for that. But that doesn't explain everything. I don't think I will ever know, apart from that feeling I have of someone outside of my core team taking more than their fair share. I know those who I felt did, but I won't name them, like I said before.

At one time when we were on tour we had around sixty people involved and we were using a big tour bus. Turpin's was costing £2,000 a week and the bus was costing £400 a day. In retrospect, you could probably see what was happening. Everything costs money. But I wasn't on television any longer and I didn't have the same big contracts I once had, yet I was still living as though I had them.

My TV shows had brought about the three Telstar albums in 1988-89 and there were also three bestselling videos to come – *The Singer, The Very Best of Joe Longthorne* and *The Ultimate Collection* during the nineties.

But my TV series, after four glorious years of great viewing figures, was over. Although television was no longer to come knocking, this wasn't to be the end of my onscreen career, as 1993-94 saw not only the release of my new album in November, but also the production and subsequent release of my record-breaking show at Blackpool on video.

My new studio album, *I Wish You Love*, pleased me for several reasons. Firstly, I was now signed to EMI, the UK's biggest record label at the time, which Tony Cartwright had negotiated for me. Secondly, of the album's fourteen songs, nearly half were collaborations written by Ernie Dunstall, my musical director, and I. Ernie was one of the industry's best musical directors, and wrote songs with Dorothy Squires. Together we penned six. Ernie was a man who really cared about his craft. We released two singles from the album – 'Lady Blue', one of the songs written by Ernie and me;

and 'Young Girl', the song originally made famous by Gary Puckett and the Union Gap in the 1960s. 'Young Girl', in particular, was a fantastic production.

We had been recording the album during 1992 and 1993 at Chris Rea's studio in Cookham, Marlow (I also played with Chris Rae, who was a lead guitarist, but this was Chris Rea of *The Road to Hell* fame) and Cranbourne in Dorset. Zeb White had been the project coordinator for the album and my ex-sound and light man was the production consultant. The album also featured four songs that have remained a regular part of my shows to this day: 'So Deep is the Night', 'If I Only Had Time', 'Mary in the Morning' and 'Say it with Flowers'.

I might not have been beamed onto people's television sets any longer, but I was getting loaded onto them through their video players via the Telstar videos. At the tail end of my record-breaking run at the Opera House in 1993, I was approached by what now seems like one of the most bizarre of sources to make a video of one of my live shows.

A man from Yorkshire introduced himself to Zeb White after seeing one of my performances, but his only previous experience in the world of filming had been with birds! And we're not talking anything smutty here, because his experience was with the feathered variety. This Barnsley man was apparently one of the leading names in the pigeon-racing game, and until he approached Zeb he had never made a video of anything other than these birds. He had become a fan after bringing his wife to see the show.

He said he wanted to produce a video of the last in the run of shows at the Opera House. I remember being slightly apprehensive about allowing him to do it. After all, he had no track record in live entertainment, but he had said that if I didn't like what he filmed and how he recorded the show, then he would just bin it.

152

To be fair to this man – who is now no longer involved with me, hence no name – he produced a fantastic video of the very last night of my summer season, and it sold in massive quantities. He went on to produce several videos and DVDs of my live shows over the years.

The *Live in Concert* video, filmed at Blackpool in 1993, was eventually released by EMI in 1994 and reached number one in the video charts where it stayed for six weeks, my first chart-topper, and it was on the charts for eighty-one weeks. We knocked Take That off the top! We followed this up with the *Live at the Royal Albert Hall* video the following year, which reached number two. I then reached number one again in 1996 with *A Man and His Music*.

There were still so many good things happening for me recording-wise and concert-wise. 1994 didn't just see my first number one video; it also saw my *I Wish You Love* UK tour with a huge tour bus announcing, 'JOE LONGTHORNE IN TOWN, ON TOUR' all over the side; and then came another very special moment for me.

I was, in time-honoured tradition, surprised by Michael Aspel with his big red book, at the Manchester Apollo, announcing, 'JOE LONGTHORNE – *THIS IS YOUR LIFE*,' which was aired on ITV on 20 March.

It was one of the proudest moments of my life when Michael stepped out on stage at the end of my concert. I was amazed. I can honestly say I did not have a clue about what was going to happen. The whole occasion was like a dream, and what had happened didn't really sink in until I saw the TV recording of the show several weeks later. The evening itself was very moving and emotional – to walk out and see all my family and friends together was wonderful, and to share it with 3,000 people who had come to see me was just brilliant. Most of all, it was fantastic to be able to share the evening with Mam and Dad. I really feel it was as much their night as mine.

Roy Walker, Little and Large, Liz Dawn and Bill Tarmey were all on the show, along with Norman Collier, Bobby Bennett, Danny La Rue and Dr Childs. Those who couldn't make it but sent their best wishes on video were Les Dennis, Marti Caine and Jim Davidson. Ray Martin, from Australia, even appeared with all of the audience from his show that day.

Danny La Rue and I were good friends, and everyone should know that not only was he a great performer, he was also a marvellously warm and generous man. He really was in a class of his own. When he passed away in May 2009, it was yet another sad loss to the UK entertainment world. There really was nobody like him and probably never will be again.

Jim Davidson and I were mates long before we ever hit television, and he has been very good to me over the years.

The producers had also dug up a clip of me from *Junior Showtime* as a barrow boy, and ran a clip from my appearance as Dick Whittington in *Noel's House Party Pantomime*. They also played part of the video of Marti and I singing 'I'll Never Love This Way Again.' I auctioned off the big red book for charity on *Richard & Judy* and it raised a lot of money for leukaemia research, something like £7,000.

To see Mam's face radiating joy and happiness throughout the night was better than anything else. Don't get me wrong, it really was a wonderful evening and I thoroughly enjoyed every minute, but it is Mam's face that sticks in my mind even now. I know Dad enjoyed it very much too.

Dad even cracked a gag when Michael Aspel said he played the piano by ear. He said, 'Yes, I use my fingers sometimes as well.' They were both as proud as punch – and for Mam, I think it then made it official that I was a star.

Even then, there was still much more to come in 1994. I had returned to headline another successful summer season at the Futurist Theatre in Scarborough, and I had also recorded with two of the leading ladies in Britain's biggest soap operas. I sang a duet with Liz Dawn (Vera Duckworth from *Coronation Street*), who also came along and said some really nice things about me at a Variety Club award I received a few years ago. We sang 'Passing Strangers', which was released as a single and made the charts. We had a few other possible songs and nearly recorded 'These Boots Are Made For Walking', but Liz had already done 'Passing Strangers' previously so she was familiar with that one.

Then I received a call from Barbara Windsor (Peggy Mitchell in *EastEnders*), who asked me if I would sing a duet with her too. We sang 'They Can't Take That Away From Me' on Barbara's *You've Got a Friend* album. Both of these songs were featured in my *40th Anniversary (in Showbusiness) Collection* album, released in 2009.

And still that wasn't all. Although I no longer had my own TV series I was hardly being neglected, as I also appeared on Cilla Black's top-rated *Surprise Surprise* TV programme.

Even without my own TV show I was busier than I ever had been! In fact, thinking about it now it would have been difficult to have fitted in the TV schedule with everything else that had been going on. Barbara also made an appearance, by video, at my Variety Club awards evening on the same night as Liz. Then, right at the end of the year I also sold out the Royal Albert Hall once again.

But 1994, for all the touring and recording, plus the big red book surprise, was the year when the kind of mess I was in money-wise started becoming clearer. I still had no real idea, but others around me could see it.

At that stage I still didn't know that I was going to be declared bankrupt, I didn't think about it going that far. All I knew was that I was working hard and, when you work hard and you can see lots of people coming to your concerts, you don't worry about the money. I was also signed to a merchandising company called Sanctuary. Everything seemed to be going alright. But one thing I had found out was where some of the money was going.

I have to say here that my family have never been responsible for any of the financial mess I was in. They have always looked after me and I have always looked after them. If you come along to any of my concerts today, you will see just how well we all work together. James tells people that we're like a jigsaw, and that if one of us is missing then the whole thing doesn't look right, but at this time we had a lot of wrong jigsaw pieces, I guess.

The first time I truly realised that things were not good was when I found that I was getting overcharged. Over the years I have since found that people don't do it to you in one big lump: they take it from you bit by bit, say through a tour or two.

But I did not let one date down in 1994, despite still living constantly with CLL and enduring more treatment. I wasn't in remission, so I was still living with the fact that I had cancer and yet managing to fulfil every engagement.

Serious money was still coming in, but the problem was that it was going out just as quickly and bills were becoming bigger than they should have been. I will be the first to admit I had bought a big house that still needed paying for. I'd bought the Rolls Royces and the Bentleys. We were taking a massive bus all around the UK with an entourage of around sixty people – riggers, caterers, drivers, the band, and I was no longer getting the TV fees which I had been used to for the past four or five years. But that was still no excuse for people shafting me upside down. I felt that I was being conned, robbed by any number of those who thought they could get something out of me. And what's more, I felt I was being conned by some of the people who had been very close to me.

James always tells me that I was never robbed. He tells me that all people did was to overcharge me and that I have no concept of money, as I keep saying, and he's probably right. But that still doesn't stop me from thinking that I had been 'done'.

There was one man, someone who is now pretty well known in TV, who I have no respect for. I went to his office one day with Big Mick Johnson to have it out with him. Mick stands 6'7" tall. He's handy having around when you need someone who, just by his sheer size, can intimidate. This TV man had three or four Page Three girls there, all with their tits hanging out, but there was no sign of him.

I knew he had been there and was still around somewhere as soon as I stepped into his room. There was a warm cup of coffee, a half-eaten apple on his desk and a jacket on his chair. He owed me money. I'm sure he was on the f★★★ing roof. He wasn't even man enough to see me face to face! Come to think of it, maybe he is one of the reasons why I'm not on TV that much.

There were still a great deal of good things going on in my life at this time, but my world was soon to go through yet another calamitous period.

In the period of 1996-97, I was to be hit with three hammer blows – bankruptcy, the return of cancer and a nervous breakdown. I think we need a break before we tackle all of that, don't we?

CHAPTER TWENTY-TWO

DRUGS
AND FIGHTS

Let's turn to drugs, stealing and fighting. And let's also throw in a few shotguns too – not mine, in case you're starting to get concerned. But before we get into it too much, let me say that no, some of this does not make me very proud, but if someone attacks any of my family I will not just stand around and watch things happen.

I said I'd tell you everything here in this book, didn't I? Apart from one or two names and allegations that cannot be printed for legal reasons, I'm not about to pull any punches either.

Yes, I have done lots of drugs. I have gambled. I have been in fights. I do still smoke, and I have always liked a drink or three.

Frank Sinatra once said about smoking, 'You die your way, I'll die mine.' Actually I've never been a great smoker, I've always dragged a bit behind!

Performance-wise, let me get one thing straight as well. I never have a drink before I go on to do a show. I might have done years ago, but I never do that now. When I get to a theatre,

I like to arrive fresh and ready to get on that stage. That's one of the reasons why I sometimes don't arrive at a venue until twenty minutes before I'm due to go on. I know there are some of my fans that still get worried when I haven't arrived and yet the interval is already underway, but I make sure that I am fit and ready, and that I look good when I go onto that stage. After all, the people who have come to see me have been home, had a shower and made themselves look good to come out for the night. So drinking is out of order until after the show.

But what about those other things? What about the drugs?

I've been on drugs since 1988, when I was first diagnosed with CLL, but in all honesty I had been dabbling with all sorts of drugs for years, mainly marijuana ever since I was in my teens, like many people of my age. I was tripping on LSD when I was seventeen in a local pub. I was doing two bottles of cider a night at sixteen. And I was driving home each night as well. I'm not advocating drugs, or drinking and driving, I'm just telling you what happened to me.

When I was living in Cranbrook Drive some 'friends' gave me speed; they put it in my tea and I became hooked on it for awhile. It was like jumping powder to me. I was off the rails every other night. I took it to keep me up, keep me going. I was doing cocaine and experimenting with lots more in the eighties too.

But you know, there's no drug in the world – including alcohol or nicotine –that can take the place of audience applause and the love and warmth I receive from everyone, but as soon as I come off that stage it's different. For a number of years I needed something to help keep me up on that adrenalin high for longer after finishing a show, and when I was at my busiest in years gone by I started taking more and more silly stuff.

I was doing Temazepam and things like that. It's now a class-A drug and you can only use it if it has been prescribed. It's a killer otherwise, and it's now banned from general usage. All of these drugs have been produced for very good reasons in the first place, and Temazepam is meant to help those with insomnia, or who are feeling overanxious, for short periods.

I would come off the stage having played to 2,000 people all standing and cheering, and there in the wings would be one of the people looking after me at the time with what they used to call 'wobbly eggs'. Each one contained twenty milligrams in liquid form, and the idea was I would take them to calm me down, because coming crashing down from the high of the applause, the standing ovation, to nothing once I'd finished was too much for me. I'd come off, insist that I had them, go back on for the encore and then, halfway through the last song, I was gone. They were all prescription drugs. Nothing was purchased on the black market.

All I do these days is smoke a little marijuana and have a beer at the end of each performance, because it relaxes me. I did an interview on the radio recently and said that I'd taken drugs purely for their medicinal purposes – but you know that was really just an excuse, it really was.

So what about my fighting?

Yes, I got into fights at school, like quite a few kids do. And yes, I did sort out Pancho when he messed up my act in Jersey – and yes, I was involved with the affray that saw me fly back from the States to appear in court. But I've had a few more hairy moments than just those.

There was one occasion when I didn't exactly fight, but I really thought I was going to land myself in deep trouble. I was seventeen at the time and should have known better.

I've never thieved at all, apart from one time when I took a torch from a shop as a kid and Mam knew straight away. Mams do, don't they? Actually, it might have had something to do with me having left it switched on underneath my jacket as well. Not very bright – although the torch was. Too bloody bright in my case!

But I came very close to being branded as a thief on one occasion when I was seventeen. A mate of mine at the time said, 'Come on Joe, we're going to go shopping.'

We went to one of Hull's big department stores. What I didn't realise was that he wasn't talking about buying anything. I found out later that my mate was what we call, in cant, a 'chorer' (Romany for thief), but honestly, on my life I didn't know what was going on. It was only when I was asked to be a lookout that I realised something wasn't right. By this time they were on with the 'hoisting'. I decided I had to get out of there, as I didn't want to be arrested for something I hadn't meant to be involved with.

I panicked and ended up throwing a guy out of the way as I got out of the store. I'd never been involved in anything like that. When I was out on the cart with my dad I'd never taken anything that people didn't want taken from their homes, and I didn't intend getting caught up in what I now knew was happening in the department store.

The man I'd thrown out of my way fell down the stairs and, although I didn't give much of a thought to him at the time, I hope he turned out okay. But really, all I wanted to do was get out of there. I didn't get out of it altogether though. I had been spotted.

I know this next bit sounds a bit daft and typically, comically me, but because I felt like I was on the run I dyed my hair from blond to black so I wouldn't be recognised. It didn't make any difference. I was still arrested, and it was as though I was admitting that I was guilty because I'd dyed it. The case ended up getting kicked out of court. It did frighten me though.

If I hadn't been frightened enough about possibly being sent down, the incident that took place down in London, which I'll tell you about next, really did frighten me. I was doing a gig in a pub I believe was called The Feathers, somewhere in London. I'm on stage singing 'Danny Boy' when all of a sudden these cars go past and shoot all of the windows out. I just carried on singing. The landlord gave the band another £150 that night, and we carried on for a while longer. And you think that kind of thing only ever happens in films!

That's the shooting over – now back to the fighting, although this is more comical than anything else.

I was back over in Hull about six years ago. There was a lovely karaoke session going on in this pub and I got up to do 'Strangers in the Night'. Then there was a bit of pushing and shoving. I thought nothing more of it.

I went outside to have a smoke, and the next thing I know there is this woman coming out of the pub, and all I see is a load of flailing black hair coming towards me. She's built like a f***ing Chieftain tank. I weigh 10st 8lbs. I can't say what happened next. Well I could, but it's probably better that I don't.

I love going back to Hull, to Hessle Road, to the pubs I used to sing in. I have a very loving family that all want me round at their houses, but I won't stop going into those pubs, it doesn't matter what happens. I love Hull, it's my hometown and it's wonderful how it has come on in recent years.

That's pretty much my fight history by the way – a few knockouts, no defeats, a few near misses. Well, I should say that's all apart from one, the big one that really did see me end up in court. We'll leave that for now and come back to it later in real detail.

CHAPTER TWENTY-THREE

BANKRUPTCY

It's funny, you know, but nervous breakdowns creep up on you. They certainly did with me. It's not just one thing. A lot of things all come on top of each other. For me it was a combination of bankruptcy, chemotherapy, drugs, money troubles, and also a car crash. They make for a pretty unhealthy cocktail.

In 1995 I'd been really busy touring as usual. There was the release of the *Live at the Royal Albert Hall* video, and in September I took part in a gala tribute to Lord Delfont in aid of the Entertainment Artistes Benevolent Fund, along with Aled Jones, The Grumbleweeds and Cannon and Ball.

I was also to meet one of the entertainment world's all-time greats. It was yet another fabulous moment in my career when I performed for the legendary, iconic comedian Bob Hope, backstage at a special night in his honour at the Palladium. Danny La Rue and Roger Whitaker were also on the bill. It was on behalf of one of Mr Hope's big golf charity nights. Afterwards, he told me how much he had enjoyed my performance and even invited me over to his home in Palm Springs.

I never took him up on his offer, but I did have a photograph taken of Mr Hope and I together. I was so proud to have been invited to perform in front of one of the biggest names ever in showbiz.

During all of this time and ever since I was first diagnosed with CLL, I had been raising funds for Leeds General Infirmary in order to help those with cancer. Little was I to know how hard CLL would come back to haunt me in the coming years. The disease really is a f***ing nightmare.

First though, it was my financial troubles that were increasing. Back in 1995 I had a house, Turpin's, that I still hadn't paid for and that was now costing me a great deal to keep up with the payments, I had massive expenses to pay out for a number of people who were overcharging me, and the money that was now coming in without the fat cheques from TV contracts was never going to be enough to pay all of the bills. It was all starting to make me ill.

Even so, I still didn't realise I was heading for bankruptcy. I was too busy taking drugs to calm me; drugs to keep me up; drugs for my cancer; drinking and smoking. I was putting so much up my nose at the time that it wasn't to be sniffed at!

When I did realise that bankruptcy was on the way, and that I couldn't spend anything because I didn't have anything, it was bloody awful. I was falling apart at the seams. So much for sex and drugs and rock 'n' roll!

Earlier, I talked about whether I'd ever lost the plot. This was the time. And just at the time I was starting to feel really bad, things were about to get a whole lot worse than they had ever been. The years of inflated costs and buying expensive items like cars and the house had now caught up with me.

It still didn't stop me from just popping into Harley Street one day though, as you do! The next bit is pretty funny. You've got to laugh, haven't you?

BANKRUPTCY

I had some bags under my eyes, or felt I did, and decided I wanted them sorting out. I also had my teeth sorted out around the same time. Anyway, let's talk about the eyes!

I'd been told that an operation to get my eyes fixed, to remove a bit of fat, would cost £1,500 and I took the money with me. They were putting me under the anaesthetic, but just before I went to sleep they told me they needed another £1,500. It was £1,500 per eye!

Jokingly, I said, 'I thought you did a two-for-the-price-of-one in an afternoon?' But they weren't joking. So I had to get onto Snowy, my man with the money at the time, who sent someone on a bike with the rest of the money in ten minutes. Eye-eye!

I was still touring all around the UK in 1996, and I made an appearance on the TV show *This Morning*. But, just five years on from my last TV series, only three years on from box-office record takings at the Blackpool Opera House, several gold and platinum-selling albums, two number one videos, and with one of them at the top of the charts at the time, I was now bankrupt!

CHAPTER TWENTY-FOUR

NERVOUS BREAKDOWN

At the meeting of the creditors I was told my total debt was £1.4 million, and that with interest it was going up day by day. The meeting had been arranged by Segal and Co. to try and arrange a VCA (Voluntary Creditors Agreement). The receivers wanted something like £15–£20,000 themselves before we even started on the rest. The Bentleys and Rolls-Royce cars had to go.

Darryl James was claiming from me; so was Bridie Reid and Sheridan's; there were quite a few more at the meeting. I couldn't believe how much was being claimed, but then again I hadn't ever realised just how bad things were. I knew now. I guess it was another case of me not knowing what was going on.

The taxman was the biggest one of the lot. Apparently, I owed £400,000 to the Inland Revenue.

I didn't want to sit in front of all these people, all looking at me, a lad from Rifle Terrace and Woodcock Street in Hull, and seeing what had come of all my hard work. I walked through the room. I wasn't going to stay. Andrew Segal, the official receiver, said, 'Joe, you've got to meet them all face to face.' But it was a bit like going into the lion's den. So I didn't stop. I just couldn't.

Rita was still at Turpin's and she offered great advice. My friends were still with me after all. And so were my family. The only thing they can ever be guilty of is sometimes going maybe a bit too far in order to look after me, like my dad used to do in my early days around the working men's clubs.

Big Mick was there too. Big Mick Johnson is another of my relations and has been around for me many times over the years. I introduced him earlier, when I visited the TV producer who I cannot name, the one who left his half-eaten apple on the table and scarpered to the roof. Mick's a traveller, lives in the south of England and has a heart of gold. He took the horses when we finally left Turpin's a few years later.

Although I'm not too attached to possessions, I must admit I was starting to think that the house would have to go. I wasn't bothered about the swimming pool or the recording studio or anything like that, but I was worried for the animals. That was the most upsetting part. I felt I had let down my animals, particularly my horse Lady Blue and a trotter I had at the time, but the pigs, the chickens and the dogs too. Walking around, seeing wildlife like the badgers and being on my own was my only real solace at Turpin's, like I said earlier, and now that all looked like it was going.

That's when it all dawned on me. It wasn't about losing the house, or how big the house was. That's when my tears fell. To see my horses have to walk out and go somewhere else was soul destroying.

I really didn't understand what was going on and it was messing with my head, to say nothing of the drugs. I knew that if I lost Turpin's I would miss my animals, my walks around the land, my Vietnamese deer. I thought about the pond, how beautiful it was. So it wasn't the possessions that were bothering me, it was the beauty of nature. This was my place where I could relax. It was my retreat where I could get away from everyone else. It was all going to have to go.

Turpin's was once featured on David Frost's *Through the Keyhole* programme. The late Richard Whiteley got it in twenty-eight seconds, bless him. He knew it was my place straightaway. I got the key that they used to give out. Now I thought I might have to give the key to the house away for real.

But Turpin's was saved for a while when a good friend from north London, Fred Nash, who was a member of a powerful business organisation and who is a very cool operator, said he would buy Turpin's when he needed to and let me stay there. 'Just keep up with your monthly payments, Joe,' is what he told me.

We kept the payments going for awhile. Turpin's was costing me £6,000 a month by then. And how did I do it? I carried on playing the concerts. I carried on touring. It's all I know and it's what I do. I've never really changed over the years. All I've probably done is matured, hopefully, as a singer and a person. I've tried to make a few shillings singing songs. To me it's still like it was when I started. I'm still singing for those fish and chips for Mam and Dad, John, Lizzie and Anne.

At that time though, it wasn't so easy to just keep going as there was so much going on in my head, either with the drugs that were helping me when I came offstage or those that were keeping me alive.

I know now that I didn't have any money, or at least what I was bringing in was only enough to keep paying what was outstanding already. Bankruptcy, or even the sniff of it, also gives the newspapers another opportunity to write about you – and of course they did, that's their job.

As I keep coming back to in this book, it is also my fans as well as my family who have always been there for me. You're going to hear that a few times more yet. They have always helped me so much that it doesn't matter what I have gone through. I had one group of fans who, at the time, were going to club together and get me out of bankruptcy. I am sure they would have done too, but that would have killed me.

They did send me money. I had to get them to stop. I really appreciated their words and gestures, but it's not what I'm here for, to be bailed out by the people I sing for – although I don't mind the odd M&S voucher!

I went broke and that's it. Willie Nelson went broke too. Lots of other singers have gone through bankruptcy. I wasn't the first and I don't suppose I'll be the last.

Some took what they could from me, that's my feeling – more than their fair share, but they couldn't take my voice and they never took my grand piano! It was a good job they didn't too, because that's where we'd hidden the money – in the piano legs! That's a joke, by the way, if the taxman's looking at this book.

Sure, I went broke, but it didn't change me, the person that I am.

Looking back, with the benefit of hindsight, it's no wonder that bankruptcy was going to come up. You cannot spend the way I was spending, or having the expenses I was carrying with the band, the tour bus and everything else that comes with it, unless you know that your earnings are going to be massive every year.

I was down, seriously depressed. It was as though I was banging my head against a brick wall. It seemed as though everything I was doing, everything I had done, counted for nothing. Apart from my family and Rita, there was nobody I could trust, nobody who was really looking after me.

Over a period of time I had now become really ill and couldn't afford to even pay household bills, let alone afford luxuries. I just didn't want to go out. It was a time when, for the first time in my life, I didn't want to be in front of lots of people.

My depression got worse and, for quite some time, I couldn't move and just stared into space all day. I was like a zombie. My fans knew that I was going through a bad time and they continued backing me. I did get bags of fan mail but I couldn't even bear to read any of it. I appreciated it though, everyone was meaning well, but by then I just wasn't right. I was too far down the road.

I overdosed.

I woke up in High Wycombe hospital, not knowing how I'd got there. I only spent two nights in the hospital, but that wasn't the end of my downward spiral.

Back at Turpin's, with me staring into space, my sister Anne was well aware I still wasn't right. I couldn't perform and I was in a terrible state, but my family looked after me, thank God, because right at that time, for the first time in my life, I just did not want to live. It was Anne who started dragging me out of it.

My GP paid me a call. I think Anne or Rita must have called for him to come, and he told me of his psychiatrist friend who flew planes. He tried to persuade me to let him refer me to the Cardinal Clinic in Windsor, where this psychiatrist practised.

I was as low as I could go. All I remember is that at one point I took some pills to help me sleep, and three days later I woke up in the clinic. Apparently, I had to be put in there forcibly, but I cannot remember a thing, only what I have been told since. The Cardinal Clinic in Windsor is a bit like the Priory is today. I was now officially having my nervous breakdown.

Finally, the pressure of what I had been going through – starting probably as far back as 1988, when I had first found out about having CLL – had got to me. But I'm a fighter. I do fight my way out of situations and, with the help of the wonderful people at Cardinal, I was able to do just that.

They started getting me right again. I tried escaping at first but then I started to come round. I was only in four days but in that time they helped me considerably. They made me start thinking for myself again, telling me that if I fell out of bed during the night they weren't going to pick me up. It was up to me. It was good psychology and set me back on the right road.

Michael Barrymore got to hear about the rough time I was going through and said, 'Come on mate, I want you on my show.' I told him that I didn't know whether I could make it because I was nearly dead. You can tell how bad I must have been, can't you?

At that time I was in a wheelchair, and I was in that bad a state that Keith had to push me around. When I got to the studio and they saw how I looked, I think they were shocked. I don't think they could believe what they were seeing.

Fortunately for me, it was Nigel Lythgoe who was producing Michael's show at the time and I believe it was Nigel who said, 'Look at him. It's not Joe.' If it had been anyone who hadn't known me, I don't think they would have even allowed me to go on.

I just looked at them and said, 'Put me on a stool and I'll sing whoever you want me to sing.' I did Johnny Mathis and Shirley Bassey. Then I sang one song as me, which was 'How Do You Keep the Music Playing?' Honestly, I don't think I have ever sung it better in my life, I put so much into it.

When it came to the show itself they put me at the bottom of the bill, which was absolutely right. I really wasn't fit enough to do a complete act. They didn't use the impressions, but they did use me singing as me and I still got my seven large (£7,000) appearance money. I needed every penny. That was a month's rent sorted.

Michael and Nigel were great in doing that for me, and so was Keith for encouraging me. God bless Michael for giving me the chance and God bless Nigel for paying me top money. It really boosted my confidence. Getting me back in front of a TV audience was just the thing I needed to get me going again. I am really an eternal optimist and they both helped in getting me back to normal. Thanks again, Michael and Nigel, wherever you are and whatever you are doing.

I have never been short of offers to sing, it doesn't matter whether I have been bankrupt, at death's door or whatever. And at the same time as I was going bankrupt, I was paid £64,000 to play Caesar's Palace – unfortunately not in Vegas, but in Luton. Once again, I didn't think about the money too much, even though it was good and welcome. I just like the audiences. It was for four nights and I only sang for forty minutes each night. My receivers even offered me £2,500 just to do a show on a boat in the Thames!

There was some good news as well though. In 1997 I was given the all-clear from cancer. After having come through the Cardinal Clinic as well, it meant I was clean both in my head and in my body. I played a summer season at the North Pier in Blackpool with George Marshall and Wayne Dobson. But how wrong can one man be sometimes? You'll find out.

Let's have another of those breaks, shall we? I know I could do with a drink after all of that. Bet you could too.

CHAPTER TWENTY-FIVE

IMPRESSIONS

I live for singing in front of people. I always have. It's where I come alive and everything else is just a prelude to that. You can see the change in me once I'm there, under the lights. Performing live on stage in front of an audience is the greatest experience I can ever get. I live to perform. Sure, I live to make CDs, DVDs, appear on television, but there's nothing on earth that matches the feeling I get when I walk out on stage. To be with an audience is something else. There is an unbelievable rush of adrenalin, a buzz of energy.

To me it's like a love affair, the audience and me together as one. It's all about love and communication – and this is where I communicate.

I'm really still doing what I have always done, right from singing on my mam's knee or for all the children at play school, outside the fish and chip shops, on tables in pubs or on a fold-down stage from a trailer at East Park in Hull.

My singing has given me everything I've ever had. Forget about the bad times, they've been and gone. I've had far more wonderful and exciting moments than I ever had bad, even though I've had my fair share of those.

There are times, and I'm sure most live entertainers would say this, where the audience sends you into another gear, something you hadn't realised would happen. That's still so exciting today, as much as it ever has been, whether it's the reaction to my hands being spread and my eyes rolling around in my head when I do Shirley, or whether it's the gyration of my hips when I go into Tom.

Which quite neatly, I think, brings me back to the impressions and how wonderful they have been to me. Without them I wouldn't have come this far in show business. They have been my passport to success wherever I have gone, and they are still doing the same for me today.

It's always been that way, and that's why I will be forever grateful to Mam for setting me on the right course when I was a little boy. My impressions get my foot through the door, and once I've done that the audience then gets to hear what I'm really like as a singer in my own right. The impressions are like my Trojan horse for getting me in anywhere, and then I storm their castle with the rest of my act. It's beautiful when it happens that way.

Sometimes when I'm in a theatre, like I said previously, I can really feel the spirits of those performers who have played there in years gone by. The world-famous London Palladium is steeped in show-business history, and when I step onto that stage I can feel the spirits of those legendary entertainers – Frank Sinatra, Danny Kaye, Judy Garland, Sammy Davis Jr., Ella Fitzgerald, Johnnie Ray. I've had some amazing nights there, and none more so than when I appeared there in 2006.

I often think that if I'd taken up purely singing straight rather than performing the impressions, I would have been more

CITY AND COUNTY OF KINGSTON UPON HULL

Win

PARKS DEPARTMENT
(Entertainments Section)

Presents the

GRAND FINAL

of the

1969
TALENT
COMPETITION

in the

CITY HALL

on

WEDNESDAY, 10th SEPTEMBER
at 7.30 p.m.

OFFICIAL PROGRAMME 6d.

NAME: JOE LONGTHORNE
AGE: 17 YRS OLD

Has appeared on Yorkshire Television in
Junior Showtime with many stars like
Bobby Bennett, Ringo Starr, Lulu, Dickie
Henderson, the Hollies etc.
Was also voted The Top Teenage Artist of
Hull and the East Riding of Yorkshire.
Has also done cabaret with stars like
Bobby Bennett and Norman Collier.
His act includes comedy, vocalist and
impersonations. A great worker who enjoys
his work.

Enquiries to: -

Joe Longthorne
Teenage Star
39 Woodcock Street
Hull

Telephone: - Hull 28781

WALKER
PHOTO BIOGRAPHY CARDS
01-636 8550

Above left: 'Look at the camera please, Joe!'

Above right: Off we go. My win in the Parks Department talent competition
helped launch my career.

Below: I have to thank my Dad for this great early publicity.

Above left: 'How much is that Joey in the window?'

Above right: In the studio working on my first album *Songbook*.

Below: I've always loved animals, and given them a home when I can. Here I am with Sugar, Rosie, Bill and Ben.

Above: This is what I call a proper day out – working with TV producer Nigel Lythgoe.

Below left: No wonder I'm smiling. I'm in the middle of my eighteen-week record-breaking run in Blackpool in 1993 at the Blackpool Opera House.

Below right: An early visit to New Zealand in the 1980s. You can see the *Canberra* in the background.

Patrons
Her Majesty The Queen
Her Majesty Queen Elizabeth The Queen Mother

we the undersigned
tender our sincere congratulations to

Joe Longthorne

on being one of the

representative artistes selected to appear before

Her Majesty The Queen

on the occasion of the

The Diamond Jubilee of The Royal Variety Performance
held at

The Palladium, London, on Monday, November 20th 1989
the performance being in aid of the Entertainment Artistes' Benevolent Fund

Life President   Hon. Chairman   Hon. Treasurer   General Secretary

Left: Performing in front of royalty was a wonderful, joyous occasion.

Right: What a shock! It was an honour to be on *This Is Your Life*.

Left: Lord Attenborough and my own dear mother Teresa at a charity event.

Right: Bullseye.
My dear friend Phil
'The Power' Taylor.

Left: You will never
guess where I was!

Right: My sisters, brother
and mother just before
my bone marrow
transplant for CLL.

Above left: Being presented with the Variety Club's Silver Heart Award was a happy, proud moment.

Above right: A day at 11 Downing Street to meet the Chancellor of the Exchequer, George Osborne.

Below left: My long-time partner James and myself during a trip to Lourdes.

Below right: At home with my baby grand piano.

Left: Have dressing room, will travel.

Right: Meeting HRH The Prince of Wales in December 2012.

Left: This was a trip to Downing Street for a charity reception for the Community Foundation for Lancashire.

Above: James and I at Buckingham Palace.

Below left: My mother, Teresa Longthorne – 'If only I could see her now, how happy I would be.'

Below right: Unconditional love!

disciplined as a singer. That's because with impressions you can always mess about a bit and make people laugh, and I've always enjoyed the freedom of that.

I love doing Shirley.

What I mean is that I have always loved her music and I hope my performance is seen as a tribute to her. Let's correct what I feel about her: I don't just love her, I adore her. To me, Dame Shirley always has been, and still is, just absolutely sensational.

There was a time when I understand that Shirley said – and I really do hope she said it this way, because it would mean so much to me – 'He does me better than I do myself.' My impression, while it does also get some laughs in the way I exaggerate some of her mannerisms, is always meant with real, unbounded affection.

Dame Shirley is by far the greatest female singer we have ever had in the UK, and you can hear some of her singing style in quite a number of the songs I perform as myself. I haven't talked with her very often but we have spoken in the past. I don't think there will ever be a time when I feel there isn't a part of Shirley in the way I perform. That first Shirley Bassey LP I bought back in 1968 was what started it all for me, in terms of my stage impressions.

Frank Sinatra came to me at around the same time. 'Strangers in the Night' had just become a big hit for him, and I could do his voice too. I ended up doing the whole of the main three in the Rat Pack – Sammy, Deano and Frank.

Sammy Davis Jr. is probably the most complete entertainer there ever has been. He was so special. He could do impressions, sing fantastically well as himself, play instruments and dance. The only one of those that I can't really do is dance.

One of my fans contacted me to say they recall having a conversation with my dad, who told them a funny story about me. Apparently, Dad had told them he once dropped me off for a dancing lesson but I didn't want to go, so I went in, then climbed out of a toilet window and went straight back home.

What actually happened was that Jess Yates (*Junior Showtime*) had mentioned to my mam that I could do with some dancing lessons, so she had taken me. Jess used to always send telegrams. She says that I lasted five minutes before coming out of the backdoor of the dance class and telling her I didn't want to be in there. I was no Billy Elliott. That was something Jean Pearce had known all along.

I might not have taken to dancing, but I have always thrown myself totally into all of my impressions and those who come to my concerts will know just how many I have done over the years. They run into the hundreds, not just singers but anyone: I've done snooker players, like Alex 'Hurricane' Higgins, Frank Spencer from *Some Mothers Do 'Ave 'Em*, Rigsby from *Rising Damp*.

My *Steptoe and Son* routine has always remained a favourite, but I particularly enjoyed the snooker routine I used to do a few years ago. I've always enjoyed putting lots of different personalities together and in recent years I launched a brand new routine revolving around David Dickinson's *Real Deal* TV programme.

Keeping up with current trends and what's happening in the entertainment scene is important, but people also want what they know and what they've liked for years. I have been told recently that Robbie Williams likes what I do, and I admire his work too. He has his own unique style so maybe I'll add him to my repertoire of 'special guests' in my shows. I really enjoy the work he has done. David Gest told an audience at a show I was in a couple of years ago that he and Michael Jackson had also watched some of my shows on DVD together.

As I've already mentioned earlier, I got rid of the props a while ago. Occasionally I've brought them back over the years, but I don't use them at all now. I just found that sometimes they were getting in the way of the impressions. I prefer to put myself fully into the character and I find I can do that, immersing myself in the person I am doing for two minutes, rather than fiddling around for props.

What I can tell you, though, is that, props or no props, I would not have had the success I've had without my impressions. I will forever be in the debt of Shirley, Tom, Frank, Deano, Sammy, Judy Garland, Tony Bennett, Neil Diamond, Barry White, Johnny Mathis, Barry Manilow and all of the rest of my 'guest stars' in my shows.

Right – after bankruptcy and a nervous breakdown it's time for some good news in my story, don't you think? Let's see...

CHAPTER TWENTY-SIX

JAMES
AND PAT

L ife has certainly played some funny games with me along the way and surely, after the bankruptcy meeting, trying to avert what seemed inevitable and the nervous breakdown, there had to be some good news on the horizon?

1998 proved to be a year of fresh starts for me, a time when several new people entered my life, and two in particular who I have every reason to be thankful for – my partner James and my very good and close friend Pat Mancini MBE, who is sadly no longer with us.

But you're not getting away with it that easily, because it wasn't a year without incident either!

During the time of my nervous breakdown, both before and after the four days I spent in the Cardinal Clinic, I must have gone at least six months without performing except for the appearance on Michael Barrymore's show. I just couldn't. Life was really that bad for me. But in 1998 I got back underway. I played a series of sell-out concerts at the legendary Green Room in the Café

Royale in Regent Street, and appeared on the *Sunday Night at the Palladium* TV show once again, also produced by Nigel Lythgoe.

I seem to recall that Nigel said to me at the time, 'Joe, for once will you do it my way?' I thought he'd meant sing 'My Way', so that's what I did.

One very famous name saw me for the first time when I played the Café Royale. Although I didn't know it at the time, he was to pay me the biggest of compliments many years later. Intrigued? Well, you'll just have to wait.

It was also the year when Garry Bushell, the TV pundit, started bashing away with stories to get me back on television. He was highly complimentary and even suggested where I should fit into any TV schedule. He reckoned I'd be great at around 10pm: 'Who other than a TV executive could wilfully ignore someone like Joe Longthorne? The greatest singing impressionist England has ever produced, and a seriously world class singer and funny too, in favour of yet another programme with people who just read from autocues.'

Garry did mention some names at this point, but I didn't think it was fair to include them here. Garry has since become a great friend and he is still telling everyone that I should be back on screen with my own programme. Who knows? Maybe this book will do some good.

You know, deals for things can be done in some strange places. Have you ever done a deal on a roundabout? I have. Well, it was actually on the revolving stage at the Palladium. It feels as though I've been on quite a few roundabouts in my life.

Another great friend of mine is funny man Johnnie Casson. He's an absolutely superb comedian and we were both on this revolving stage, appearing as part of Bruce Forsyth's seventieth birthday show. On the bill with us were M People, Danni Minogue and the star of the show, Miss Diana Ross. It was Sunday, 15 March 1998.

As the stage was moving around, Johnnie and I were talking and I asked him whether he fancied doing the next summer season with me in Blackpool. I didn't know Johnnie particularly well at that time, although I had met him years before when he was drummer with The Diamond Boys at Keighley Variety Club. He had made his name on TV's *The Comedians* show, but had also played with another very popular band called The Crestas, who once opened for The Beatles.

We did the deal there and then, whilst the wheel was going around! Johnnie is now one of my best pals and we're currently appearing on tour together as I write these words. He really is a diamond himself, such a generous and unassuming man. He can make me laugh at the slightest thing.

I was still living at Turpin's. Rita was still around too, but we were nearing the end of our time together. It seemed like she had always been around, helping me out of situations, offering advice. She was always there to come back home to.

I had enjoyed living in this fabulous house in Berkshire, but I hadn't enjoyed some of the paparazzi or some of the people who just wanted to see where I lived. I'll always try my best to have a nice chat with someone, but my privacy was constantly being invaded.

More and more people were coming to Turpin's to have a look, often using a neighbour's garden to get closer. In the end I had the view into my land from his blocked off. The neighbour concerned became a bit stroppy and told me I'd spoilt his view. I just told him he needed to understand that, every time I went out for a walk, there were camera flashes going off. 'I can't have it,' I told him, and went on to say that I reserved the right to put up a fence.

He had been a flight bomber, some sort of squadron leader, and gave me that 'Do you realise who I am?' routine. I just told him straight, no airs and graces, 'No sir, but I know I'm proud to be a traveller.' I felt sorry that I'd rowed with him. He'd been decorated for his services during WWII, like my dad. However, he still went to the newspapers about the fence. He also went to Esther Rantzen and her TV programme, *That's Life*.

That was hardly the big incident though. That's still to come.

When I came up to Blackpool that year I had no money. All I had once again were pretty much the clothes I stood up in and whatever I would earn during the season. And most of that was going towards paying the monthly rent at Turpin's.

I stayed in Great Eccleston at digs, about six miles away from where I was appearing. I stayed on a farm with a man who became a really good friend, 'Tatie Alan' (Alan Thomasson). He helped me out through those times when I had nothing. Alan provided potatoes to most of the fish and chip shops in Blackpool at the time, so I suppose that was another thing that had come full circle. I was back with the fish and chip shop people I'd started with when I was little.

Although I now live in Blackpool, I hadn't originally wanted to stay in the town where I was performing, which is why I ended up in Great Eccleston. In a way it's a little bit like putting on the show in Scarborough, but staying up the coast at Ravenscar. It allowed me that space.

I managed the season okay but I was starting to get worse again health-wise. I didn't feel particularly good. The money situation was still not good either. I also hadn't quite come clear from the nervous breakdown at that time, but I had got back to putting on my show and I was at least able to pay for things.

After such a bad time the year before, the nervous breakdown and the bankruptcy meeting, my life was suddenly to get a lot better – although typically not without incident.

We're getting close to it now! Hang on to your stockings!

I was at a 'stage night', one of those nights where all of the entertainers who are in town doing summer seasons all get together. It was sponsored by *The Stage* newspaper. I was still ill but making a recovery. I was chatting with Chubby Brown near to the bar when James walked by.

You can call it whatever you like but I was drawn like a magnet towards him. I asked him where he was going and I thought he'd said he was going to have a dance with his wife.

We didn't get together there and then on that night. What happened was he came to see me where I was appearing on the North Pier. He'd given up his ticket to see *Cats* to come and see me. He gave me a little peck on the cheek and we've never looked back. We clicked; it's remained that way.

He couldn't drive when we left Blackpool and Great Eccleston behind to return to Turpin's, so I tried to teach him but we weren't very successful. Put it this way: the big oak tree that had been there for hundreds of years didn't last that long with James at the wheel and me as the instructor.

I suppose we became – what do you call it these days? – an item, and I'm happy to say that we've now been together for nearly twenty years. James has been with me all the way, through everything that has been thrown at us, and I love him dearly. He is my lover, my best friend and my very official partner.

James and I are a bit like chalk and cheese. When I first met him he was twenty years of age, and the first thing I wanted to know was what he liked doing. He said golf – he was a one-handicap golfer at one time, a left hander, one of the best in the area – and I just thought, *Bingo!*, at least we wouldn't be in each other's pockets because I can't stand someone around me every second of the day. I said that we'd look for the best courses for him to play, but the way it's turned out is I've screwed up his game, as he looks after me so much that he can hardly fit in even a single round now.

Nobody else, apart from my mam, has cared for me quite

as tenderly as James. He's there every time I need him, every moment when I am really low or tired. He doesn't do it to win any prizes or to show others. He does it all just for me. There are plenty of times when he has had to put me to bed, tend to me when I've been in one of those desperately low periods and make sure that I am looked after properly. I have a wonderful family that also does that, but James is so very special to me. He's there for me every inch of the way. I think I'm going to cry after writing that!

It's at this point I should really mention Fran Cunningham. Fran is one of the nicest, kindest, most warm-hearted ladies I have ever known. She was with me in Blackpool for quite some time up until a few years ago, and she helped enormously. Thanks, Fran.

Very soon after James and I had got together, I asked him to also be my manager. He was reluctant at first, which was only to be expected because he hadn't been involved in the entertainment business, but he has a beautiful mind and is a very astute businessman. I could see he had that in him at only twenty. He is also good at buying and selling anything and can very quickly tell you what most antiques are worth.

He's shrewd – not a yes-man. He will say 'no' to people, and to me, which is important. Sometimes people will only tell you what they think you want to hear, but not James. He does it all nicely with me though. I've never had that kind of management in my life until he walked in.

What that has enabled me to do is to get on with what I do, to perform and entertain with even more confidence. I think we've already established how rubbish I am with things like finances.

James resisted managing me at first because he had never done it before, so he watched how others did it for a while to learn the trade. He worked with those who were managing me to get things sorted out in his own mind, but he now handles it all with the team we have around us. He tells me it took him five years to get used to the environment, that it was like an apprenticeship for him, but he's now not just my manager but a very well-respected young man in the entertainment world. He has also managed all of the merchandising, including the sales team and the printing of the brochure for David Gest on his UK tour in 2010.

We have had some very good people who have helped me too – people like Jean Parkes, who I mentioned much earlier, and her husband Mal Ford. All of the help I have received since 1998, when James came into my life, has brought me to the feeling that my finances are now being looked after correctly. Whether it's working with other promoters, booking theatre dates, talking with the Variety Club, setting up deals or even making my supper, James does it all.

What James saw straightaway was that I was not always getting the monies I was entitled to. As he puts it, if I was doing a concert where it had been a sell-out and £25,000 had been taken on ticket sales, I would be getting only a very small proportion of it. He's the one who always tells me that nobody was robbing me at any time, they were just taking what was there and, if they weren't questioned, they would continue taking what they could.

James and I lived together at Turpin's for around three years. After nearly twenty-five years, Rita finally moved out of my life not long before James arrived. I'd told James that I had a relationship with this girl and that we had been together for a long time.

Looking back, I don't think I really handled the situation very well. Rita always was a wonderful woman. She never swore even in the most passionate moments, and I still love her. It's one of those horrible modern-day things where we are all frowned upon for saying we love more than one person at a time. There was a song called 'Torn Between Two Lovers'; that's exactly where I was coming from. While I've said that James had cared for me as tenderly as anyone ever had, it would be wrong to say that Rita had cared for me less.

Getting together with James, and Rita leaving, were still not THE INCIDENT of 1998. What happened with both of them was very important, but THE INCIDENT was something else, involving blue flashing lights, blood, fighting and THAT court case!

I guess you're ready for it now.

It happened on the night James and I were officially an item for the first time, and what happened that night saw me up at Preston Crown Court nearly two years later, on a charge of assaulting two punks after a five-hour drinking session. That's how it was put on the BBC News website. I don't deny the drinking, by the way.

What happened was this. We had just finished a charity show for Lord Delfont at the Opera House within the Winter Gardens complex in Blackpool. It was more of a comedy night than anything else, but I had my band on with me and I was headlining. There was a young man called Dave Spikey on the bill who went on to achieve great success with Peter Kay in *Phoenix Nights*, as well as packing theatres throughout the UK with his own one-man shows.

I'd come out in my dinner suit, with James and Keeley, my niece, and a few of the others from the crew. By the time I had finished signing autographs and meeting and greeting people, we couldn't get a drink at the theatre bar so we went outside to a local bar where we could get served. It wasn't a particularly upmarket place, The Regent, not at that time anyway, but I wasn't bothered. It was somewhere to drink.

The main bar was packed, so Frank, who ran The Regent, opened the other bar for us. So I'm sat there in this bar in my dinner suit, all done up to the nines, looking like a penguin. We were there a while and I had drunk quite a bit, but I still knew what I was doing. These punk rockers were there. I know you can't always judge a book by its cover but you could on this occasion. They were taking the p★★★ out of me, probably because of the way I was dressed, but also, so they ended up saying in court, because they said I was 'bragging about my wealth'. Their words, not mine.

If only they had read the newspapers, they would have known how wrong they were. I might still have been living at Turpin's but none of it was really mine anymore. I remember mentioning a swimming pool in some way, not to them, but they obviously heard and they started having a go at me about it.

How it all kicked off was that Keeley went to the Ladies, and when she came back we were outside. She had scratches all over her. Her gold crucifix had come off its chain and she had clearly been assaulted. There was blood on her neck from where they had obviously attacked her. Like I've said all along, if anyone does anything to any member of my family we do something about it. That's how the fight started.

The punks said they hadn't done anything to Keeley. My niece has always been able to handle herself, like the rest of the family. She knows a thing or two about protection.

What happened next was quite a fight, with fists and kicks flying everywhere, and then the police and an ambulance arrived. Because we had blood on ourselves we were bundled into the ambulance. Keeley and I just sat there for a few minutes, getting our breath back and 'manging' in cant (speaking in Romany).

All of a sudden, the doors of the ambulance flew open and we were dragged out to be put in the black Maria. We swapped with the punks, with their bright orange and purple hair. They went in the ambulance. It was unbelievable, you couldn't make it up. All we had wanted to do was go for a quiet drink after the show, and we ended up making a visit to the cop shop.

Keeley and I were locked in a cell, over in Bonny Street nick in

Blackpool. Very quickly, the word got around to all of my fans who had been at the show and were still in the area at the time. They all came down to the police station where I was being held and demanded that I be let out. If ever there was a case of 'fan power' for me. this really was it.

Inside I was screaming, 'Get me out of this f***ing jail!' Outside all the girls were screaming, 'We want Joe! We want our Joe!' I don't think Bonny Street had ever heard anything like it. Not for a singer anyway.

It was Jean Parkes who got me out that night. Jean was working for International Artistes at the time, and they had booked me for the summer season in Blackpool on the North Pier. She paid the bail and got both Keeley and me out. Keeley had broken her arm during all that had happened, so she should really have been in the ambulance after all!

Keeley ran the merchandise side of my concerts for a number of years. She doesn't now – that's where Michael, Keith's son, has taken over in recent years. Keeley now has a very loving, adorable family. She still comes along to some of my concerts when she can.

You may by now be wondering what happened to James that night. All I can tell you is that the prosecution alleged there was a mystery 'third man' who was also involved with the fight that took place. I can't tell you who that person was, because it all happened so quickly, but whoever it was they really helped out.

The next day the national and local media was full of 'TV COMIC IN PUNCH UP' stories. I hated to be labelled as a comic. I'm a singer, an artiste, a performer, an impressionist, but not a comic.

As I mentioned earlier, the court case didn't take place until around twenty months later, which meant I had it hanging over me for all that time.

But we've a bit more ground to cover before we get to that – and it's pretty important, because this is where the lovely, magnificent, sexy and beautiful Pat Mancini MBE makes her regal entrance in my story.

I was first introduced to Patricia when Johnnie Casson and I were appearing at the North Pier in 1999. It was the early part of the year and it was another great friend of mine, James and Johnnie's, the lovely Ann Marie Slack, who brought Pat and myself together.

Pat was the proprietor of the extremely well-liked and well-known Queens Hotel on the seafront in Blackpool, and had recently lost her husband, Rudi, when we met. She was still in mourning for him and had been struggling to come to terms with things, but we had an immediate connection. She reminded me a lot of my sister Lizzie. We had just finished on the Pier that night and went back to the Queens. We were in the cocktail bar, which is really nice and secluded. It was Ann Marie's idea, she thought us being there might help Pat.

In her own book Pat tells it like this:

'... they persuaded me to go downstairs and have a chat with them. I was all in black and desperately down. I'd never met Joe before but I'd enjoyed his show very much and I thought, being in show business, he might like champagne. He looked at me and he said I reminded him of his sister. We got chatting and it was like the endless feeling of grief was lifted off me. I can't describe the feeling exactly because it was a bit unreal. My emotions were all over the place at the time but something in Joe's personality rang a bell with me. Something happened that I can't really explain. We just talked and gradually I felt a little bit easier about myself for the first time in months. After he went I felt quite different. As I walked back up the corridor to my flat in the hotel I

started to sing for the first time since Rudi had died. I sang
"I Wanna Be Where You Are" (one of Joe's). It's one of my
favourite songs.'

Pat's book is called *Queen of Blackpool* and that's exactly what she
will always be to me, despite her passing. It's a great read and tells of
how she came from nothing to running this famous hotel on
Blackpool's seafront.

We had a fantastic night and Pat came along to one or two of
my shows after that, but little did James and I know just how much
of a part Patricia was to play in our lives. I hold her close to my
heart today. Along with James, she's been my best pal.

We were still on our uppers in 1999. We hadn't been thrown
out of Turpin's, but we just couldn't afford to live there anymore.
We needed to be nearer to where the action was in terms of
summer seasons, but we also didn't have enough money to pay for
accommodation.

In desperation we turned up one day at the Queens Hotel, but
Pat wasn't there. Ironically, it was she who was in Las Vegas – not
me! James and I didn't have anywhere to go, and one of Pat's staff
managed to get a message to her in the States about our situation.

She rang back saying, 'Tell them they can have anything they
want and can stop as long as they like.' It was so kind of her, such
a marvellous gesture. But it didn't end there. Pat had also recently
purchased a house on the seafront. It had been intended for her
and Rudi to live in and was empty at the time. We stayed in the
hotel for about three or four weeks, then moved back out to
Great Eccleston for a short while, before moving down to the
seafront house for two years until we were back on our feet. Ann
Marie also came to our rescue during that time too. She let us
stay in her apartment with her.

By now Pat knew what I had been going through. She knew

about the cancer, the nervous breakdown, my impending court case and the bankruptcy. She knew all of that. She didn't have to help us in the way she did, but I am so grateful for her kindness, love and friendship.

So let's just take stock here.

In the past year I had been locked up for an affray, was due up before a judge in court again, still couldn't afford to pay off all my debts that had been lingering on since the creditors' arrangement in 1997, no longer had TV contracts to fall back on, was still not completely clear of how my nervous breakdown had affected me, and was getting closer to saying a final goodbye to my lovely home in Berkshire.

You would think it would be a sad time wouldn't you? But you know, it really wasn't. I had James with me. I had wonderful new friendships with people like Pat, Ann Marie and Johnnie. And I had others too who were to be incredibly helpful – in many ways it was like coming onto the next chapter.

Now there's a good link, because that's the end of this one. We won't take a break this time – unless you want one; if you do then let's just charge our glasses this time – because I'm on a roll now.

CHAPTER TWENTY-SEVEN

IN COURT

I'm not one for looking back and regretting things that have happened. You move on – and that's what I was doing in 1999 and 2000.

Funnily enough though, my first studio album since 1993, released in 1999, was titled *Reflections*. It was another release from Telstar, the last of my four studio albums with the company. There were twelve tracks in all including 'Mack the Knife', 'We Don't Cry Out Loud' and 'I Will Drink the Wine'. Quite appropriate if we've all just recharged our glasses!

It didn't make an impression on the albums chart but it has still sold well over the years. It was released that May. I was back on television again in 1999 and appeared on a programme called *The Big Stage* on Channel 5. But one of my favourite TV appearances of that time was when Chris Evans' team contacted me to appear on *TFI Friday* with David Bowie. You know the rest from what you read earlier!

If this all sounds to you like things were picking up a bit then you would be right. I was feeling far better. I was with James, had a great new friend in Pat, a new album out and I was back on television. Things were looking up. I was also back at the North Pier for the summer with Johnnie. International Artistes were the agency who booked me onto the Pier at the time. I was getting some work through them and Tony Clayman was promoting me.

Of course, there were two major problems on the horizon. Actually, there were two that I knew about and also one that I didn't! We're now into the year 2000. There was the bankruptcy, the official one this time. I have only been actually declared bankrupt once, contrary to what some have reported in the press over the years; and there was the court case at Preston Crown Court for the affray outside the Regent Hotel.

But even before all of the three major problems, there was another! It involved my brother John and I being questioned by the Thames Valley Police over an alleged incident. This is how it came about:

We were getting closer and closer to the official declaration that I was bankrupt and a local garage owner came to Turpin's. He had come to take back the slate-grey Mercedes S280 I had at the time, but things got out of hand and both John and I ended up being questioned at Maidenhead Police Station.

The official bankruptcy was only a matter of months away, and so was the affray court case. It seemed for a while as though I might be in court more than Andy Murray or Roger Federer!

In the end it was the court appearance that came first, followed hot on its heels by the declaration of bankruptcy. But that wasn't the end of my problems either.

If bankruptcy, a voluntary creditors' agreement, a charge for affray and a nervous breakdown hadn't already been enough for me to cope with, there was even more still to come. I told you earlier that the problem with CLL – or non-Hodgkins' lymphoma, as it is sometimes referred to – is that it isn't there one minute but is definitely back on the scene the next.

I think you can pretty much guess what happened next then, can't you? That's right – it returned in March 2000, twelve years on from when I'd first found out I'd got it, and just three years after I'd proudly announced in concert that I was living proof cancer could be beaten, there it was again. This time it was far worse than before. I needed more chemotherapy.

I had thought it had gone, but with this disease you do have periods when you feel perfectly alright. Somewhere in my head, I had let myself believe it had gone. I was a week into my UK tour when I realised I wasn't feeling right. I went to my local doctor, who referred me straight back to Dr Anthony Childs. I think because I was seeing doctors less and less, I had felt that everything was okay. I had been feeling so good.

I died inside for a short while when I found out. When I left hospital I cried my eyes out. *Here we go again* was all I could think.

That evening I cried on the way to my show at The Grand in Blackpool, but somehow I managed to block off all of those bad feelings. I'd fought it once before, I would fight it again – and go on fighting, no matter what it took. I have always loved what I do and I will do it to the best of my ability for as long as I can. There would be no nervous breakdown this time. I think after you've had one of those you do see the danger signs in future.

I now had good people around me, people who cared for me, people I could trust. Sure, I had a few of them around me when I was going through my nervous breakdown, but this time it was different. I felt better able to cope.

I started the treatment again that same day. I undertook six months of intensive treatment that year, while also fulfilling all my engagements here and abroad. There were times when I felt as though I'd been to hell and back. Sometimes I felt as though

I'd done fifteen rounds with Mike Tyson and then started all over again. I would take the pills that I'd been given and ten minutes later I'd be seeing double and would have to go to bed, because I was feeling lousy.

From the resumption of my treatment and a UK tour, I then went straight to court. If ever I realised just how much my fans thought of me, it had been when they all turned up en masse outside Bonny Street police station two years earlier, but they topped that with what they did throughout my case at Preston Crown Court!

There was nothing anyone could do about my illness, but the fans really felt that there was something they could do about my being in court. Some were there in court every day, including Fran. Others took shifts on it. I'm not sure how they managed to wangle all the time off work that they may have had, but their constant appearance was a great comfort to me. Every day there was a queue to go into the courtroom.

Pat, lovely Pat, made sure that I looked my best in court. She took me to Marks & Spencer's just before I was due to go in for my first appearance, and I came out looking and feeling a million dollars. She had told me I couldn't go to court in the way I was dressed at first.

We arrived at Marks & Spencer's at nine o'clock that first morning of the trial, and Pat gave me £300 to kit myself out. I came out wearing a navy blue pin-striped suit, pink shirt and shades. Pat says it was like someone going through the smoke they used for the *Stars in their Eyes* programme, with the same person you have just seen in his normal clothes looking great as he comes through it.

The trial was supposed to last just three days, but it went to six, and over into two weeks. My barrister cost me nine grand to fight the case. He told me that he wanted the money before he went in.

I think he knew that I was going to be declared bankrupt, since it had been reported in *The Lawyer* magazine, and understandably wanted to make sure he was going to get paid. So I rang Tony Clayman, my promoter at the time. I told him that unless I got the nine large ones for my barrister he wasn't going into that court – wig or no wig. We got the money, and we were underway!

In court the prosecution asked me, 'Mr Longthorne, did you kick my client in the head repeatedly?' I asked the jury what 'repeatedly kicked' actually meant. I said that there was no way anyone could have gone from our fracas with just a bleeding nose and be in the newspapers the next morning if I had 'repeatedly kicked' him. If I had done that then his head would have caved in. I asked the judge, 'Your honour, can I demonstrate a "repeated kick"?'

It had been devastating for me to see what had happened to Keeley and I really didn't think we had a case to answer; we had only protected ourselves from people who I believed were intent on making trouble. We had only been in the Regent because I couldn't get a drink at the Winter Gardens. We hadn't gone looking for trouble.

I took over the courtroom for a matter of seconds. 'Here's what a repeated kicking is, your honour. Listen to this. Imagine if I'd kicked him like it has just been said,' and I almost kicked the witness box out. I really showed them what a repeated kicking would be like. Then I turned back to the jury.

'Ladies and gentlemen, he would be dead. He wouldn't have been able to sell his story to the front page of the *Daily Star*.'

Although I was confident that Keeley and I had done the right thing, I was still very relieved when the verdicts were read out and we were cleared of assaulting the two punks. The jury took two and a half hours to return the 'not guilty' verdicts, and they were the longest two and a half hours of my life.

JOE LONGTHORNE

The solicitors, Budds, had done their homework and found a taxi driver who had witnessed what happened that night. In his statement the taxi driver had said that the only person doing any kicking was someone in white trousers. That couldn't have been me as I was in my tux and suit, all black. I was in the clear.

All of my fans were clapping. Pat had organised the champagne again and, when the jury came out, I asked whether they wanted a drink. So in May 2000, Keeley and I were finally clear of all charges. We were not guilty! The incident had been hanging over us for twenty months.

Next up was the bankruptcy.

I told *HELLO!* magazine in an interview that appeared later that year, a few months after I had been declared officially bankrupt, that I had tried my best to stave off going bust. It was eventually my creditors that had demanded it. Once again, I couldn't believe some of the bills. We had one from the accountant who said I owed £50,000. Bridie Reid's bill was still there, and the Inland Revenue bill was £500,000. I know that others might say I should have looked after my finances better, but you know the drill by now. It's not what I do.

Andrew Segal, the supervisor of the official bankruptcy petition that I had avoided earlier by entering into the voluntary agreement, was the man who arranged for it to take place properly this time. Tony Clayman, my promoter, told Segal's that I had tried to meet the terms of the voluntary agreement, but that I had been unable to keep up with the payments that were required. They were just too much for me.

No matter how much I scrimped and saved, struggling to pay off my debts, I just couldn't clear them. I was paying back £7,000 a month by performing as regularly as I could, but it wasn't really making any impact on the million or so that I owed. I had kept Turpin's during the past four years, but now was the time that we just had to sell. I sold it for £500,000, and since the buyer had no reason to be in straightaway, James and I were able to carry on staying there for a little while longer.

The bailiffs had come to the house to claim what they could. but by the time they arrived everything had gone apart from the piano. Like I said earlier, they should have looked in the legs!

I also told *HELLO!* that I would be breaking open a bottle of champagne on 15 July 2000, which was the date when I finally became clear of debt. At last! I'd got two monkeys off my back – the financial ruin and the court case. Maybe now I could return to a normal life – or as normal as my life gets.

But no. That wasn't all. Within hours I was back on yet more gruelling sessions of chemotherapy, as I continued my personal battle with lymphoma.

I was feeling good about getting back on my feet financially and being cleared of any charges in Preston Crown Court, so that helped with the return of cancer. As well as all of the help I was now getting from everyone around me, including my wonderful fans, it was probably the reason why I was able to cope better this time around.

In the space of six months right at the start of the new millennium, I had been through more dramatic events than some might go through in years, but at least now I was able to deal with it. When you've come back from really dark moments like I'd had with the nervous breakdown, maybe it makes you stronger inside. At least that's how it felt for me.

I invited Pat to come on tour with us for the rest of the UK dates – and she did! We had a great time and went all over the country together, Pat, James, me and the band. It was to be the start of some funny and amazing stories as we travelled around the world together. The first of those went like this:

When we were on the UK tour in 2000, we had a couple of

days off down on the south coast. I got it into my head that we should hire a boat with a radar on, so that we wouldn't get lost. I thought about us going to Jersey, as you do, just for the day!

Did we have any sailing knowledge between us? No, but surely if a boat has a radar, everything would be alright, wouldn't it?

I had been told that all you had to do was point the boat's radar to Jersey, press a few buttons and we'd get there! Simple, really. It sounded so easy. I thought we had organised a boat, and so the next day we arrived at the harbour armed with stuff for a great day out. You know the kind of thing, sailing essentials like champagne. When we got there we couldn't believe the boats! One was being painted, one was in, and all the rest were booked out.

We quickly forgot about anything to do with radar. Pat describes the boat we saw as being like Popeye's from the cartoon series, with a blue funnel. It was just an old fishing boat.

Ever the optimist, I still fancied a go. It was just like having an old caravan to me. Needless to say, we never got to Jersey. I think we made it about 200 yards outside of the harbour before we turned back. Not exactly the world's greatest voyage.

But I was to become a captain in another way that year. My summer season saw me on the North Pier again. Johnnie was back too. He'd had a tough time of it the previous year, because he'd needed a heart bypass operation during the run. This time he was fine. We also put together a charity show called *All Hands on Deck* that featured me as the Captain and Johnnie as the ship's cat. I would dress up in my captain's hat and outfit and go onto the pier, shaking hands with people who were coming to the concerts. I really felt like the pier was my own personal liner. I was a bit like Alec Guinness in the film *Barnacle Bill*, where he tries to make sure a dilapidated pier is saved from being demolished when he registers it as a foreign cruise ship. Sometimes, when the sea was a bit choppy, it felt like we were sailing across to the Isle of Man.

I was not feeling too clever at times during the season, as I was still fighting the lymphoma and, when I came offstage, I was so tired. All I wanted to do was relax. It was a long walk off the pier of a night after we'd finished, so I started setting myself up for the night in the dressing room. I stayed there quite a few nights and turned it into my home during the run, but the company that ran the pier decided I couldn't stay on there each night. I think it was something to do with the insurance only running up until midnight.

It was quite enjoyable really, living on the pier. I could have carried on doing it. I would pop downstairs every morning to see the milkman. He would always come on board my 'ship' to deliver to me. I'd also hang out my washing.

Jean Parkes and I struck up a friendship during that time which remains to this day. Jean was working, like I said earlier, with International Artistes and when the company who had the North Pier wanted me to get off they sent for her.

Why would I want to move? I didn't see why I had to leave the pier each night. I was tired, I wasn't going to do any harm to the place, but apparently I had to go.

Jean's visits became a nightly ritual. I wouldn't move from there until she came, then Jean would be sent for and she would have to come and get me at about three in the morning. We would walk off the pier together. Jean tells me she ended up just staying in her tracksuit until she got the phone call. I thank Jean now for what she did because, bless her, she was putting herself out to do it.

One afternoon when I was on the pier, Michael Grade came up and had a long chat. He owned it at the time but told me he was moving into television. He'd been interested in what I thought about him letting go of it. His uncle, Bernard Delfont, would have done a back-flip in his grave if he'd known. The company ended up selling it to First Leisure.

Later that same year saw me heading back to Australia, my first time since 1993. We played Perth, Brisbane, Twin Towns, Sydney, Melbourne and Adelaide in theatre and concert venues. All of the troubles I'd had in the past few years were gone and we all had a fantastic time. There was James, Pat and the band. We went to Thailand for a week first and then on to Australia for five weeks. Pat had said she was only coming for the first two weeks, but she stayed for the lot.

Patricia and I went up to the top of the Harbour Bridge in Sydney. I told her I'd only gone there because I didn't think she'd do it. It was a marvellous experience. When we got to the top, Pat asked where the shops were.

I have always loved Australia, both the country and its people. My fans over there follow me everywhere when I'm on tour, a bit like they do here in the UK. They're so supportive.

When we arrived in Sydney I was asked to do a breakfast TV programme. I had to be up by seven o'clock but I'd only been to bed for an hour. I have to admit I felt a bit jetlagged, but I wasn't going to turn it down. They wanted to record it live under the Sydney Harbour Bridge, and they wanted me to do not just any impression but Pavarotti as well as Dame Shirley.

Pavarotti at seven in the morning? Did they not know my lifestyle, or how much it takes to warm up to that kind of performance? I would never start a show with an impression of Pavarotti, but I did the impressions with no music, no backing, nothing. Pat was amazed, she was sure I'd fall on my arse with it.

But isn't it funny how small the world really is? I know everyone says it, especially with the internet these days, but it was brought home to me on one of our visits to Australia. And it wasn't in the most pleasant of ways.

Do you remember me telling you that my sister Anne was incarcerated in Rampton for a while? Well, we were in Fremantle one day. We were all sitting together – me, the band, James, Pat. We were drinking champagne again. Well, someone has to drink it, you know.

Anyway, this woman on the next table, which was full of more mature ladies, had heard us talking and told me that they were all from Nottingham. She went on to tell me that they all now lived over there. I get a lot of people coming up to me to ask for an autograph or just to chat, so I thought nothing of it. Then I heard one of them mention Rampton.

That was it. My ears were well and truly up. I looked around and asked whether what I'd heard was correct. 'Did you say Rampton? The hospital for the criminally insane, a mental institution?'

When they nodded, I told them that my sister had spent a bit of time in there. I mentioned her by name to see if there was any reaction, to see if any of them knew her. Anne had told me she wasn't very happy with the way she had been treated at times. What I suddenly wanted to know right there and then was if they knew anything. I was hungry for information.

Maybe they didn't know; maybe they hadn't all worked at Rampton; anyone who works there has to sign the Official Secrets Act, but if I'd found out that one of them was responsible for anything out of order I'd have blown up right there and then.

Who would have thought it? I'd come thousands of miles to be sat with these people, who were probably very decent and honest, but just the mere mention of the name Rampton had been enough to make me think that way. The world really is getting smaller.

My interview with *HELLO!* magazine had taken place during the time of the court case, but the story didn't appear until later that year. Pat had come with James and me back to Maidenhead, to Turpin's. I took her breakfast in bed.

I think she was a bit shocked when she went into one of the rooms the next day and found nothing in it but floorboards and a sliding window. She says she was even more shocked to see a big Welsh Cob, a goat and my dog, Henry, all inside it!

My Welsh Cob, Rosie, appeared in *HELLO!* looking in at the house through the window. I had three horses all together, including a thoroughbred called Sugar and Lady Blue. *HELLO!* also used a picture of Pat and me.

Pat stayed at Turpin's for nearly a month, and it was to be the last couple of weeks James and I spent there. I remember Pat saying to me at the time, 'Joe, don't you ever go out?'

I told her that when I was at home I generally didn't go anywhere, and that's true. Because I'm on the road as much as I am I just like to stay at home when I can. I don't go out unless there's something special. I'm the same today.

But I did have something special lined up for Pat, I took her to see Dame Shirley at the Festival Hall in London. We went in a Rolls-Royce, not mine of course, and had a fabulous evening. I wasn't particularly well that night but we still had a great time. Well, who wouldn't when you are going to see such an incredible woman, especially when you're with an incredible woman as well!

Considering the year had included a court case, my bankruptcy, the return of lymphoma and even more treatment, it still hadn't been a bad one. I'd come through the court case unscathed, free of all costs; I was now free of debt and, thanks to Pat, was living in her house up the coast in Blackpool; and I was coping manfully with my illness. I'd done a UK tour, a summer season and an Australian tour.

Maybe everything was not quite well with my world, but it wasn't at all bad. I'd got James, I had a wonderful friendship with Pat, and Jean had looked after me really well on the North Pier.

In fact, Jean had looked after me so well that I wanted her to manage me, and eventually she did. I first asked Jean at a Christmas function in 2000. She told me that she was reluctant to take me on because she didn't want it to spoil the friendship we had developed. I respected her for that, and I also respected her because once again, like James, she wouldn't just tell me what she thought I wanted to hear. She told me things straight.

It did lead to a few problems along the way, as she had thought it might, but we are still friends today, and her husband Mal is a superb, straight-as-a-die man as well as a fine musician. They are both very professional and that's exactly what I needed around me.

Around this time I also had Chimes International as my booking agents, with Robert Pratt looking after my tour dates. Everything and everyone was now in place, better than it had been for years!

CHAPTER TWENTY-EIGHT

THE MUSIC HALL TAVERN

I was back on track. Not only did I have some great friends and business-minded people around me who thought more of me than to 'take more than their fair share', they also liked and respected me.

James and I were building some proper friendships with people who cared about us, friendships that have more than stood the test of time, and we had also been royally looked after by Pat. We were no longer on our uppers.

2001 was a great year for me. I was signed to a new record company, Ritz Music Group, and in the early part of the year we produced a fantastic live recording of one of the concerts up in Aberdeen, simply called *Joe Longthorne Live in Concert*.

Peter Faint was my musical director at this time, and he produced the CD with me. Some of the players on that tour were amongst the best I've ever had the pleasure of working with. There was Lewis Osborne on lead guitar, Peter Brent on bass guitar and Stephen Power on keyboards. The rest of the band was brilliant too. The album contains one of the best mixes of me singing as myself as well as quite a few impressions, and of all my CD releases I think it's also the only one that includes my version of 'He Ain't Heavy, He's My Brother'.

There was also my first ever DVD-only release. All of the previous films of me in concert had originally been released on video and then transferred to DVD. This was called *The Genius of Joe Longthorne*. I was concerned about the title. I mean, what right have I to release something proclaiming myself as a genius? But the others around me liked the title. The recordings had taken place during my shows at the Grand Theatre in Blackpool the previous summer.

Jean was now managing me. She got the Friendship Club back up and running again; Geraldine Vine has also now run it for a number of years. Today, my official website has over 40,000 registered users and a regular newsletter is sent out to all Friendship Club members.

While Robert Pratt and Dave Halford of Chimes International were looking after most of my engagements, Jean had picked up some work for me back on the cruise ships. This brought about a series of adventures – and of course a few misadventures along the way.

In 2001 we played on the QE2. We joined the ship in Singapore and got off in India, but that certainly didn't pass without incident either! Before we go any further, I wasn't involved in what happened. Not personally anyway...

What happened was that I couldn't take the band, just Andy Mudd, my musical director at the time. Andy is great. It's his studio that I use sometimes for recording. Andy is another of my great group of friends too.

We had done okay on the ship, but Andy didn't think the musicians backing me were suitable. I didn't either. The band onboard the QE2 had its own musical director and Andy told him what he thought of it. The other MD didn't like it.

When Colin Handley had been my MD on previous cruises I'd done years ago, and he didn't think one of the musicians was up to the job, he would just tell them they weren't needed the next night, but that's not Andy's way.

The next morning I was summoned to the Captain's office to hear what had happened. We were getting off in India anyway, which was the next stop, and so did the ship's musical director.

We even caused a bit of a stir in India as well. Again, it wasn't me! Jean was with us on the cruise and had forgotten about covering up. She was wearing a strappy top when we got out of our car at the airport. I told her to cover her tits up! I ended up throwing my coat over her.

Then they wouldn't let me through customs wearing my hat. I couldn't see why I had to take my hat off when all of these Indians could go through wearing their turbans, and I said so. We were all frisked as a result of it.

Back on home soil, it was time for me to bring my own version of variety to Blackpool, in the form of my own club. I have never been frightened to try new things, and 2001 saw the launch of Joe Longthorne's Music Hall Tavern with its official opening the following year. It was something I wanted to make a go of, my own venue, but even some of my best friends were telling me not to bother. They would say, 'Why do you want to sell beer, Joe, when you can entertain like you do?' I just thought it would be a good idea and that I would enjoy it.

Pat told me not to get involved; she had told me it wasn't big enough to make money from. James saw it the same way, but do I ever think of the money? All I ever think about is whether it will be good fun or not. I think we established that quite some time ago, did we not?

The building had a curved entrance on the corner of Church Street and had previously been the Gas Board showroom. I would play there every Thursday evening with a five-piece band led by Andy. We had live music on every night and Mal Ford, who is an accomplished keyboard player and played in several Midlands bands, as well as being a band leader in his own right, performed on a Saturday evening. Every night's entertainment was free entry, except for the night we performed when we charged £20 on the door.

We had some good nights while it lasted, but unfortunately it didn't last long. It just took up too much time and Pat was right, it wasn't going to work financially. While it was great to have our own venue, the problem was that people expected me to be there all the time. But I was still also working hard on tour. The tavern had been a really nice idea though, and is another part of my life that was particularly special for me. It also brought, as you might expect with me, a few laughs and gaffs along the way.

There is a feeling in the entertainment world that the bigger you get, the bigger the light show. I think we just might have taken that a bit too far in the Tavern. Read on!

One of the funniest moments ever was when Patricia and I went to Manchester on a mission to kit out the Tavern. I was after some chandeliers, fantastic lighting for the tavern that would give us the wow factor. We got to the store and started checking out the lighting on display, but I didn't know how it would really look back in the Tavern, so Pat said we should get down on the floor.

So there we are, Pat and I laid together in the centre of this store head-to-head, and there are people walking around us and over our bodies. Pat just said, 'There you are, that's what it will look like,' and we just stayed there laughing for what seemed like ages. It still makes me laugh to think about it now.

We ended up buying three of them: two the same size that we

had just seen and a bigger one the manager said we could have for a lot less than its original price. We didn't see the bigger one on display and that was probably for a very good reason, as we were to find out when it arrived in Blackpool.

You have never seen anything like it! You couldn't even get it through the doors! The salesman had said it was bigger than the others on display, but hadn't told us just how big it was!

We just figured that the huge box would probably contain a reasonable amount of packaging. It couldn't be as big as the box it was delivered in, surely?

Wrong. It was massive. I might have wanted to create an impression with the lighting, but this was way beyond all of that. If we had put this up then customers wouldn't have been able to even walk under it, and with its size I'm pretty sure it would have brought the ceiling down. Now it's one thing 'bringing the house down' when you're performing, but not doing it for real! This would have done exactly that. It was the size you might expect in a cathedral.

There was another problem as well. Because I had been declared bankrupt in 2000 I couldn't be the licensee. When breweries saw that the place was to be called Joe Longthorne's Music Hall Tavern, they didn't want to supply us. It was all to do with the bankruptcy, so we were in danger of being a bit like that Irish song, 'The Pub with no Beer'. Jean came to the rescue and ran it for me with Mal. She'd been a licensee in the past, so she managed the whole building with Fran working behind the bar.

I don't regret the idea one bit. I would have liked to see it carry on, but it just wasn't viable. One good thing it did was to give others a chance to perform, but what I found was that when your name is attached to something like that, the people who come inside really want to see the man whose name is outside.

On a Monday night we had Jubilee Music Hall Night with Eric Hamilton, Maureen Nolan Senior and Connie Hall. Tuesday was cabaret night with different singers every week. Wednesday was Cabaret Showtime with Pete Oliver and the Choir Girls. It was me on Thursday, then Friday saw a Summer Star Search Talent Contest where we gave cash prizes every week. We had some great talent that came through, including Lady Elvis. Saturday Night Live! was Mal, along with pianist Andy Knight, and they hosted an open-mic spot. Sundays featured the vivacious Vicky le Plume. Something for everyone, every single day!

I'd still like to have another go at my own venue one day, but as Bobby Ball said to me recently, 'Joe, what do you want to run a club for? That's for entertainers who are finished. You're in the prime of life right now. Why do you want to bother with selling drinks when you can be selling out theatres and arenas?' Pat said something of the same.

It's probably best I have people telling me the way they do now. Jean and Mal have been great friends in that way too. By now they were 'Jean and Mal', running a company called Personality Artistes. Mal had been looking after bands like The Platters for a long time. Between them they were not only managing me as a performer, they were also making sure that I wasn't going bankrupt again and had set about rebuilding my reputation.

Understandably, my career had suffered quite a bit during the various traumas I had been going through, so there was a bit of work to do but Jean was a great help to James and me, as James began taking more of a management role and, together with Mal, really helped me get back on my feet.

Of course, in managing me the way they did there were one or two moments when those who had found it easy to bill me 'more than their fair share' also found that was no longer possible. Jean tells me that some of these people made their lives hell at the time, but they came through it.

'We only pay on quotes,' is what Jean used to say to me. 'We don't pay any extras.' Apparently, certain people would turn up months after a concert had been played, demanding additional payments. What Jean always said to them was that they should have put it in their original quote. I don't pretend to understand any of it really. All I knew was that Jean and Mal were looking after me, and that the pair of them were, and still are, true friends.

In 2002 the Tavern had opened and then closed. We had put on music every night but it just wasn't working. We'd had a gala opening night in June, and I had played there every Thursday with Andy and the rest of the band, but we had to come out of it. Actually, we received an award for it too. We came second in the Blackpool Tourism awards in 2002 for what we had achieved, or perhaps what we had tried to achieve.

That same year we played an October season at the Opera House in the Winter Gardens complex once again. We broke more box-office records, this time for the top-selling show of the year.

It was also the year when my songs started reappearing on a variety of new compilation albums. There were three released that year: *Love and Reflection* through the Demon Music Group on Music Club; *You're My World* through Snapper Music, issued under licence from Telstar; and *Christmas Time Is Here* through Delta Music. It looks like I had more record labels than anyone in the industry that year, without ever having to go near a studio.

Spencer Leigh, one of BBC Radio Merseyside's presenters, wrote some lovely words in the sleeve notes of the *You're My World* CD: 'Joe was once appearing at the Floral Pavilion in New Brighton. When he arrived, the compère, Billy Butler, asked him if he could do John Lennon. Joe had never sung "Imagine" before, but that night he did a perfect copy as a tribute to the late Beatle in his home town.'

I might not have been recording new albums, but it seemed as though I was getting pretty good at re-releases.

Jean and Mal even helped James and I move house. She says that's just what they do, her and Mal, try their level best to help. Just like when she used to come on the pier to take me home, Jean has always gone beyond the call of duty for me.

One of the proudest moments in my life was when Jean asked me to give her away when she married Mal in 2003. She had come with us when we toured Australia again, in November and December 2002. This time there was James, Jean, Andy Mudd, Zeb White and me. It was another wonderful time, with sell-out concerts wherever we went. We played right across the country from Perth to Sydney, including Adelaide, Melbourne and Canberra. It was a six-week tour playing two concerts a week.

The tour also allowed me to once again make the most of this beautiful country. But our next destination was one that I had been aiming at ever since Chicago.

It was Vegas!

This is the place I regard as the pinnacle of my area of show-business, in cabaret entertainment. Any top tennis player wants to play at Wimbledon; any top boxer wants to fight at Madison Square Garden; any footballer wants to play at Wembley; any jockey wants to ride in the Epsom Derby; any golfer wants to play at St Andrews; and any snooker player wants to play at the Crucible. For me, Vegas is the place to play.

Jean and Mal had got me there. Their contacts had got me close to 'the Strip', even though it wasn't what I had imagined. It might not have been the best known of Vegas' clubs, but it was still Vegas.

Unfortunately, I wasn't feeling too good around the time of my engagements, but they still went well and I received quite a bit of TV and radio exposure. I think it was CBS, one of the US's biggest networks, who interviewed me.

Jean and Mal were married at the wedding chapel in the Little

JOE LONGTHORNE

Church of the West in Las Vegas. Jean looked fantastic and it was a very real honour to give her away. As well as Jean, Mal and James, there was also 'Tatie' Alan, his wife Sylvia and quite a few from the Friendship Club.

We would have stayed in the States for longer. Jean and Mal had also organised a lovely house for James and me in a really great place called Spanish Trails, but I really wasn't too good at the time, so we decided to come back not long after the wedding. I was full of flu and I also needed more treatment.

That wasn't everything though. As Pat always says, things just happen when I'm around. This time it was another crash, but it wasn't financial.

I'd decided to hire a car. The one I took was green. Now Mal is a pretty superstitious man, and as soon as he saw it he said that green was a bad colour. He could have told me beforehand!

I drove it from the hire company driveway and that was it. *Bang!* A truck wiped me out! It hit me, we spun. I had 'Tatie' Alan and Sylv with me in the back, Jamie in the front. I swerved to get out of the way because I'd seen it coming, but it was coming far too fast. In the end it only clipped us, but its speed was enough to make the green car a write-off.

As if that wasn't enough, we also had a near-miss with another plane on our flight back from Vegas. We were coming in to land at Heathrow on a foggy, blustery day. I looked out of the window and there, right in my vision, was another huge plane. I saw the tail end of the plane veer away.

It wasn't a happy way to end our time in the States – I decided there and then that the next time I wouldn't be hiring a green car!

CHAPTER TWENTY-NINE

THAILAND

James and I were on the move again when we came back from the States.

The beautiful house Pat had bought as a place for her and Rudi to live, away from the Queens, had been purchased just before he passed away. Pat had no interest in living there after that. It was up for sale before we moved in. We were lucky that it hadn't sold at the time, as it became our home for several years. It's a lovely place just up the coast to the north side of Blackpool.

Thanks to all of the people who were now working with me, our financial situation was a good deal better. We were now able to afford to buy again, and we bought a house away from the seafront in Blackpool. I was also back on another UK tour and was due to start my summer season, this time back at the North Pier in July.

Tours of Australia, appearances in Vegas (albeit not on the Strip), successive years of UK tours and Blackpool summer seasons had seen me in work throughout the period when Jean and Mal –

as well as Dave Halford, by now running Artistes Direct – were looking after me. Everything appeared to be on the right track.

But trouble was lurking just around the corner for me once again.

This cancer thing is such a killer, but it's not just that, it's also such a lingering illness. It has affected, and continues to affect, millions of people throughout the world. It affects everyone – those who have it, their loved ones, their family and friends. Everyone knows someone who has it. I'm lucky, I'm still here and I've come through, but many have not.

May 2003 saw the next stage of my lymphoma develop into full-blown leukaemia. I'd lived with the prospect of my death since 1988, but now there had been an acceleration in my illness. My treatment was stepped up once again.

It was also around now that I stopped driving. I'd had my latest bout of chemotherapy and was out in the car. I clipped a wing mirror. It was enough for me to realise that I was now a liability on the road – nothing to do with drink driving, nothing to do with being irresponsible, I just felt it might be better if I didn't drive anymore.

I got through the UK tour and the summer season, but it was becoming an effort to cope once again. I was feeling more and more tired. The chemo was slowing me down.

That's when James and I took ourselves off to Thailand. It's another of my favourite places and I've been there a few times over the years. We went elephant trekking and saw some wonderful shows. I felt so relaxed, which was the general idea of going there in the first place. I was taking my medication and enjoying the break. But disaster was to strike in a different way as we were about to fly home.

I lost James.

I hadn't misplaced him. We hadn't fallen out. I just didn't know where he had got to. I wasn't concerned at first. He had packed our cases and gone for a drink. I'd stayed at the hotel because I wasn't very well. I was changed and looking forward to going home, watching *Die Hard* on the hotel's in-house movie channel. This next part is so heart-rending…

After James had been gone around an hour or so, I started to get worried. Where had he got to? I watched *Die Hard* again; still no James. He'd now been gone for hours and I'd had no contact with him at all. *Die Hard* started up again for its next showing. I started panicking. Our flight had been booked for 2.30am and we were already going to be running late. I wasn't bothered about missing the flight; I was bothered about James. Where was he?

I'm dying inside now, not just from the leukaemia but my heart is beginning to break.

In desperation I rang the Bangkok hospital. Thank God he wasn't there. I got someone to take me on the back of a motorbike, checking out all of the bars that we had been to since we'd been there. I looked in every one of them that I could, but it was now about six in the morning and many were closed.

In the end I asked the man on the bike to take me to the nick. It was now nine in the morning. I was just starting to think about what I could tell his dad and his brother. I really was that worried.

When I went through the gates I saluted. It was the king's official birthday! I asked whether they had anyone who had been locked up during the night as I was looking for my friend. Thank the Lord he was there.

It turned out James had gone to a so-called Irish bar for half a Guinness and his drink had been spiked. He says all he can remember about that night was seeing me. He asked me why I was crying when I saw him. I just said it was because I was so happy to see him.

He was in a pretty bad state and looked as though he'd had a kicking. It also looked as though he'd been bitten as well.

Finding him was one thing but getting him out was another. At first I thought the man in charge of the clink was asking me whether I was trying to bribe him, but I wasn't. It turned out he was asking for a bribe. Eventually, James and I left – thankfully together.

Why is it that whenever we leave anywhere there is always drama? India, the States and now Thailand, but there was far more drama to come in the next year and a half.

Now you're probably thinking that you haven't had another of those breaks for ages. I think it's about time we had one, don't you? Then we can tackle the period that led to the biggest challenge of my life. It's the story of how I came back from the dead. Drink anyone? This time you'd better charge your glasses because we're entering tearjerker territory once again. I did tell you this was a rollercoaster ride, didn't I? We're about to fall off right now. But first, here are some of the people who a singer cannot do without...

CHAPTER THIRTY

MUSICIANS

I told you earlier that the first time I was backed by Maurice Merry and his Merry Men in Scarborough, I knew that the show was mine. But that's not trying to be clever about it. I just understand the value of having good musicians.

You can have bands with lots of musicians, but if they're not on the money you can tell the difference. I can hear when someone's not up to scratch, or playing a wrong note, instantly.

I've played with the best. It's hard to mention everyone here, so for those who have played with me and not received a mention, I hope you won't be offended.

My current musical director is Steve 'Stretch' Price. Steve is such an outstanding pianist and he marshals the band brilliantly. If you're reading this having never seen him before, there is a good reason why he's called Stretch. He's a really, seriously tall bloke!

The rest of the band in recent years has featured drummers Paul Smith and Elliott Henshaw; bassists Si Goulding and Richard Hammond; lead guitarists Lewis Osborne and Alan Wormald; and the fabulous John Morton on keyboards.

Andy Mudd is a great professional and is doing his own thing again at the moment. I'm sure we'll play together again. We have both had good times and bad. He's like family. He comes from Halifax originally, and Roy Walker became like a dad to him when he first started in show-business.

But what of all those others I've played with?

From my TV show days, I would have to mention Ernie Dunstall once again, one of the greatest musical directors, with whom I wrote a number of songs. Colin Hadley was also another of my all-time favourite MDs. He has also sadly passed away. As well as Ernie and Colin, I really need to give a mention to all of these: Alan Rogers, Trevor Brown, Alan Ainsworth (once again), Steve Sidwell, Dave Arch and the great Don Lusher, one of the world's finest trombonists. There's also the fabulous Derek Watkins, who played trumpet.

Lewis Osborne played on the *Live in Concert* CD released by Ritz. He was an amazing young lead guitarist who made it all the way from a little village near Bristol to the London stage. He started with me when he was sixteen years old, and he's involved again today.

Chris Rae played guitar on so many of my recordings. One of my other favourite lead guitarists would have to be Ian Aitken, who played for me on 'Always Something There to Remind Me'.

As well as Paul and Elliott, I have always been well blessed with fabulous drummers. Brett Morgan played for me in the eighties; and there's Graham Ward, who went on to work with Tom Jones and George Michael. Graham has to be among my favourites. He developed one of the oddest of obsessions: on tour he became addicted to bingo. We used to play it on the tour bus to win the boxes of chocolate that fans had brought for us. Graham was just mad for it. And then there's Welsh drummer Harold Fisher, another great musician.

There have been so many great players. I count myself extremely fortunate to have been backed by such gifted performers, and I never, ever take for granted the hours of hard work they put in while I am not there. Nor do I take for granted the work put in by my sound and lighting crew, particularly the man who was with me for many years from the early days in Hull. Zeb White also put so much time in for me.

Today it's Paul Philips and Cliff Mair who are at the helm, and they do such a terrific job. Then of course there are the amazing backing singers, currently including the wonderful Tracey Jordan and Fiona Ford, who have been such an important part of my shows too. Everyone is important to me. It's a real team effort.

They all spend hours sound-checking and rehearsing, so that we can achieve the standard of playing and performing that we all strive for when onstage together. It is a very real pleasure to work with each and every one of them.

Right, that's your latest break over! Are you ready for the onslaught that comes next as I hurtle towards that moment when all looks lost for me? Good! Then I shall resume. I have to say that you might be ready for this next part, but I'm still not. This is the part that really hurts, even now, no matter how many times I think of it.

CHAPTER THIRTY-ONE

ANYONE GOT SOME BONE MARROW?

While 2003 had seen me diagnosed with leukaemia, it wasn't until July 2004 it was confirmed that I needed to find a donor fast. That's when Dr Kelsey told me that a bone-marrow transplant was my only hope of survival. He'd said the chemotherapy and the drugs would keep things at bay in the short term, but it was the transplant that was the key. In fact, if a suitable donor could be found, the really great news then might be that I would probably make a full recovery, and that I would not have to live with this thing hanging around my neck twenty-four hours a day, as I had for years.

Wishing and hoping is one thing. Finding a donor, and then a match, is another. But then we found out about a wonderful charity, one that I now help in any way I can.

But before we get to the drama, there were still plenty of other things going on. I had shows to perform, DVDs to release and money to raise for charity.

On the performance and merchandise front, we were back on the DVD trail in 2004 with the release of *A Year in His Life*, which was split into three parts and featured rehearsal and concert footage from Sheffield City Hall; part of the concert at Leeds City Varieties (where I had performed in my *Junior Showtime* days); and the Friendship Club party at the Hilton (it used to be called the Dragonara) in Leeds. There was also rehearsal and concert footage of my summer season at Blackpool Opera House, and several interviews with Granada and Yorkshire Television recording my ongoing battle against this horrible disease.

We released both *A Year in His Life* and the DVD of the charity gala concert on behalf of the Sheffield Children's Hospital and Jane Tomlinson's appeal at Sheffield City Hall, which was titled *Joe Longthorne... with Love*. I wasn't too happy about all of the footage on the Sheffield concert because of the size of my glands at the time, but my fans thought it was just great to have another memento of me in concert. In my heart of hearts I knew there would be better concerts to come, if only I could pull through what was happening to my body now.

People tell me the best production of all was the DVD that also appeared on the Biography Channel on the Sky network – *If I Never Sing Another Song* – made by the Vegas Films production company, written and produced by the wonderful Paul Iacovou.

Little did the TV company know at the time that my life was to undergo another rollercoaster ride in the months they were filming. It is a beautifully shot programme that I believe captures the real me more so than any other.

Our spring tour took in thirty-seven shows in just fifty days. We travelled over 7,000 miles on that tour alone, mainly because the treatment I was receiving at Blackpool meant that I needed to be there three times a week and each session took around eight hours. It was the kind of logistical nightmare that makes some shake their heads in despair, but James sorted it all out. It really was a Herculean task at times.

I was determined that we would get through all of the dates on what was a sell-out tour. There was one night when we finished in Southend, drove back to Blackpool that same night, went to Victoria Hospital in the morning, took a flight from Blackpool to Biggin Hill then drove around the M25 to Dartford.

Zeb was tour manager, and he was to remain a close friend throughout the next year as I fought my personal battle against this illness, with the help of the finest doctors, nurses and hospital staff you could wish for. This was the time when James and Fran had to look after me all of the time. I was barely surviving. The combination of the treatment plus the fatigue from the concerts, where I never gave less than 100 per cent, meant I was constantly tired.

Joe Wildy, one of my fellow entertainers who has played in Blackpool and on tour with me, said at the time, 'I don't know how he does it [meaning me]. It's been a terrible strain for him. How he's managed to get through it. It must be willpower.'

When I wasn't going straight back to Blackpool for treatment I would sleep in what became known as the 'Joemobile', the tour bus.

What particularly annoyed me when we got to Billingham Forum, where we were to play two nights and is captured on film for all to see, were the swollen glands in my neck. On the *If I Never Sing Another Song* programme, I show how bothered I was about them:

'It's these bloody lumps, like bastard boiled eggs aren't they?' I wasn't happy about them at all – although I quite like eggs, but I prefer mine poached or scrambled. Little did I know that they were to end up the size of cricket balls.

I was still able to make jokes on stage about what I was going through. I told one joke about a nurse who got my name wrong. She called me Mr Long Horn.–"'Oh," I said, "you've seen me without my clothes on then!'"

The Friendship Club event which was held at the Hilton in Leeds saw the auctioning of three of my suits, and with further contributions this total was swelled to just under £4,000, which again was divided between the hospitals in Leeds and Blackpool. This was where the key that I had been presented with from the *Through the Keyhole* TV programme was also auctioned off.

The same evening as the Friendship Club party, we performed at the world-famous City Varieties Music Hall in Leeds on my birthday, 31 May, and by then we had raised £7,000 for the Leeds General Infirmary. We presented the cheque to Professor Childs. We also raised a further £1,000 for the MacMillan Windmill Appeal at Blackpool Victoria Hospital.

I had got through the spring tour with only one or two cancellations, which were more due to the treatment not being completed in time for me to get to a venue than anything else. I really had tried my best to fulfil all of my engagements, but the treatment had occasionally made life too difficult. I was reported as saying in May 2004:

'I have the steadfastness to go forward and give it a f***ing good fight. Going on stage is like therapy to me. I've now got to get through this summer's run. The last thing I want to do is let anyone down.'

Three weeks into the rehearsals for the Summer Spectacular, it was time for Dr Paul Kelsey to deliver the verdict. I had been taking thirty-five steroids a day and had needed regular four-pint blood transfusions during the twelve-week course of treatment, but it hadn't been successful.

Dr Kelsey told me that my white blood-cell count had stabilised and was just above the danger threshold. That was the good news.

The bad news was that he decided I should undergo six chemo-therapy sessions over an eighteen-week period at Blackpool Victoria Hospital, immediately after the close of the summer season's shows, and that a bone-marrow replacement operation was not just my best way forward, it was now my only option if I wanted to live for anything like a decent time.

I put it this way at the time: 'The doctors choose what to do. It's a bit like chess. There are many possible moves but one wrong one and that could be it, checkmate.'

My family were first in line to see whether they could provide a suitable match as a bone-marrow donor, but none of them fitted the bill. My fans were next in line. They have never ceased to amaze me with the loyalty, tenderness, love and care they have shown me over the years. If it's money I'm short of, they'll send me that too. Bless them all. They've probably a lot less than I've had. If it's part of my body that needs replacing, they'll even offer me parts of theirs!

Sometimes it's not always possible to tell everybody just how much you think about them, but every one of them has a special place in my heart. And one of them might have had a special place inside my body too, because hundreds of them registered with the Anthony Nolan Trust to see whether they were a match.

I had added my name to the Anthony Nolan Register as a possible recipient, and my fans had followed suit as possible donors – of course, not just for me but because of being made aware of the fabulous work the trust carries out every day. How wonderful is that? I started working to raise funds for the trust, which I had not heard of until then, immediately.

Due to the treatment I was going to have, it was quickly decided that my next Australia tour, which had been scheduled for late 2004, would be rescheduled. Around this time, Dave Halford had to do so much cancelling of tours and gigs, but he remained faithful to me throughout the time that followed and was there for me as soon as I was back, fit and able. His people at Artistes Direct are really very professional and ensure that I get to venues right across the UK.

Just before I started the summer season in 2004, I auctioned off most of my gold and platinum discs and special awards received over the years on eBay, in aid of Cancer Research. There was the Best Newcomer Award of 1983 from the Variety Club of Great Britain and the Variety Club of Jersey Award I picked up in 1980. I really felt I ought to be doing something more, and these awards were one way in which I could further contribute. I really didn't think I needed them anymore and the money we raised (over £10,000) was far more important. A number of my fans followed suit by also auctioning off their memorabilia for charity.

I was all set for the Summer Spectacular at the Opera House to be just that, and we had a fantastic line-up with the Stardust Dancers, singer Kiely Hampson, violinist Gary Lovini, the always wonderfully entertaining Johnnie Casson and Tony Jo as compère. It opened to fabulous reviews and a sell-out audience. I couldn't have wished for better.

It was scheduled for a nine week run (19 July–19 September), five nights a week, and negotiations were underway to extend the season by a further two weeks. I fancied breaking my own box-office record that year.

But I was suffering. During August I struggled with severe back pains and those damned swollen glands. I was still giving it my very best shot every night, but my body was rebelling. It was as though it was shouting at me that it had gone far enough. I just couldn't perform. It had got to the point where I was performing, then immediately being wrapped up in cotton wool and put to bed, sleeping until seven o'clock the next evening and then coming to do the show.

Normally I would have spent time with the fans after each show, but I was using up so much energy on stage that I had nothing left to give afterwards. I just went straight home after each concert, so I was only awake for the time I was performing.

I had performed thirty-five shows of the Summer Spectacular when it all caught up with me at last. I couldn't stand throughout my performance, so I had an armchair brought onto the stage. My glands were also getting larger and larger, and inevitably I became too weak to perform at all. I was so disappointed – not for me, but for the legions of fans. I knew this was a really serious time. It was the worst I'd ever been.

Dr Paul Kelsey and his team quickly decided that, although my blood count had remained stable during the Summer Spectacular concerts, the best course of action to deal with the swelling of my glands was to start my treatment earlier than originally planned. To be fair, I don't think Dr Kelsey wanted to leave the treatment until after I'd finished the Summer Spectacular in the first place, but he knew how important the show was to me.

So there I was, on 7 September 2004, admitted back into hospital for my first week of treatment. I was due to be in for seven days, with the Summer Spectacular still being performed minus me. My intention was clear. I wanted to be back on that stage performing again before the season ended, preferably as soon as possible.

But it wasn't going to be that simple.

I had been told it would be like committing suicide to go on stage. At that moment, Blackpool Victoria Hospital was where I needed to be and James called it a real life or death decision.

There was a story doing the rounds at the time when I was admitted that I had collapsed on stage during the last concert, but that wasn't the case. I had collapsed several times offstage, but never on it.

I always told my mam, 'There's always people worse off than me.' And I truly believe that. All of the affection I am constantly being shown by my fans is really wonderfully uplifting. They follow me throughout not just the UK tours, but Australia, Cyprus, Spain and Vegas. How can I ever be worse off than others with that kind of support?

I was determined to get back in the action as soon as I could, and on 18 September I returned – for one night only, the last night of the season. Word quickly got around that I was back and once again we had a complete sell-out. Everyone turned up – of course the fans, but also many other stars from the world of show-business. I was grateful to them all for showing their concern.

At the show we also managed to present cheques to Macmillan Cancer Relief and Cancer Research. The lady who received the cheque on behalf of Macmillan Cancer Relief said some beautiful words on the night that made me feel very humble:

'Ladies and gentlemen, life is not measured by the number of breaths you take, but by the number of times your breath is taken away. Joe, you're truly inspirational. You're the finest ambassador for those living with cancer and you take our breath away a million times.'

It couldn't help but bring a tear to my eye. I'd never seen myself in that way – being an ambassador – I've just done what I feel is right.

While my treatment continued, there was at last some fresh hope on the bone-marrow front. And it was really fantastic news.

Originally it had been thought that there would be even less of a chance of finding a suitable donor from outside of my family, but the reason why the Anthony Nolan Trust exists is to ensure there is a big enough pool of people to improve the chances of finding a suitable match.

Let's hold on for that fantastic news just a bit, whilst I tell you why we should all be supportive of the work of the Anthony Nolan Trust. I told you this wasn't a me-me-me book, and this is what I meant. It's important this, it's the bit where I get on my soapbox:

The important things in life are people, those who are your family, friends, fans, and those who make sure you can carry on living.

Amazingly, given all of the monies our government puts into war efforts and paperwork, the Anthony Nolan Trust receives no direct government funding. The Air Ambulance is the same by the way. These amazingly vital, lifesaving bodies are simply registered charities that rely on the public and private companies to fund their tremendous efforts. The Terrence Higgins Trust, the leading HIV and AIDS charity in the UK, is another.

Personally I think it's criminal in this day and age that we spend so much of our time on other things when just a small proportion of what is spent elsewhere could improve so many people's lives, instead of living with the fear that every new day could be their last.

I was going to leave the next bit until the end but, in case you forget by the time you finish the book – and there is a lot more to come yet, quite a bit of heartache and then some of the best moments in my life – here is what you need to know if you feel inspired to register. And I hope most sincerely that you do:

To find out more about the
ANTHONY NOLAN TRUST
Contact: 020 7284 1234
Or visit: www.anthonynolan.org.uk
The Terrence Higgins Trust urgently needs your support too.
Whether you want to give money, time or both:
TERRENCE HIGGINS TRUST
Contact: 314-320 Gray's Inn Road, London WC1X 8DP
Please do what you can, even if it is simply a donation. They

are always looking for more bone-marrow donors in order to help people like me.

Now let's turn to just how amazing the trust turned out to be for me!

The Anthony Nolan Trust found seven donor hopefuls from its worldwide register of nine million people. That's why they need so many people on the register. It really is over a million-to-one shot that you find compatibility.

One of the seven was from South Africa, another was from Germany and one was a girl from Wales. Professor Guy Lucas told me that the German sounded probably the best bet because of their techniques over there. I think he might have been watching too many of those TV advertisements about German cars,

Vorsprung-Durch-Technic and all that! Anyhow, he said that they were settling on this young lady from Wales. I'm told she was only twenty-eight. I've never met her, but of all the people I have said I am grateful to so far in this book she has to be right up there at the top – apart from my mam and dad of course! You saved my life, thank you, whoever you are, so much!

Of course, finding a donor, a suitable match, is one thing. Going through the procedure is quite another, but we were on our way.

Have I mentioned gangsters yet? I mean THE gangsters? Which UK gangsters do you know? Yes, it's them, or at least one of the twins.

Well, it's about time I did mention them. Now this is a break that I bet you weren't expecting. And it's all true. You might need an even stiffer drink this time!

CHAPTER THIRTY-TWO

REGGIE

On my cherished grand piano at home stands a sheaf of papers. They are not the works of Don Black, who I admire greatly, nor are they any of the other great songwriters of the past century such as Sammy Cahn, Cole Porter, George Gershwin or Lennon and McCartney.

They are the works of a man who was better known for his partnership with his twin brother. I'm talking about Reggie Kray.

Back in the 1990s I received a call from a man called Frank Fraser, who simply said, 'Reg wants to see you.'

I knew the Krays liked my music because I'd heard that Ron had wanted me to sing at his wedding. It didn't happen, but it was then that I knew they both liked my work. It turned out that Reg had been writing quite a bit in Maidstone prison with another inmate, and when he was to be released he planned to have a recording studio in his new home. He had already written his autobiography and a book of slang, but this was different. He had been collaborating with another inmate on lyrics with a view to him and me turning them into songs. There is one called 'Butterfly' that's on the top of the pile on my piano now.

When I went to see Reggie I was amazed at his appearance. He was wearing overly thick spectacles and he could hardly hear me. He couldn't do anything, probably couldn't even see anything whilst he was wearing them, and yet there were still extra guards on duty for my visit. I spoke to the wardens about the spectacles he was wearing and the fact that he needed a hearing aid; apparently, the week after my visit he had new specs and a new hearing aid.

I'm not going to comment on why he was in prison, that's not my place. All I knew was the man I saw in front of me that day didn't look as though he was being treated properly. The next day I got a call from Frank Fraser again, who said what I had done was a 'wonderful gesture'. To me it was just common decency.

I talked with Reg about his mother, whom it is well documented that he and Ron loved more dearly than anyone else in their lives. We talked about the film that the Kemp brothers had starred in, playing Ron and Reg. He liked the film, but the one thing he was bothered about was the way his mother had been portrayed:

'Our mother never swore as much as she did in the film. I'm still a bit upset about the way they did that.'

Then he said, 'I'm sending you some lyrics.' And that was it. One day I hope to release them on an album called *Inside Out*, with all of the funds going to Reg and Ron Kray's charities.

CHAPTER THIRTY-THREE

BONE MARROW: THE PRELUDE

I liked the idea of having my bone marrow coming from Wales; after all, it was the land of Dame Shirley. But there was plenty to go through before I even came close to receiving it.

Following that final appearance in the last night of the Summer Spectacular 2004, my life for the next year was to be one long round of chemotherapy, treatment, double pneumonia, a state of unconsciousness and hospitals. I honestly don't know how I came through.

There was just no way I could perform, and everything in the diary was shifted so that I could concentrate on one thing only – finally beating this disease. We had to reschedule the charity concert I had been looking forward to in my home city of Hull in December, where I had hoped to play for what could have ended up being my last ever time.

DVDs were released along with further compilation CDs in late 2004 and the early part of 2005. It was the closest I would get to performing for some considerable time.

BONE MARROW: THE PRELUDE

When I first met Professor Guy Lucas, he explained to me that I had run out of options. I only had one choice and that was the bone-marrow transplant. He also told me that all he could offer me was a hard time. He said he had heard I was a bit of a character – although it could have been another word that I won't use here. I soon knew where I stood with him. He was in charge. He told me that I could either 'go forth and multiply', in as pleasant a way as possible, or I could do it his way.

It was in October 2004 that I found out about the number of possible donors. By now I was underway with what turned out to be a further twenty-four weeks of chemotherapy, taking me through until February 2005. There had been a hope that the bone marrow transplant would take place following the course of chemotherapy, but the news I had been waiting for wasn't good – I still had to wait.

You can't keep me away from singing for that long. Since I was now simply waiting and I was feeling good again, we announced that I would be performing three shows over Easter at the Paradise Rooms in Blackpool. They were scheduled for 26–28 March and I played them all.

While I had been looking forward to performing again and felt better than I had for a long time, I was also nervous. But I needn't have been because the audience was fantastic. All of my fans were there again over the three nights and some came to all three – they really helped me through.

It was just after the Paradise concerts that I was very nearly in paradise myself! There were compatibility tests to undertake that were to last a further three months, but it looked like we were getting close to the match I needed.

That was the time when I found out about the seven hopefuls, including my young lady from Wales. The news was that the transplant looked odds-on for later in the year.

When the curtain fell at the Opera House for that last night of the Summer Spectacular in 2004, I thought it might be the last concert I would ever play. But since that time I had managed to fit in a date at a club called The Willows, the three sell-outs at the Paradise Rooms, and had also been booked to appear at the same venue twice a week throughout the summer. I was feeling stronger again and actually felt sharper in those three days at the Paradise Rooms than I had for a year or so.

In 2004 there had been some nights when I had only been on stage for thirty-to-forty minutes and felt completely drained. That isn't like me. I want to be out there for as long as I can. I don't want anyone feeling short-changed. But now things were looking up again.

I was told all along the way that having the bone-marrow transplant was not the end of it. There was far more to go through, as my body might reject what had been administered. In short, my chances were not brilliant and I could die just from the procedure itself. All I could do was put my trust in them and that's exactly what I did – up until that moment when I could hear those voices around me losing their faith, which is where we started this book.

How right they were. Not in losing their faith, but in warning me of what might happen.

I had also been told I would need six to twelve months in order to recover. But before all of that, and just a month or so after coming out of chemotherapy, I was told it was time to start a new round of it, so that when they undertook the procedure my body was completely free of cancer cells.

Professor Lucas had promised me a rough ride and this was only the start of it. You might think that some rollercoasters you have been on made you feel sick or dizzy. Let me tell you that, although my life had been like living on a rollercoaster for many years, it was now time for the big dipper!

When you go down a dip you inevitably come to the lowest point – and I have come to that a few times in my life. The nervous breakdown was obviously one of those, but this illness has sent me down quite a few dips. I have suffered from depression regularly and there have been times when, because of what I have been going through, I felt as though I just wanted it all to end.

The after effects of chemotherapy, as anyone who has had to undergo it will verify, are like the worst hangover you can ever have – and believe you me, I've had my fair share of those too.

When I am unable to perform I begin to wonder what my life is all about. It is what I was made to do. I know a lot of young people say that today, when they are trying out for TV programmes, but it really is what my life has been about.

I have often said this, but the people who suffer the most are those around you. When you're depressed you are feeling sorry for yourself, but that only makes things worse for your loved ones. In my case that's James, my family, my friends and all of my fans. They all look after me in whichever way they can.

I've not made too many mentions of my faith up to now, but I do believe in a higher authority. I'm not too religious, but I am a Catholic and I do believe in Jesus Christ. I'm not much of a good-doer, but what I do have is faith in the creator, whoever that is. I can't claim to know what he or she looks like, but I do know God is all. I couldn't tell you any more apart from that I believe there is one. I do go to church, but not regularly. I take mass. I'm not a Bible-thumper but I do believe that the Bible makes sense of our lives.

James also brings a great deal of sense to my life. As he will tell you, that is often just commonsense too, but he has been wonderful for me from the moment we got together. I owe this young man so much – I couldn't possibly ever repay him. He knows everything about me; he understands everything that has happened in the past twenty years; and most of all he has been there for me every step of the way.

I don't think I could have come through all that I have without his constant support. Is this getting too mushy? Well, I don't apologise for any of it.

James is a diamond. I do an impression of Neil Diamond, but James is the real gem. He calms me down when I'm overwrought and emotional; he won't let me do anything that he thinks will do me harm. If he thinks I'm doing too much he will tell me to stop, to rest. But most importantly of all, he is always there by my side. He doesn't make a big play of it; he doesn't want to be in the spotlight; all he is doing is looking after me in the best way he can, and that's good enough for me.

How's all that for mush? Well, it's not mush to me and I mean every word.

We were talking about being on a big dipper, weren't we? Well, with no immediate prospect of a transplant in sight and buoyed by the success of my three nights in the Paradise Rooms, the summer season was booked and Dave even added dates at the Royal Concert Hall in Glasgow. This big dipper of mine was starting to go up again.

My long-time show-business friend Engelbert Humperdinck was keen to get me back to Vegas, and if anyone had the contacts he would have them. He was going to play a series of concerts in Paris and he talked about me joining him to play over there. It was all dependent on my next series of tests.

Typically for me, they didn't go my way, so the Paris idea was shelved. By now I had a pretty long shelf to keep all of what had been put on there.

My last performance before the ordeal that would see me in a hospital bed for nearly four months was once again at the Paradise Rooms, on 30 May. We had it filmed and the DVD could even have been my epitaph. The place was packed; it was a wonderful evening that included my sister Lizzie getting up to sing 'Crazy', written by Willie Nelson but always associated with Patsy Cline. Lizzie sang it beautifully, like the professional I always thought she could have been. I did tell you that all of my family were great singers, didn't I? It was another massively emotional night for me.

I told everyone that night, 'I am looking at the next few weeks as a journey. I have had a great and wonderful time. When I get through this next period of treatment and time in hospital undergoing the bone-marrow replacement, I'll be back in top form and top style – and I hope my hair will have come back again too!'

My hair has gone five times over the years through all of the chemo I have had, but each time it has always come back.

Never was I to sing my final song so meaningfully. I think everyone felt what I was really feeling in the room when I sang 'If I Never Sing Another Song'.

There were hankies out everywhere, tears running down people's faces. I think we all knew that this was it. This was the big one. My big dipper was about to go down – would it come back up again this time?

CHAPTER THIRTY-FOUR

DEATH'S DOOR

Two weeks after the May concert we were finally underway. Would I ever come out of hospital alive?

Well yes, I would actually. As it happens, within a day! But that's because we hadn't reached the full-on procedure stage just yet. This was the preliminary. We were pretty much at base camp before taking on Everest – and I'm not talking about buying double glazing.

On Wednesday, 15 June 2005, I was admitted to the Manchester Royal Infirmary to have what is known as a Hickman line inserted into my chest. It was to ease the administration of the treatment, and I had been told that if there were no complications I would be discharged the following afternoon.

Step one was a success.

I went back on Monday, 20 June, after a lovely evening that had been laid on for James and me at the Lowry Hotel in Manchester by one of Zeb's colleagues. We had been booked into the Presidential Suite, and I remember the suite had a Yamaha grand piano. It was another wonderful gesture. A Bentley had also been laid on for us, to and from the hotel.

When we arrived at Manchester Royal Infirmary the following morning at eight o'clock I was ready. All I felt was that this was it: I'm here now, so let's get on with it. After all, I'd had long enough to think about this moment. It had been on the agenda for what seemed forever. At least, one way or the other, something was now going to be done.

At this point I have to thank Zeb again, because it was he who kept the fans in touch with what was happening to me during this time. We might have had our differences from time to time, but he really did stick close by.

At first I was receiving various chemotherapy treatments. I received two separate treatments in one day – ARA-C and Campath – and Lord, did that hurt. I was also on morphine to counteract the back pain I had been suffering. I was, so I'm told, holding up well after the first seven days of treatment, but remember this was only the chemotherapy. We were nowhere near the transplant just yet.

In fact I was in such good spirits at the time that I was already talking about when I would be performing again. I had felt that New Year's Eve would be as good a time as any, with a big 'Welcome Back' party. It's the only way I could really cope with what was going on, by constantly looking forward.

Professor Lucas told me I had been doing well and that the next step would be a smooth infusion of stem cells the following day, 29 June. I had lost my appetite by now and had come down from 12st 7lbs to 11st 7lbs. I was reliably informed that would come down even further.

This was the real start of my countdown to the operation. Dr Paul Cahalin, who had been looking after me at Blackpool Victoria Hospital the previous year, was drafted in to the Manchester

Royal Infirmary team. I was now receiving a powerful drug called Melphalan, along with others, which was intended to bring my immune system down to zero. The idea was to lessen the chance of infection when the bone marrow was infused.

While all of this was going on I was receiving good luck messages from all around the world, from fans and all of my pals in showbiz. Among them were one from Andy Williams and another from Engelbert.

On 29 June, the bone marrow transplant was administered. It lasted around the length of one of my concerts, between an hour and a half and an hour and three quarters. There were more drugs to follow after the transplant, including antibiotics, but I was doing well.

I should have known that things would get worse, just when I felt a little better. It's the way it has always been for me with this awful disease.

Five days after the transplant I contracted GVHD (Graft Versus Host Disease). I was now in the real danger zone. After all those months of preparation, my body looked like it could be rejecting what it had been given.

It wasn't all bad news. I was told I was making good progress regardless of the GVHD. We were now in mid-July, it was hot and portable air conditioning was needed. With the good progress I was making, there was talk of moving me to Blackpool Victoria. But it turned out to be far too early. I wasn't out of the woods yet by a long way! In fact I'd only just entered the darkness of the trees. The worst time of all was to come pretty quickly now.

Just after receiving a report about how well I was doing, I developed a chest infection and I understand that my odds of surviving were halved at that stage. The bookies would have had a field day with me.

My whole body was starting to shut down, and by the end of

July I was deeply sedated on a ventilator. I couldn't do anything but lie there now.

I now know just how much all of the dearest people in my life were going through: James, my close friends, my family, and of course my fans. Candlelit vigils were being held in churches up and down the country.

James has told me that at one point he honestly thought that was it. He spoke to Pat in desperation and in floods of tears. He told her I was on a machine and that he thought I was finally dying. Of course, he was still with me even then and he never left my side. There was nothing I could do except, somewhere deep inside me, fight my way out of this. I believe I did it through my faith.

It was a really bad time for all of the people closest to me. All of my family were there now. My dear sweet mam was in bits. I think she'd nearly had enough herself. Pat had come and she couldn't believe it was me. There I was, this blown-up man; the drugs had done that to me. She knew all of the scrapes I'd been through over the years and had seen me bounce back from them all, but even she didn't think I could get out of this one.

The three Fathers came, including Father Geoff – a bit like 'We Three Kings', except they didn't bring me any gold, frankincense or myrrh. Instead they gave me 'last orders'! Well, I knew I wasn't Jesus, but I had expected a little more hope than that! The funny thing was that, as soon as I saw them, something inside me told me that I wasn't dying.

Professor Lucas came back from his holidays and was apparently as surprised as anyone to see me still alive. When he had gone, I don't think he thought I had any chance of survival. He knew that what had been done was all that he and his team could do. The rest was up to me and my body. Fortunately for me, I had a bit more than that. I had faith, plus the prayers of everyone around me, and those praying in churches or in their homes. It worked for me.

But even that wasn't enough! It was time for my sister Anne to leap into action. Anne took over from the nurses one day when she saw that my blood pressure wasn't right. My temperature was 104. Anne dragged the pillowcase from under my head and had it filled with ice. The more ice I got, the more my blood pressure came right.

Of course, I couldn't have told you about any of this at the time. I was unconscious for weeks, so a lot of it is from what others have told me. What I can tell you is that the thoughts going through my head were those we started with at the beginning of the book.

I couldn't move, but there were times when I could hear things, or at least you think you can. I was sure that someone was talking to John Boy, telling him I would be going at six o'clock. 'We can't do any more,' was what I think I heard. At one point I really think they were going to switch me off.

By now, although I couldn't move, couldn't speak, couldn't communicate, I was fighting so much inside of me. I had double pneumonia – bad news at the best of times, critical for me at this time. But still they were pumping me with drugs. Everything that could be done was being done to keep me going.

My fight was still going on, even if they couldn't see it, but I was fast approaching the time when it was all becoming too much even for my faith.

That's when I thought I could hear them say the words, 'He's dead. He's dead. He's gone.' But I wasn't! I wanted to scream at them that I was still here. That's when I gave myself up. This is when I said to myself, *My Jesus, this is it now. I'm f***ed.*

He understands any language and I'm going through too much pain to care about being right. I'm dying. I've been on this slab for six hours, all of these people are trying to help but I'm now in too much pain. That's when I thought, *Dear Lord, if you've any decency about you take me now.*

But then I heard a phone call. That's when I believe I heard the thing about not being touched with a bargepole – and that's when I changed my tune too. That gave me the spirit I needed.

I just thought, *Jesus, help me now.* I didn't see his face. People say they do, but I didn't. It's just a feeling that he was there.

We're still not even at the stage where I was back with my eyes open just yet. I remained unconscious for a fortnight. Two whole weeks taken out of my life! I suppose it was still better than being taken out completely.

A breathing tube had been inserted, but it was between my vocal cords. Now there was a concern amongst my nearest and dearest that even if I did recover, I might never be able to talk again, let alone sing. Maybe the last song I had sung at the Paradise Rooms was going to become prophetic?

They moved the breathing tube from where it went through my vocal cords to directly into my trachea. Apparently, I was now also starting to produce healthy white blood cells, but the regular blood transfusions I needed were still taking place.

August had been almost nonexistent for me. I had now regained consciousness and was through the worst of it. I tried to speak but couldn't. That was worrying. I had been told that I shouldn't attempt to speak straightaway, but you do want to try. I couldn't help it. I didn't expect to be able to sing like Mario Lanza, but I so wanted to sing again, or at least know that I could.

The very least I wanted to say was, 'Mine's a half of lager!'

At one time I was using an alphabet chart to spell out what I was trying to say. James, Zeb, Anne and Pat all tried their best to lip-read too. James put his mobile phone to my ear so that I could hear Mam's voice again. It was such a wonderful feeling. I had been through hell and was still in a lot of pain, but I had come through it all. Professor Lucas had told me only three out of every ten who endured what I experienced made it back to life.

Things started coming back to me slowly. When my hair first grew back I looked like Saddam Hussein. Not a good look!

The first thing I saw when the pipe was taken out of me was this beautiful nurse. I fell in love with her instantly, and yet I never knew her name. I was too weak to ask, but she was around me all of the time. She really looked after me and was my very own personal Florence Nightingale.

By September I was well enough to be transferred from Manchester Royal Infirmary, where I had now spent twelve weeks, to Blackpool Victoria Hospital where I took up residency in the Macmillan Unit for three weeks, before returning home for the first time in four months.

I recorded a message on my update telephone line, promising all of my fans that I would be back on the road just as soon as I could. My voice wasn't brilliant at the time. It was weak and croaky, but I just wanted to let them know just how much I felt their prayers and good wishes had helped me.

While I was in hospital I kept thinking about when I might be back performing, but even at home I was still in the hands of the doctors. By now I was bored. When all you have done for the past thirty-five years is to earn a wage singing for your living, constantly preparing for the next performance, it is hard to accept the fact that you need to just stay at home. But that's what I needed to do right then if I wanted to make a full recovery.

My first consultation following the operation was in November. I had been going in for weekly check-ups at Blackpool Victoria and was still having regular blood transfusions. As you might expect, I was a bit apprehensive. In fact I'd had trouble sleeping the night before. If it had been bad news I don't know how I'd have felt. But it was good news. I was on the mend and my white blood-cell count was now normal.

There was a charity show to be held in my honour in December, but the specialist advised me against going. I wasn't going to sing but I knew that, if I had gone, I couldn't have resisted getting up. I didn't go, but I was there! I had recorded a message on video.

It was a good job I didn't go either. In the first week of 2006 I was back in hospital again. Was there to be no end to this?

This time it was nothing to do with the bone-marrow transplant. I was suffering from the effects of dehydration. It wasn't a relapse and the cancer hadn't come back. We were ready to roll. I was ready to get back on that stage at last. It was the best news I have ever had!

CHAPTER THIRTY-FIVE

THE COMEBACK

Nervous breakdown. Bankruptcy. Cancer. A bead up my nose. I'd come through it all. It was now 2006, and I was about to start making that journey once again through my singing career – the journey that, after everything, is still on the upturn.

Are you ready for the rollercoaster to start gathering pace once more? Well, now is the time!

We were underway by April. It was Easter again, just a year on from all that had happened, and I was back in the Grand Theatre in Blackpool. I was back doing what I was made to do.

Glasgow, Motherwell, Sheffield, Bradford, Whitley Bay, Darlington, Billingham, Telford, Worthing, Southend, Swansea and Purfleet were all on the tour schedule, along with many more to follow. It wasn't the biggest UK tour I'd ever done, but it was a start. Dave Halford of Artistes Direct had been guarded in not giving me too much too soon, and with James now having taken over managing me fulltime we had a fantastic time. The tour finished back in my home city of Hull at the New Theatre, and I was also back at the Paradise Rooms for a summer season, performing every Friday and Saturday.

It really was such a marvellous time for me. Everywhere I went the audiences, my fans, were on their feet giving me a standing ovation before I'd even started singing!

I've always received so many flowers at my concerts for so many years, but now I could have replaced Interflora. It confirmed to me what I already thought: everyone coming to the concerts had been going through my pain and trauma with me.

But there was one extra special concert that really marked my comeback that year, and it was my return to the London Palladium. Chris the Greek was the man who made it possible. I'd first met Chris way back in 1977, when I was appearing with Jim Davidson down in London, at The Frog & Nightgown in the Old Kent Road. (It's now a nightclub called Virgo's.) Chris told me then that I was going to hit the top. I remember saying, 'I'll see you again one day,' to him. I didn't realise how long it would be. It was twenty-eight years.

Chris and I had not been in touch since that time, but he had contacted me while I was preparing to go in for the bone-marrow transplant. His track record in the music industry has included working for Harvey Goldsmith and putting on stadium gigs for world-famous singers like Marvin Gaye, Stevie Wonder, Lionel Richie and the Commodores, and Diana Ross.

How we got together to organise the Palladium concert was that Chris was putting together a charity night for a man called Joey Pyle (another gangster), known as 'Big Joey' in the London underworld in the sixties, who had motor neurone disease. Joey had been best man at Ronnie Kray's wedding.

Apparently I was one of Joey Pyle's favourite performers. Why am I so popular with gangsters? Reggie Kray, Joey Pyle, the Richardsons, they have all been amongst my fans.

Joey had wanted me to perform at his charity night but I was dying at the time, so it was a little inconvenient! I sent one of my gold discs for the auction they were having.

James then rang Chris when I was making my recovery and, knowing how clever he is at arranging things, asked him whether he could sort the Palladium for us. He did a marvellous job. It was a sell-out.

I had appeared there many times during my TV career days, but usually as one of several stars on variety shows. This time it was my own night, and I was even more determined to show my fans, and the whole of the entertainment business, that I was well and truly back. It was 10 September 2006, and it was another performance captured on DVD for posterity. It really was a remarkable and inspiring night.

The standing ovations I received before I came onto the stage at every concert in the provincial venues were tremendous, but they were nothing compared to what happened at the Palladium. It felt as though for five minutes everyone just stood there applauding, before I'd even opened my mouth! There was so much love in this historic theatre that night.

What was even more marvellous was that, for the previous eight months, the Palladium had been home to the multimillion-pound production of *Sinatra*. What an honour! It might not have been the great man himself but it felt good, Mr Sinatra and then me. It still brings a smile to my face thinking about it now.

Chris the Greek became part of the team for a number of years after that concert. He came up to Blackpool, came on tour with me, and for a long time he never went back to London. His lovely wife, Marilyn, had to come up and see him here!

Now I know what you're thinking by now. There's just bound to be some bad news along the way. Surely I couldn't go a full calendar year without something?

Unfortunately, you're right – but it wasn't anything to do with my state of health, state of wealth, a nervous breakdown or fighting this time. The touring was going well. All of my dates had been packed out – and then my dad died. It was early in December.

Dad, as I said at the start, was such an important part of my life. I know that might sound obvious, but it's really not the same for everyone. Some people in this life never get to see their father, let alone have someone as supportive as my dad was to me. Mam set me on the road with the advice she gave me, but it was Dad who took me to all of those clubs throughout Yorkshire and the North East when I was younger. He looked after me, nurtured me and fought for me.

Those were great days, when I was leading such a simple life really, performing wherever it was possible to sing. But it wasn't all about the singing. Dad was much more than that to me. When he died I thought about those days when, even at the age of three, I would go out on the rag-and-bone cart. We would be singing songs together even then, as we travelled around Hull.

Mam said that I had inherited my musical ability from both of them – him and her. She said that Fred could make a piano talk, which he could, and that when he was in the Royal Navy he used to entertain the rest of the crew similarly to the way I do today.

Dad had been diagnosed with prostate cancer four years earlier, but he never made a thing about it. He was always more concerned with my illness. Lizzie said at the time that it had broken his heart that he hadn't been able to come and see me in Manchester Royal Infirmary the year before, but he was too ill himself. He died at the age of eighty-four in Hull Royal Infirmary.

It doesn't seem enough to leave it at that, does it? So I won't.

My dad was a fantastic man. We had our moments along

the way, like dads and sons often do, but he was always there for me, always believed in me and, like I said earlier, he was the man I respected more than any other in the world – and he still is. There you are, Dad. I'm sure you heard that somewhere, I certainly hope so.

CHAPTER THIRTY-SIX

LIFETIME ACHIEVEMENT AWARD

If 2006 had been a triumphant return to the stage, then 2007 was about to see us move back to a massive tour schedule. I really was determined to show everyone that I was back to stay!

I felt that everything was now in place properly, for the first time in my life. My voice was 100 per cent. The absolutely stunning Joe Longthorne Orchestra now had such a terrific sound that we were a major force to be reckoned with against any other live performance band. I'd have backed the boys, 'Stretch', Si, Paul, Alan, Andy and the rest, against anyone!

But it wasn't just the onstage side of things that was spot on. James had become the superb manager I always knew he would be. Since he took over managing me, it is no surprise that my career has been back on a continuous upswing. Television appearances started to come my way again, after a long time in the TV wilderness.

But things are not just all about me and James either. What we have is a real team effort. My family, including my brother John, my nephews Keith and John Boy, and Keith's son Michael, all play their part. At this point I must also mention my niece Julie, who cut and styled my hair for many years. She's now involved in the film industry in London.

John Boy has been with me since he was about fifteen. We're like glue and we stick together no matter what. One day, a long while ago, I smashed up what I thought was James' phone in frustration. Then I found out I'd smashed up the wrong one. It was John Boy's! He just laughed because he found it so comical.

John Boy's a bit like me. He will chat away with anyone. When he was in his teens, he was with me on the *Canberra* as we were going to Australia; even then he was able to have a proper conversation with an eighty-year-old judge on the ship! He's a great chess player as well. You need great concentration for that, and he's got it.

There's also Dave Halford of Artistes Direct, whose management agency books all of the theatre dates, liaising closely with James, and Jean Parkes is still handling some bookings for me too, we keep in close contact. It took nearly forty years, but I now have a team around me that not only understands me, they also care about me. We work together as a family. And in 2007 that meant we could shift up a gear or three, heading on up for overdrive!

Following on from 2006's twenty dates, we started a forty-six-date UK tour in Glenrothes, Scotland. Dave Halford said he'd only anticipated it being around twenty dates once again, but the tour just grew. We finished in July, but there was even more to come.

Paul Iacovou, who had made a highly-acclaimed documentary about me in 2004, through Vegas Films, was back again, this time following me on the *You & Me* Tour and putting together another DVD. Once again, it was another quality production and it led to what was to be an extra-special time, with an extra-special award coming my way in June 2007. We'll get to that pretty soon.

Dave had promoted the tour and he spoke on camera about how it was very rare to see a performer who is simply loved the way that I am by my fans. I have always felt that love from all of the audiences at my shows, and I try to give that same love back with every song I sing. It is always nice to hear someone say it though, especially a tour promoter like Dave who has seen so many performers in his time.

The *You & Me* DVD is another of my personal favourites, mainly because it catches me in a very natural way. There are some wonderful moments captured on it too – and one of those involves 'Stretch'. Just listen to his playing on 'You'll Never Know', which Paul Iacovou and his team recorded when we were playing at a private function that year. As Frank Sinatra said about one of the songs on his own *A Man and His Music* album, 'The way it was being played even a mynah bird could have had a hit with the song.'

Don Black paid me possibly the biggest compliment ever that year. He was even good enough to say it on the DVD programme for posterity. It brings tears of gladness and humility to me every time I think of it:

'Instantly you realise his voice is from the gods. It's a different kind of talent. It's so in-your-face. It's so obvious that he is special. When I first saw Joe, I got goose bumps. When I come across talent, to me that is the greatest aphrodisiac, just phenomenal and Joe is a remarkable talent. In this world of *Pop Idol* mediocrity he shines like a beacon. He is a great, great talent, but he should be in Vegas, he should be on Broadway. He should be lighting up the West End, but life isn't fair and he's had a lot of bad luck. When I have sat at a concert with Joe Longthorne singing those hours just fly by. He's very, very special and in today's world I can't compare him to anybody because all the great people have gone – the Sinatras and the Dean Martins and Sammy Davises. They no longer exist and Joe is up there with those kinds of people.

'When I sit and watch Joe singing my songs it's obviously an extra special kind of thrill, particularly "If I Never Sing Another Song". It has an extra meaning because of what he has been through with his health, so when he sings, "If I never sing another song, I'll get by, but I'm not sure how," it really is quite heartbreaking. He's earned the right to sing that song. You have to have gone through a troubled life to sing that song.'

When you hear sentiments like that from the great man himself, who has written so many fantastic lyrics, that is the kind of thing that makes me feel so humble. As a singer you are really only as good as the songs you sing and the people who perform with you. That's why Mr Sinatra always used to make a point of mentioning the songwriters in every song he ever sang, and always made sure his band was credited. I try to do the same.

The tour also culminated in the recording of my first studio album for nearly a decade, when *You & Me* was released the following year through Union Square Music.

I felt so fresh and reinvigorated after the bone marrow transplant. It was as though all of those years of living under the fear of losing my life were now finally behind me. My dad always taught me, 'Joe, don't take a backward step. Sometimes take a sideways step, but never a backward one.'

Now, about that special moment! June 2007 saw another wonderful experience for me. While I've always looked forward, this was one night when I was able to look back on my life a little, as the Variety Club of Great Britain honoured me once again, this time with a Lifetime Achievement Award at the Palace Hotel in Manchester.

Lyn Staunton, the Development Director for the Variety Club, told us of a problem they were having with putting on the event. They usually had around 350 people come to a 'do' like this, but within a very short space of time they had been inundated with requests and over 500 had been accepted, with a waiting list growing by the day! I understand the waiting list was up to 250! My heart was bursting with the knowledge that so many people wanted to come and see this lad from Hull pick up this special award. I also knew that the more people that wanted to come, the more it would mean for the charity as well.

And it wasn't just my loyal fans from all over the world that wanted to attend. There were many of my friends from the world of show-business too: Ricky Tomlinson was there (I have even been mentioned twice in *Royle Family* scripts); Roy Walker; Lord Jeffrey Archer; the then Deputy Prime Minister, John Prescott; Liz Dawn; Roy 'Chubby' Brown; Frank Carson; Don Black; Engelbert Humperdinck; Barbara Windsor; the late Mike Reid (*EastEnders*); Cannon and Ball; Johnnie Casson; and the widow of Sammy Davis Jr., Altovise Davis. They all gave their own personal tributes. The Lord Mayor of Hull at the time, Brenda Petch, was there to deliver some very kind words from my home city. They all meant so much to me.

Freddie Starr delivered a surreal tribute. In fact it was so surreal that Chubby mentioned it in his own very kind words to me: 'Is Freddie Starr a full f★★★ing shilling or what?' Now Chubby sometimes gets a bad press because of his blue act, but he is one of the nicest, most considerate men in show-business. He's from Middlesbrough originally and like I said earlier, I was on the same bill as his pop group when I was starting out in my career. We have been great pals ever since.

After his first few gags, he turned really serious, probably the most serious many of his fans will ever have seen him. It's time to grab your hankies again. This is what he said:

'I'm not a religious man. But seeing is believing. I've probably prayed twice in my life. One [time] was when Joe went in for his operation. We were sat in the car, me and my driver Keith. Joe had gone in for this bone marrow. You hear people saying only one in ten survives, you know, and I prayed for him, because I love him, everyone in this room loves him, that's why we're here. I went to his first show when he came back and he sang "If I Never Sing Another Song" and there wasn't a dry eye in the house, including me, we were all in tears. He is a fantastic entertainer, a giant in the entertainment world.'

Professor Guy Lucas was there too. This was the man who had made sure I could get back on the big dipper of my life. He had taken time out from his vital work in saving other people's lives to be a part of this evening. There are some times when 'humble' isn't the right word. Surgeons, consultants, doctors, nurses – what I have learned is that they are the most important professions in life, not singing or writing, or performing, or any of the other jobs we all have. These are the wonderful people in our lives, the people who help us carry on living and let us achieve whatever we want to achieve. Without them I would have been gone a long time ago.

It was that night that I also found out just how worried even this great man had been for my voice, although he hadn't shown it at the time. Usually it is other people giving me a standing ovation, but that night I didn't even care if it was only me who stood up and applauded this wonderful, wonderful man. I gave Professor Lucas my own personal standing ovation. James stood too; then everyone else.

Ricky Tomlinson made sure that people knew this really wasn't all about looking back though. He wanted to tell everyone that I was back, not just the way I was before but better and bigger than ever:

> 'Joe, I just want to say lad, it's easy when you're a star, you're right up there, money's rolling in, elation's rolling in and there's people surrounding you and giving you compliments. But when things go bad, both in health and in work-wise, it's only a superstar that can get up from the ashes and make it again, bigger and better, and become more loved, that's you!'

If I hadn't been filling up before, I was overflowing now! Barbara Windsor was next. She couldn't make it to the 'do' but she did send a really heartfelt message:

> 'Dear Joe,
> 'I am absolutely devastated I can't be at your tribute dinner. You know how much I love you. You know what a fan I am of yours. You are one of our greatest performers in this country – the consummate performer. When I did my album I said to my producer, "Can you please, please get me Joe to guest on it?" and you did. You shot down and did it all in one take – and we had a ball.'

All of the messages and speeches meant so much to me, especially the one from Altovise Davis. Now this was some compliment!

257

'Dear Joe,

'You are a true showman following in the steps of all who have been honoured with this accolade, and I know [I am] speaking for the Sinatra and Martin families when I say you are singlehandedly keeping variety alive and well over there in the UK.

'I only wish you had been around in Las Vegas in the 1960s at those legendary performances the boys gave at The Sands. Had they known about you, they all could have had a night off together and let you perform the entire show!

'Enjoy the evening and I know Sammy would have been so proud of you.'

'God bless,

Altovise Davis.'

I was actually turned down by Frank Sinatra one time, you know. Frank Warren was putting on the great man at the Excel Centre in London's Docklands, and he had sounded me out about being his support act! But apparently, from what I heard, Mr Sinatra didn't want another singer on the bill. I came that close, but not close enough.

Engelbert went even further with his praise, but you're probably starting to think I'm going on a bit about all of this now, and I really don't want this to turn into that 'me-me-me' thing I was mentioning earlier. So let me finish this section off with what Lord Archer said. For me this was yet another example of how what I do onstage seems to reach all walks of life, from the normal, every-day folks like me and my family to great authors such as Jeffrey:

'Many years ago my wife and I were dining at the Café Royale in London when I heard this voice, I just simply got up, left the room, moved up one floor and listened to one of the greatest talents I have ever heard in my life. Many of your fellow professionals have stood on this stage tonight, Joe, and they have talked of you with affection and respect because they have worked with you.

'I represent the millions of people out there who are simply fans. We are the people who know how good you are. I tell you how you judge a fan – and I'll ask you in this room. How many of you have a Joe Longthorne recording in your car so that it's always with you? Hands up! [And Jeffrey put his hand up immediately.] I've got in my car Ella Fitzgerald, Frank Sinatra, Bobby Darin, Tony Bennett and Joe Longthorne. And the reason I have Joe Longthorne next to those four is because he's damned well as good as those four.

'When I listened to those who have come up on this stage it became clear that all of them have had their ups and downs to fight in this remarkable profession which you belong to, Joe. But yours has been more extreme than any of us – debt, illness, you fight everything. And I think it's that persistence, that determination that is an inspiration to us all. Ninety-nine people out of a hundred would simply have given up. Many of the reasons so many of your friends are here tonight, and the reason you have not only survived but come through your problems, is because you don't give up.

'And in between, with all that happening, you've still continued your charity work. And that is why, and one of the many reasons why, the Variety Club honour you tonight. Joe, when all of us are gone and long forgotten, there will be a new generation that will still play your records, there can be no doubt about that.

'Have you noticed how the great stars, whatever profession they are in – Sinatra, Fitzgerald, Bassey, Olivier, Gielgud, Guinness. That is how you think of them. But the difference with you is that if you look at the sign up there, Joe, the word JOE is bigger than the word Longthorne. And I'll tell you why. It's because all of us believe we know you, all of us believe you're a friend, and all of us want you to go on forever. Good luck!'

Right. Hankies away now, let's get on with what the Variety Club is all about and the good work that is done by people like Professor Lucas. I said the next bit on the night when I accepted the award. So let's have no more about me just at the moment. These are my words, but don't just think about me here, think about what I'm saying, please:

'In some way the Variety Club doesn't shout about what it does. It doesn't scream and bawl, it does it in a really fantastic way and it is first and foremost with charity in mind, looking after the children. What a terrific organisation it is. Then there's the great Professor Lucas, surely these are the people we have to admire, we have to look after, and make sure they get the right funds. Raising money is really what tonight is all about.'

I said I was 'goosed' for words, which brought a big laugh – and thanked everyone for the award. I told everyone this was one award that wouldn't go on eBay!

It was the most fantastic night. We raised a record figure of £40,000 through the auction that followed, with Lord Archer in charge. My big darts mate, Phil 'The Power' Taylor, who I also speak with regularly, paid thousands for a very special, diamond-encrusted watch. I just had to sing after all that, didn't I? So I sang five songs at the end of the night, when I have to say I was a little the worse for wear.

LIFETIME ACHIEVEMENT AWARD

Here's another little note, just so that you're getting the idea of where I am coming from with this book. It's another advertisement, but I'd like you to keep this in mind:

The Variety Club of Great Britain

Formed: 1949.

Purpose: To make a real and lasting difference in children's lives.

If you would like to make a difference or would like more information please contact:

VARIETY CLUB OF GREAT BRITAIN

4th Floor

St James' Buildings

79 Oxford Street

Manchester M1 6FQ

Tel: 0161 236 0500

Email: varietyclubnw@btconnect.com

Web: www.varietyclub.org

CHAPTER THIRTY-SEVEN

CYPRUS AND DON BLACK

All of Blackpool's main entertainment venues have been wonderful for me – the record-breaking 1993 summer season at the Opera House in the Winter Gardens complex; the North Pier, where I have had some brilliant times as 'the Captain'; those emotionally-charged nights both just before and following the bone-marrow procedure at the Paradise Rooms; and then there's the Grand Theatre.

The Grand Theatre, like the Palladium, is a Matchem's theatre. It may not have the same size of stage or auditorium as the Opera House, but it has an amazing atmosphere and I have had some perfect nights there. I played there in 2007 through September, with yet another full production show. It was a fantastic season and we had a great line-up. Maurice from The Grumbleweeds was compère; we had the lovely and brilliant Leanne Fury and the comedian Carl Schofield, who had even come up with a very funny 'rap' all about me!

Later that year we were back at sea for more adventures. We had been booked to play on the Royal Caribbean, but that's not where we were heading. And again we didn't start from the UK. That would have been too easy!

We had flown out to Norway – well, it is quicker than walking you know! We were boarding the ship in Bergen, which was then sailing to Amsterdam and then back to Harwich. Simple, you'd think, but not if you're with the Joe Longthorne touring party.

Norway was good, but it's very expensive. Eight quid a pint! I know that I'm not very good with money, but surely that was far too much! At that rate I'd be back in financial trouble before long. The food was great though. I love fish. I had crab and just about every form of seafood I could get, but I didn't eat the whale sandwiches. They do have them.

Now remember, this was me on a cruise, in foreign parts again. It couldn't all go that easily, could it? Well, it was soon to get complicated.

We got off in Amsterdam and that was our first mistake! Chris the Greek and the lovely, adorable Marilyn, Chris's wife, decided to go off and do a bit of shopping. Then they both ended up joining us in a café where 'Don't Worry 'bout a Thing (Three Little Birds)' by Bob Marley was being played. That's because we were in the world-renowned Bob Marley Café.

To cut a long story short, we all ended up a bit the worse for wear, if you understand where I'm coming from. If you don't understand, then I think the phrase 'we were stoned' will do.

We'd been on the 'happy cake', and on the way back to the boat we nearly knocked five bikes over and were close to being killed under four trams! I was then attacked by some dogs as we were going back to the ship, interfering bloody beagles, and Marilyn nearly didn't get back on at all!

Once we'd got to Harwich, we picked up the next set of passengers and sailed to Lithuania. It was hardly the Caribbean, but it was a tremendous time on board and the people we played to were fantastic.

Two more compilation double CDs were released in 2007 – one titled *The Ultimate Entertainer*, which includes one CD of my live show material where I sing as me and another CD which features all of my 'special guests'. This is the only time in my career that one whole CD has been devoted to just that. The other double CD was released through Demon Music and titled *Joe Longthorne – The Essential Collection*.

More CD releases, a Variety Club of Great Britain award, cruises, constant touring and summer seasons – who needs television! It would be nice though, so don't start getting any funny ideas that I don't want to be on it. Remember that *An Audience with…* idea, if any TV producers are reading this.

Writing this book has also been a major undertaking, and I couldn't have done that without the man who is now another of my good friends; Chris Berry has put together this book from all of what I have told him. He comes from Hull too, so he understands our home city, and he's a singer who works very hard at his craft too, so he understands some of what I have gone through as well. He is also a very talented writer, and the way in which we have worked on this book together has been great therapy for me. Thanks, Chris.

But we're not finished by a long way just yet – oh no! It's time for that rollercoaster to get under way again.

Two more releases were on their way– first there was yet another compilation double CD, this time titled *The Joe Longthorne Collection: All the Songs I Love* on H&H Music. Then there was that first all-new studio album in a decade, *You & Me*. I cannot express to you just how much I enjoyed putting the album together, and I need to thank both Andy Mudd and Colin Skinner here for all of their help in arranging all of the tracks between them.

The title track, 'You & Me', is my favourite on the album and has been recorded by Frank Sinatra and Peter Allen, who are both no longer with us. Everyone knows Mr Sinatra, but the passing of Australian-born Peter Allen, who I mentioned earlier during the 'FAVOURITES' section, and who wrote this song, was also a sad loss to the music world. He wrote some great songs, as well as being a fantastic singer.

Another of my favourites on the album is 'If', written by that brilliant singer-songwriter Bill Gates! Those of you who come to my concerts will understand why I've put it that way. I know it was really written by Gareth Gates – the one who finished second in *Pop Idol*!

The 2008 tour was even bigger than the previous year. This time we started out around Easter, as we had done each year since the bone-marrow transplant, and continued right through until November. We also played every weekend in Blackpool on Friday and Saturday from the beginning of August to the beginning of November.

I was particularly happy to be playing Blackpool in 2008, because I had heard that the North Pier's future was in serious doubt. This fantastic and historic period piece is one of the oldest pier theatres in the country and has seen some of the world's finest comedians and singers tread its boards.

Of course, I also have a very strong emotional feeling for the place as it was here that James and I first got together. It was also here that I spent those evenings as 'Captain' of my own ship. This wonderful theatre sits at the end of an uninterrupted 500yd-long pier, and it was here that I first came into contact with the beautiful Pat Mancini MBE, and where Jean had helped me off each night. How could I not want to help this place after all it had done for me, after all it had given me?

It was also here that Johnnie Casson and I struck up such a

terrific friendship. That's also why it was really good to appear with Johnnie again in 2008, along with a full production show involving the Joe Longthorne Orchestra, dancers and a variety of female solo singers, including the lovely Leanne Fury, the charismatic Carol Kaye and the terrific Tracey Jordan.

I hadn't known it at the time, but Don Black's very kind words the year previously were also to translate into an invitation from him to play at his special seventieth birthday tribute show at the Palladium in August 2008. Now when Don Black invites you to play, you just do not turn him down. Don has won an Oscar, several other Academy Award nominations, and been responsible for some of the most amazing lyrics ever written: 'Born Free'; 'Ben' (for Michael Jackson); 'As If We Never Said Goodbye' (from *Sunset Boulevard*); 'Diamonds Are Forever'; 'If I Never Sing Another Song' – the list goes on and on.

It was an absolute honour to sing for him, and of course I just had to sing 'If I Never Sing Another Song'. We brought the house down with it and that's when Michael Parkinson, who was MC, said, 'we cannot possibly follow that,' and the show went into a break. It was a great feeling, especially as on the same bill were people like Gary Barlow, Lee Mead, Lulu, Mica Paris, Elkie Brooks, Marti Webb and Craig David. The whole evening was recorded for BBC Radio 2's *Friday Night Is Music Night*.

Don says that the first time he remembers seeing me was when I was in a cabaret show. With him at the time was Charles Strauss, who wrote the musical *Annie*. They were both, in Don's words 'blown away' by my vocal range. Apparently, Charles still goes on about my 'machinery' today.

The Don Black Tribute was one of the two massive live highlights for me in 2008. The other was thousands of miles away on an island in the sun. This time though, there was no Rupert the drunkard Bear; no Pancho 'Overtime' Villa, no fog machine problems and no Demis Roussos costume – although we were nearer to his homeland than Jersey.

There have been those who have been so very kind over the years, telling me that I have a voice given to me by the gods, and in September of 2008 I was to sing to them! Now don't start thinking I'm getting ideas above my station at this point. It's just that I had been booked to play a quite extraordinary concert in Cyprus, an open-air, evening performance at the world-famous Kourion Amphitheatre that dates back to 500BC.

I have never played a place like it before in my life. I have played the Royal Albert Hall and the Sydney Opera House, as well as several other amazing venues, but this was simply magical. It wasn't just the setting that did it for me though, with the amphitheatre looking out to the Mediterranean, it was the fans once again.

We had completely sold out the show weeks beforehand, as families and parties of friends had planned their holidays around coming to see me, as well as getting some sun of course. I just loved the evening and would play there again tomorrow. It was all organised by our 'Man in the Med', Paul Iacovou.

There were no support acts, just me and the Joe Longthorne Orchestra, and when I went into the audience partway through what ended up being a two-hour show there was just so much warmth there – and yes, I know we were in Cyprus which is a warm place anyway, but I think you know what I mean.

I knew then that the past three years since the bone-marrow transplant had shown not just me, but many more, that I was now on a roll. I was fit and hungry for more, and more, and more.

CHAPTER THIRTY-EIGHT

BENIDORM

In November 2008 we headed for the Costa Brava for a very special one-off concert at the beautiful Benidorm Palace. This proved to be another spectacular night as we took out the whole band and put on yet another stunning show.

We had the three amigos back together for this trip: Pat was there with me and James. And there was, of course, a problem or two along the way. Pat always said that, no matter where she went with us, there has always been some kind of 'iffy' moment. Well, this one had all the hallmarks of those days when I used to pull a fast one to get out of some scrape or other with my sound and lighting man.

You see, after a concert I do like to wind down. Mr Sinatra called it 'boozing time' and I'm no different. I like a beer or two, or three. I also like chatting with people and generally just having a good time. I guess to some it's a bit like I've finished my job for the day, now I can relax and enjoy. It's just that for performers, that happens at a different time to others. That often means I don't get up, or don't want to get up, until the afternoon.

It's a routine I find hard to shake off, so I stick with it quite a bit when I'm not performing as well. Unfortunately, it was not a routine that went down too well with the hotel.

The day we were meant to be coming home, I couldn't get out of bed as I was that tired. I knew we could always get another flight so that wasn't the issue, but the manager of the hotel wanted my room. Patricia, who knows one or two things about hotels, knew they had 200 rooms so she felt they were being a little bit stroppy.

The other two amigos, as well as Chris, start telling the manager that I wasn't well, and so the hotel called our bluff by saying, 'If he's not well you will have to get a doctor.' I really wasn't feeling very well. I had a hangover.

They get a doctor. He arrives a quarter of an hour later and James comes up to the room with him and wakes me up. I may have already opened my eyes on several occasions slightly before this, but who's to know! James can talk us out of any situation.

I tell the Spanish doctor that I just can't get up. James explains that I've been working the night before and that I'm totally exhausted. He tells him I need at least another five hours' kip. The doctor then goes down to the manager and says, 'This man cannot be moved for five hours.'

We missed the plane but at least I was fresh when we did leave. I don't know what convinced the doctor the most – my act, James' act or the 100 Euros we bunged him along with a copy of my DVD! It certainly made Pat laugh anyway.

I've played the Benidorm Palace quite a few times, so maybe it's time I played Morgan Tavern, which is where they film the Neptune's Bar scenes in the *Benidorm* TV series. I just love the show and it would be great to be in it sometime. My favourite character has to be the hairdresser Kenneth, played by Tony Maudsley. I love the way his mouth drops when something goes wrong. Johnny Vegas has recently livened it up again as 'the Oracle'. If it were possible, I'd love to be in it.

CHAPTER THIRTY-NINE

FORTY YEARS

The year 2009 saw me back on mainstream TV for the first time in many years. It was also the year when I was finally 'spotted' by the US, through Mr Sinatra's manager, Elliott Weisman, and almost got to 'The Strip' in Vegas. It was the year that saw me sing for three quite different legends at their own Variety Club of Great Britain award evenings.

It was also the year I celebrated forty years in show-business with yet another massive tour of the UK, and dates in Spain and the Emerald Isle. We once again had a tremendous summer season at the wonderful Grand Theatre in Blackpool. That year also saw me performing on David Gest's special Soul Spectacular at the Opera House.

We started the year with a little holiday. We knew it was going to be a busy first six months otherwise, and we'd had yet another long year prior to it, so James and I needed a break. We'd originally thought of going to Morocco, then we changed our minds at the last minute and decided on Amsterdam. Not much of a difference there then! It was freezing. I was going to put a word in front of 'freezing' but I don't think you need me to tell you any more!

Our next destination was Thailand. The world really is a small place these days, as I said before, and as if to prove it Jimmy White was there too. Jimmy is a mate of Chris the Greek, and when he found out we were in Bangkok he drove over. He'd just won a tournament over there. We had a great time together and it was a lot warmer than Holland.

The three Variety Club award functions I sang for included an award evening for Tommy and Bobby (Cannon and Ball) at the Reebok Stadium in Bolton; Engelbert Humperdinck's Lifetime Achievement award at the Palace Hotel, Manchester in March; and this was followed by The Bee Gees' Silver Heart award in April at the same venue.

Tommy and Bobby's night was full of fun and laughter, as you might expect with anyone who is anyone from the world of comedy present. Engelbert is one of the most consummate performers I know. The feeling between us is definitely one of mutual admiration. I brought the Joe Longthorne Orchestra with me and they played for 'The Hump' too. We also sang together. Engelbert has always been so encouraging to me and it was a wonderful moment in my career when I was introduced to Mr Weisman, who had purely come over to see Engelbert collect his award.

I was back in Manchester just weeks later to sing for The Bee Gees. Once again I took the band, and they not only backed me but also played for Ronan Keating, Richard Fleeshman, the legendary PP Arnold and the amazing Bee Gees themselves! Ti Amore, a group of four sensational tenors from Hull, was also involved. I sang the two songs I mentioned earlier, 'I Started a Joke' and 'Morning of My Life'.

The 40th Anniversary Tour saw me perform nearly 100 dates from March until December, taking in theatres, hotels and even a castle. Craig Y Nos Castle in the Swansea Valley in Wales deserves a special mention.

There was another double CD compilation out in 2009, but this time with a big difference! It included a double DVD package and the whole thing was called *Joe's 40th Anniversary Collection*. It included 'Wonderful Tonight', the first time I had ever recorded the song, and it features many songs from throughout my career, including the duets with both Barbara Windsor and Liz Dawn.

CHAPTER FORTY

BESTSELLER AND SILVER HEART

After years of thinking about it and many people suggesting I should do it, I finally found the man who could write my life story with me. I could never have written it on my own and hadn't felt comfortable with others who had approached me. The difference with Chris is that he is also a singer; he comes from Hull too, so he understands where I have come from; we share a faith, and he's a great writer. Together we spent hundreds of hours trying to get everything into the book, all the highs and lows.

And we haven't finished yet by the way, because this is still only 2010 that we're talking about. What you're reading here has been updated and edited from the book that was first released. Rightly so – five years is a long time in anyone's life, but in mine? Well, it's a whole other lifetime!

We worked on my story throughout 2009. As you will see, that old rollercoaster just carries on going up and down, but I have to say it has been more up than down in recent years.

James gave our 2010 dates the title of The Book – The Official

Tour, and once again we set off on a massive run of performances throughout the UK, with Chris also singing a variety of hit songs and those he has written himself.

Just ten days before the official book launch I was to be honoured once again by the Variety Club of Great Britain, at the Hilton in Blackpool where I received their Silver Heart award. It was another tremendous evening with Cannon and Ball on top form as they took over the stage.

Bernie Nolan looked fantastic and said some very kind words. It's so unfair that she has now left us; Johnnie Casson had us all in stitches; and Frank Carson, who has since become another sad loss, was also on top form. Jimmy White arrived on cue, but said he needed a rest! Snooker lovers, eat your hearts out.

Special thanks must go to Marj Boyer, chairman of the Variety Club for the North West and all of her team. We even managed to get hold of the very first copy of the hardback edition in a special case for the night. It raised £3,000 for charity.

Fittingly, the very first event where the books were on display was back in my home city. I was one of two special guests at the Hull and East Riding Literary Luncheon, with the other being Pauline Prescott, wife of John, who had just released her book. She's a really wonderful, charming woman and it was a delightful event.

The book launch was set for Monday, 29 March, 2010, and in the ensuing fortnight I saw so many fans at Waterstones and WH Smith bookstores in Hull, Manchester, Blackpool, York, Sunderland, Glasgow, Stockport and anywhere else we could fit in with the tour. It was disappointing not to be able to include every region of the UK, as I know many fans were asking whether I would be able to conduct signings, but I'm afraid I can't split myself into two or three.

We were booked on to several TV and radio shows, including a breakfast TV interview with the lovely Lorraine Kelly and a great live show with Sir Terry Wogan on BBC Radio 2. It was just like old times and I think Terry was a little taken aback by the noise made by the fans. You know who you are; thank you from the top and bottom of my heart. Terry even said that he felt it was as though it wasn't his show that day, and that the Joe Longthorne Friendship Club had taken over the studio.

I also made a number of other appearances on TV stations, including *Calendar* on ITV, at the TV studio in Leeds where my broadcasting career kicked off with *Junior Showtime*. Presenters Duncan Wood, Gaynor Barnes and Christine Talbot are a great team and Christine has had her own personal battle after finding out she had breast cancer. Happily, she's come through.

The book launch went so well that after just two weeks of its release we found out it was a bestseller! It topped two of the Amazon charts for biographies under Entertainment and Cabaret. It also remained top of the Cabaret chart for ten weeks. While we felt that my life story may have had all the hallmarks of a bestseller, it was nice to see it for real. We're hoping to make it back to the top with this book too!

Having promoted the book and received the Variety Club award, it was time for the tour to get underway in April and we took in nearly every venue you could think of: from Hastings to Hayes; Truro to Torquay; Dartford to Dundee; and South Shields to Southsea. It was exhausting and there were times, I will freely admit, that I just wanted to go home. Let's just say I had my moments when it would have been easier to walk away from it all than to be cooped up in a car for hours on end. That's also the reason why we have different transportation and accommodation today. More of that later.

There are also many times when I wonder about our booking agent's sense of geography. Our tour schedule can see us in the

North East one night but in Kent the next. It's crazy. We were seriously considering using Sherpas for much of the tour!

Summer season was back at the Grand Theatre in Blackpool, a beautiful auditorium where I always feel at home. We had a great run and that also led to my first appearance at the Indigo Room at the O2 Arena in London.

In October 2010 I was back working on behalf of the Variety Club once again, as Neil Sedaka was honoured with his Silver Heart Award at the Palace Hotel in Manchester. But still we weren't finished. There were concerts right up until Christmas and yet another New Year's Eve Special in Blackpool. And the book sales kept on coming.

After such a busy year I was all set for a break. Not a lucky one, just a holiday break this time, and some quieter moments for myself with James. It really was a brilliant year though, and one I will never forget. It seemed as though everything was looking good. But you know me by now and how my life goes; surely there had to be something that wouldn't quite work out and would go against me? You're not wrong. Now where's that drink gone? You might well need it again here. Oh, and grab another box of Kleenex while you're at it. We've a few 'moments' to come.

CHAPTER FORTY-ONE

CRASH AND LOSING PAT

You know, just when you think you're on a roll again there's always something to bring you back down to earth. For some people that happens with little things, but it's never been that way with me. In my case they've always got to be great big problems, something mega-dramatic.

I suppose, with the amount of travelling I've done over the years, there has always been a greater chance that I could be involved in traffic accidents along the way, but mercifully I'd got away with very few until 2011.

Way back in 1995 we'd had a close shave in a helicopter. The *Daily Mirror* reported it at the time: 'Comic Joe in Copter Crash – Entertainer Joe Longthorne cheated death last night when his helicopter crash-landed in a field.'

Hilarious! That doesn't tell the tale at all.

The helicopter was flying myself and Big Mick Johnson from Turpin's to a concert in Birmingham, when all sorts of lights started flashing and I told the pilot he would have to land in a farmer's field. We landed amongst a herd of bemused cattle and a few red-faced country gents, or 'joskins' as we call them in cant, armed with what looked like trumpets. It was like a scene from *The Beano*! These 'trumpets' were what others would call blunderbusses. It was as though we had to prove to the local gentry that we weren't aliens.

As we had been coming down to land in the field I wasn't sure we would be able to make it, so it certainly shook me up. But we weren't hurt and made for the nearest public house, nerves still jangling.

But what happened in 2011 was very different. This wasn't any kind of scene that you could laugh about later. It was the real near-death thing.

I was in the back of the Mercedes, with John Boy driving and James sat alongside him in the passenger's seat. It had been a long drive in awful conditions; a five-hour haul from Portsmouth up to Alvaston Hall in Cheshire. Another logistical masterpiece from our booking agents! Keith was following in the car behind. It was a customary night-time drive, just another in our regular touring season before settling in Blackpool for the summer.

I always sit in the back of the car – unless I'm driving, because otherwise that would look a bit daft wouldn't it? I had my earphones on, listening to some music, and was having a can of lager. I couldn't have told you where we were. I never can. I just try to relax. We could have been heading for Fife or Forfar for all I knew, but I found out later we were only fifteen minutes from the venue when our world very nearly came to an end, yet again!

No one can exactly be sure about what happened next, but what I can tell you is that this time I really did think we were out of here, me, James and John Boy. What we now know is that the car turned over three times as we continued travelling up the road.

I now understand what some people say when they tell you that your life turns into slow motion at the time. That was certainly true for me. I was bracing myself for the impact as our car became a ten-pin bowling ball, holding on for dear life. Fortunately, I was wearing my seat belt and the air bags worked too, otherwise that really could have been the end of all of us.

The first thing I was fully aware of when the car came to a standstill was that we were upside down. It's quite a sobering experience when you realise you've come that close to losing your life but you're still here – albeit the wrong way up. I was now thinking very clearly. The car wheels were spinning and the car had taken a hammering. It was unbelievable. There was creaking of metal, the smell of fuel and, for the briefest of seconds, everything went quiet as though we had frozen in time.

Then I remember hearing screaming from James, and not without very good reason as it turned out, but I couldn't hear anything from John Boy. At least by hearing James I knew he was alive, but what about John? Fortunately, it wasn't long before he came round too.

Sat there in what was now not just a mess but a possible tomb, I remember thinking to myself there was steam all around us and this thing could blow. *Get out! You're not going to die here. Get out now!* But I couldn't because of the air bag. It had pinned me in place as it had been designed to. Thank God for German engineering! I could still hear James screaming and wanted to help him as he was hurt badly.

I'm sure Keith expected to find three dead bodies when he pulled over with his son Michael, but we were all still very much alive – even though James, particularly, was in excruciating pain.

Ambulances and fire engines arrived at the scene very soon and the paramedics took over. As ever they were excellent and we were soon despatched to the local infirmary. We all ended up in Leighton Hospital, Crewe, where we were looked after very well.

I managed to come out of the evening's drama with whiplash, a broken rib and a broken nose. I also had some other facial abrasions and my neck in a brace. It was a lucky escape.

James wasn't quite so lucky. He suffered a shattered ankle. His golf, the sport he loves, has suffered and I feel so bad about that. I know the accident wasn't anything more than just that, but for James to lose out on playing the sport he's very good at makes me feel guilty. He was kept in hospital for a fortnight and, for once, it was my turn to visit him. John Boy was also injured, but not too badly.

Once I'd rested up for awhile, I was soon back on stage at The Grand in Blackpool for another summer season; but very real tragedy was about to strike again, and this time there was loss of life.

My dear friend Patricia Mancini, MBE, passed away on 21 July 2011, aged seventy-two. I cannot begin to tell you how much more this hurt me inside than the physical pain from our car crash the month previously.

This lady had been our rock. James and I both loved her dearly and we still do, but we had known the end was near. A year earlier she had been diagnosed as having a malignant brain tumour, and it had been just a matter of time. In November 2010 I had asked the Variety Club if they would consider honouring the work she had done in looking after entertainers through her hotel. She had been responsible for helping many others, not just me. It was my way of trying to give Pat something back for all she had done for us. She had a heart of gold and worked hard for lots of charities. If anyone ever wanted anything, Pat would be first in the queue to help.

The Variety Club thankfully agreed, and were delighted to

honour her with a special Show Business award, something normally only given to those who perform. I know she was suitably thrilled and enjoyed a wonderful night, but I also saw tragedy in her eyes in the final months. She certainly didn't want to go. She loved life and she put up a real fight.

I know not a lot of people want to die, but for Pat it was really annoying. She had enjoyed everything she achieved, and she'd come up from nothing over in Manchester to be 'Queen of Blackpool'. She wasn't going to let go in a hurry. She knew she was going, but she was mad about it.

Her funeral took place at Our Lady of the Assumption Church, and we all attended – myself, James, Johnnie Casson, Bobby Ball, Roy Walker, Chubby Brown and countless others whose lives had all been touched by this marvellous woman, who will forever remain one of the loves of my life.

If it hadn't been for Pat, I certainly wouldn't have been able to rebuild my life the way I have since I met James. And I certainly wouldn't have been back on the ocean waves, cruising and singing once again, as I was in 2011. And I wouldn't have been appearing back in London's West End for the first time in a while, in September of that year.

Patricia, you will always remain in our hearts. We love you very much.

Appearing at Leicester Square Theatre was the first of a number of high spots that followed since the crash and Pat's passing. I'll play anywhere, but playing the West End is always special, and my good friend Jeffrey Archer even managed to get along. This is how he very kindly reviewed my show on his personal blog. I don't even know what one of those is, but I'm assured it's all aboveboard!

'I dashed back into London last night to attend Joe Longthorne's concert at the Leicester Square Theatre, with my old friend Patti Boulaye. Joe was on top form, and the audience clearly loved every moment, giving him a standing ovation three times during the performance. Joe has one of the most loyal fan bases of any artist I've ever known, and if it were not for so many sadnesses during his life, I suspect he would still be filling the Palladium night after night.'

I think a thank-you is called for there. Thank you so much, Jeffrey.

CHAPTER FORTY-TWO

MBE

At the end of 2011, James and I were both exhausted. We had managed another whole year of touring, summer season, cruise ships and the West End. It was a very pleasing exhaustion. We had played everywhere and the audiences had been marvellous.

James had arranged a break for us, and on 3 January 2012, we flew out to the United States. We went to Fort Lauderdale, which is known as the 'Venice of America'. We've a great friend, Len Rawcliffe, who lives there. My friendship with Len goes back to 1993, when he was with his partner Jimmy Porter. We've been close pals for all this time. Jimmy and Len started a cafeteria in Blackpool bus station and ended up owning a hotel. They worked their way up like Pat Mancini.

The idea was to get away from it all for three months. I liked the idea. We enjoyed ourselves immensely, but after about three minutes I wanted to be up and singing again, that's one withdrawal I can't deal with. There's only so much champagne and lobster – and mushy peas – that you can eat you know! I'm one of those people who, if I go to a party, I will die if nobody asks me to sing.

We were invited to a charity show at a theatre in the town, and you can pretty much guess the rest. I'd listened to a few of the others but was itching to be up there myself. The next thing I know, there is a microphone being passed to me and I'm there on stage. I decided to give them my impression of Barry Manilow singing 'Can't Smile Without You'. It wasn't the way I perform it back in the UK, it was the full-on impression without making too much of a joke about it all. At the end of the song the place went up in the air. What a feeling!

That performance led to a meeting with Billie Wells of Wells Entertainment, based at Lighthouse Point in Florida. Billie is a wonderful woman who is an agent and promoter for Jack Jones, Gloria Gaynor, KC and the Sunshine Band and Kool & the Gang, to name but a few. Maybe something will come of that meeting one day, but really James and I were there to take a break rather than make a break.

The views we had of the Atlantic were simply stunning and, like anyone on holiday when they like a place so much, we ended up checking out property. It's a great place to live.

When we returned to the UK three months later, I was refreshed and ready to swing right back into action. Andy Mudd and I had been working on putting together a new show with no band, but just the two of us and two pianos on stage – and a new album of all my own songs released just before the new tour started in April. Its title, *Lady Blue*, was taken from one of the songs I wrote a number of years ago that appeared on my *I Wish You Love* album.

It was such a thrill singing my own songs once again. It's very personal for me. These were all my own work, along with Ernie Dunstall, Lewis Osborne and Barry Mason. They'd all been locked away awhile, but it was great to see them fly again and it's a really pleasing feeling, like old friends coming back to me.

And the 2012 tour couldn't have started in a better setting – Grimsby! Now there's nothing wrong with Grimsby at all, but when your second night of the tour is a return to a sell-out Leicester Square Theatre just six months after you've appeared there, then that is something else. It set the tone for what was an amazing first half of the year.

I enjoyed the shows with Andy immensely. Having a piano available to me on stage can lead to some very comedic moments. Yes, I'm concentrating on what I'm singing, but having the piano available adds to my versatility. Andy and I worked very well together and it's always lovely to see his family. He's a very capable musician.

As we were travelling back from a concert that April, I received a call from James. He wasn't with me on all of the shows that year. He told me we had received a letter addressed to me from Buckingham Palace. My first thought was, *What have I done now?* I couldn't believe it when he told me that I was to receive the MBE.

What a wonderful thing. It is in honour of my charity work, raising funds for the various charities we have supported and continue to support. I've been in show-business for a long time and I am so honoured and humbled by this award. I see it as a kind of ambassadorship. I've always enjoyed not just raising funds, but also making people aware of the needs of others. I've done it all my life, giving to others who are in need where I can.

I should also mention at this point all of those who have come along to my concerts over the years, as they have also contributed to my work in raising funds and awareness. Well done everybody. The Friendship Club has done a fantastic job over many years and continues to do so.

The official announcement of the Queen's Birthday Honours

List was made at midnight on the Friday evening/Saturday morning. I was playing the Swan Theatre, High Wycombe on the Friday evening and the Wyvern Theatre, Swindon on the Saturday. As soon as I put my foot on the stage on Saturday night, the roof went off! There was a standing ovation without having to do anything.

I try to be a guy who just goes about his business, but it would be wrong to say receiving news of the MBE hasn't given me a real sense of pride. The most important thing, though, is that this award is a tool that can be used to raise even more funds for charity and greater awareness of the plight of others. We've since set up the Joe Longthorne Foundation, the umbrella name for the funds raised for the various charities I'm involved with. The MBE has certainly helped us push on with the good work even more.

But before we get to my very nice day at Buckingham Palace, it won't perhaps surprise you to learn that it wasn't all without a little bit of pain, when I managed to break my foot!

That summer saw a return to The Grand Theatre in Blackpool and a season with my good pal Roy Walker. We'd first met many years ago in a working men's club in Coventry, and of course we'd performed on the same bill in Scarborough and Bournemouth. I have the highest regard for Roy. His wife Jean passed away through cancer in 1988, and he lives not too far from us.

So how did I break my foot? As Roy might have said, 'Say what you see, Joe.' That might have helped me avoid my latest minor catastrophe. I'd bought these red shoes that looked great. They were a bit expensive but I had to have them. I tried to wangle a deal out of the lady in the boutique in Bournemouth where I saw them, but she wasn't having any.

Back in Hull a few weeks later, having had a drink at the Vauxhall Tavern, one of my favourites, I was walking back to where I was staying with one of my nieces when I totally missed the kerb, and *crack!* I had a cast on it for six weeks. Obviously I could still sing so that wasn't the problem, but it was a pain in more ways than one!

We held a charity fundraising event around that time called the Joe Longthorne Celebrity Invitational Golf Day. This all came about through my good friend, the tremendous comedian George King, who has also toured with me. George worked so hard on pulling the event together and we raised £10,000 to help Bryan House in Blackpool, a care centre for special-needs children.

I won't go on too much about the actual day itself when I received the MBE from HRH the Prince of Wales, because I don't really like to, but it was a good day. We stayed at the Royal Lancaster Hotel that looks over Hyde Park. We went to the palace in a massive white Rolls-Royce, thanks to casino boss Paul Stone. I remember it took us a while to get through bomb squad regulations and all sorts of things, and that it was a freezing-cold day: 13 December 2012. The worse news was that when we got inside it was even colder! I could have done with a brandy to warm up a bit, but there was none of that. But the funniest thing was they had one of these old electric three-bar fires. Do you remember them? I do. My dad used to set it at what everybody knew as 'miser rate'! This was the same type of fire! I love the Royal Family to bits but they could do with getting something sorted there.

I was in awe of the paintings though, and managed a few words with HRH Prince Charles. We talked about charities. He comes over as a very warm, considerate, caring man.

I'd had a great 2012. It couldn't last, could it? There had to be something. It turned out that there were two problems looming on my horizon.

CHAPTER FORTY-THREE

TERESA

James and I had gone back to Fort Lauderdale for another winter break before getting on with the 2013 tour, but I'd known for a while that Mam was ill and she had been deteriorating for some time. While we were in Florida, I kept in constant touch with her and could tell she was fading. It made me think that I should have been back home. We'd always had this pact where one would look after the other when the time came. It was on its way.

We came back from America to play The Hippodrome once again, and then the Potter's resort complex in Norfolk. Mam had been moved to the Castle Hill Hospital in Hull, and I sensed the time had come to do something. We didn't exactly kidnap her from the hospital and take her back to Blackpool, but it might have looked that way as we stashed her into the camper van we had at the time.

I just felt that it was time to look after her and that I could do it if she was with me in Blackpool. My thoughts kept going back to those days all that time ago, when she worked in the fish house in Hull. She spent sixteen years in there in freezing surroundings, and the least I could do was keep her warm, have a laugh together and enjoy the time she had left.

We had a glorious summer. Lizzie, Anne and John would have done the same, if they'd been in my position of being able to offer her what I had. Lizzie wasn't too well at the time; Anne had her hands full and John didn't know what to do, except love his mother. They all came over though.

Alzheimer's is another sad disease. Everyone needs so much help and I found that you don't argue when a sufferer disagrees with you over things. You don't answer back or correct them. You just carry on. We had so much joy in those last months. I'd put on all her favourite songs and we'd sing together. She had a wonderful voice. She loved Max Bygraves and Issy Bonn.

The time was soon to come, and one night when she was doubled up in pain we called for the ambulance. She was taken to Victoria Hospital and, at 2am on 11 September, we got Father John out of bed to come to her.

John and Anne were both there with James and me, but I felt sad that Lizzie couldn't be with us. It wasn't her fault; she wanted to be there but, like I said, she wasn't well.

Now one of the amazing things with Alzheimer's sufferers is that sometimes they can suddenly remember things clearly. Mam went through every single word of the last sacrament with Father John. She kept up with him every part of the way and afterwards he said, 'Well, I've never known that happen before.'

I thanked him for coming and for blessing her, but he said, 'Joe, she blessed me.' Teresa Longthorne, our mam, passed away 11 September 2013, aged eighty-nine. We love you, Mam. Always will.

CHAPTER FORTY-FOUR

BEATING CANCER... AGAIN

2014 was meant to be a nice, relaxed year. By that I don't mean it was set to be a do-nothing year, but certainly James and I hadn't planned it to be a do-this, do-that year. One of the things I was looking forward to was spending summer at home in Blackpool with James, my lovely dog Kenny and the chickens. Have I mentioned them before? We have all sorts of variety of chickens, and they are great fun to watch and very therapeutic too.

It was going to be about having friends over and performing at Viva! a couple of nights a week. Viva! is the recently-opened show bar of our good pal Leye D. Johns, who had toured with me a couple of years earlier, and it has won some prestigious awards already. I must also mention comedian George King here too. George has also toured with me in recent years along with Chris Berry and Johnnie Casson. They are all lovely men and true professionals who know how to entertain.

We'd had some really busy years and it just seemed right to relax a little more. We flew off to Tenerife for a break in January.

I performed while over there, as you might expect, and there was another tour with theatre bookings looking really healthy. It was maybe going to be just as busy as normal, looking back, but we were happy with the way things were shaping up. I was back at The Hippodrome in April, and we'd gone down to London in the new motor-home that James had bought for us at Christmas 2012.

Now let me just tell you what this motor-home does for me. We'd had a smaller one before but this one is just great. I'd become very weary of stopping in hotels all the time when on tour. We'd usually arrive in the early hours of a morning after having played a venue, and then drive to the next town on the agenda. The motor-home we have now means James and I can have our privacy and independence. Anyone who has a motor-home, caravan or tent will know what it's like. It's good for my nerves and it also means we can take Kenny with us.

You can go just about anywhere with a motor-home; we even parked up in Covent Garden when we played The Hippodrome. What a great feeling to be in your own home in the middle of London! I'd love to play a West End season and just be able to get into our motor-home after each performance.

So there were plenty of nice things going on in 2014. One of those was a charity show at the Palace Hotel in Manchester, where I was performing for the Christie charity, which is all about helping those with cancer. Little did I know that, within two days of that concert, I would be once again a victim of this horrible disease. The concert, held on 26 April, was another fantastic fundraising night, and both Roy Walker and Jimmy Cricket were on with me.

But two days later a rough area on the right-hand side of my mouth was being checked over. Strangely, when I was in America three years previously, I could feel that something wasn't right but now my mouth felt like it was on fire. Once the biopsy results came back there was only ever going to be one result. Whatever it was inside my mouth was cancerous. At first I just thought, *No, no, no, not again!* Then I started laughing. It was out of disbelief really.

We found out the results through a charming man, Dr Shakeer Akhtar at Royal Preston Hospital. He went through my options – radiotherapy, chemotherapy, do nothing (not really an option) or cut it out.

I went for cutting it out. You've got to fight, haven't you? It's what's in me, and I just decided there and then to go for it. I must admit I had started thinking that I would be okay dealing with it, because of having gone through things like this before, and that this would be relatively easy against what I'd suffered during the aftermath of the bone-marrow transplant. But I was wrong.

The best way I can describe it is that it's like going into your favourite store and everything has been moved about. It was entirely different to what I had experienced with the bone marrow, because with that the discomfort is that of the donation.

Anyhow, I thought I'd fight it and ended up going through a ten-and-a-half-hour operation on 2 July. I wish I knew all the names of those involved, because I would really like to thank them all.

I sang immediately after the operation and, in my head, felt ready to get going again straightaway. But getting back on the road wasn't going to happen for quite a while, as much as I wanted to.

After about five or six days of being in the hospital, I wanted to be outside again. James had brought the motor-home and had been sleeping in it, so that he was close by throughout the time of the operation and during my recovery. So I decided to visit him! But I soon went back when I felt a pain coming on. I think it's an instinct to try to get your life back to normal after any kind of operation, and to have my own luxury motor-home outside waiting for me was a real help.

I think the operation took more out of me than I'd expected,

293

and any hopes I'd had of getting back on stage within a couple of weeks, or even months, were not realistic. It was only near to the end of the year that I felt ready to get going again. But that doesn't mean I wasn't getting things done. It certainly wasn't the type of year I'd planned, but of course I'm glad I came through it.

One of the things people kept asking me was had I had a good rest? I said it's not about rest, it's about recovery. For me it was all about getting back to the point I was at before the operation, and even better both mentally and physically.

I am eternally grateful to Darren Day, who stood in for me at Viva! Darren is such a genuinely nice man and a top performer. He's an extremely versatile entertainer with a voice that has just got better and better, and he does some great impressions. All my fans loved him too. Thank you, Darren.

Okay, right, let's get this show back on the road! Before we do, here's a little-known story about my ear. If you're going to get a drink right now try a lager, you'll see why!

CHAPTER FORTY-FIVE

LEFT EAR

It has been common knowledge among my fans that I suffered from occasional deafness in my left ear. I can't prove how it happened, but what I can tell you is that I was smacked on it one time in my teens and I felt it go *gong*. I've been in and out of hospitals over the years and had several operations to try and rectify it. When I was recording my TV series, the studio had to be tailor-made for me because there were times when my ear would just not be right.

Performers have this saying about never leaving anything in the wings. That means that you never give less than 100 per cent, but looking back there were probably some times when I sent a ghost out instead of me because of my ear. Thankfully, it's not affecting me now, but that's another one of the problems. When it comes and goes, I'm just never sure when and if it's going to come back. It's like some form of Chinese water torture and it's been quite concerning.

I don't normally chat about it at all, because it's just something else that I have to deal with from time to time; but if someone has seen me and noticed a change in my performance, that's perhaps why. I've had times when it hasn't affected me for six months, but then it comes back and stays awhile. It's the last thing I need when I'm on stage, I can tell you that. But it's also important to mention because others who suffer from it might find it's the same for them. I hope that if you do, there is a way out of it for you.

One of the remedies I have found useful – and don't try this at home, as they say – is, when I've come offstage, to pour lager into the ear. I don't know why it works, maybe it's the bubbles or something, or maybe it's like that advert in that it refreshes the parts other beers cannot reach. Who knows? All I know is that each time I've tried it, it has worked for me.

For me as a singer, only having one good ear sometimes has meant that I don't feel anchored. It's as though my nerves have switched off and all I can hear on the left side is a muffled bass sound. When I came back on stage this year after last year's cancer operation, I wasn't worried about my voice because I knew that was fine, but I wasn't sure whether the ear had gone again. Fortunately, it hadn't and so now, with the cancer dealt with and two good ears, new albums, new book, new tour, the Palladium, TV appearances, maybe *Benidorm* too if Derren Litten is reading this, and even the film that has been mentioned, it's time to hit the road again, wherever it takes me next.

CHAPTER FORTY-SIX

BACK ON
THE ROAD

New Year's Eve 2014 was the first time in a long while that I'd sung back in front of my fans. It was just one song but it was the start. My first theatre show was in February 2015, at the New Alexandra Theatre in Birmingham, followed by Cliff Pavilion Theatre in Southend. It was like coming home, back to where I belong.

I will go anywhere and perform wherever people want me, and this year we're back on the road with a full UK tour, dates abroad and the London Palladium concert to celebrate my sixtieth birthday. I honestly feel I am singing better than ever, and because I'm free of the problems with my ear, as well as getting shot of the cancer again, I am really happy right now.

I'm as ambitious today as I was before the TV shows. I'm ready to show anyone what I can do and to tear places apart. I have some great new songs, and some that are classics that I've taken on, such as Frank Sinatra's 'The Best of Everything' and Frankie Laine's 'That's My Desire'; then there's 'I'm Not Anyone' that we picked up from Sammy Davis Jr.'s amazing rendition of it; and like I said earlier, we're also doing 'Make the World a Little Younger', another Shirley recording. There's 'Gypsy Song' too, which Dorothy Squires recorded, written by her husband at the time, Billy Reid, and 'Yesterday' by The Beatles.

I have an amazing band with 'Stretch' at the helm, and for the Palladium concert we will have a 32-piece orchestra – now that's my kind of band! And I really mustn't forget the amazing Tracey Jordan once again. Our duet on 'You Don't Bring Me Flowers' has been one of the highlights of the show over the past few years. Tracey, you are a wonderful singer and it is a joy to work with you.

Like many other performers, I've been asked to go 'into the jungle' or into the *Big Brother* house, but they're really not for me. My place is on stage or on screen, doing what I do, and with people like Eric Hall with me now, you never know what might happen. This could all be bigger than ever!

But before we get ready to start the next chapters for the next book – and the film, and the *Benidorm* TV show (ha ha, hope you're reading this, Mr Litten) – there are two final statements that I really must make. The final chapter I'm devoting to just one person, but here I want to talk about and to my fans, my friends. You see, that's what all of you have become to me.

It's important to reflect on what you have. God knows, during the things I've been through I've been forced to reflect many times. I know some singers and bands say they are nothing without the fans. I never look at it like that. All I know is that the people who have followed me, not just around the UK but all around the world, may just have been fans years ago, but now they have turned into great friends.

I feel that they look after me. I don't know what to call it, but it's as though I have many minders, people who care for how I feel. Their love is an abiding joy to me. I truly can't say enough here to thank them for that love; they've always been there for me, they're here now and I know they always will be. Now that is a tremendously warm feeling. Thank you everyone, you know who you are.

And now to the man who deserves the most thanks in the world.

CHAPTER FORTY-SEVEN

JAMES

I've said enough times that this was not to be a 'me-me-me' book, and fittingly I'd like to say a few words about the man who I have always been proud to have as my partner.

James is a wonderful man with a big heart. We're actually quite opposite but respect each other immensely. He likes his golf and is very good at organising everything. He's not a show-business person even though he does love the finer things in entertainment, like musicals and opera.

Living with someone like me or any singer or performer can be difficult, but our relationship has grown through the years. He's a great man and together we have shared an amazing rollercoaster ride since we first met in the nineties.

I have a photograph of James and I when we first met, and I look as pleased as Punch. It says to me, *Here we go*. Well, we've come a long way since then, and James has been with me every inch of it. We've lost some good friends during that time, none more so than Pat Mancini, and we've had our share of life's ups

JAMES

and downs, but I still love him dearly. And he loves me. He's a great calming influence on me too, and I always feel more settled when he's around.

There are many old sayings and the one that rings true for James and myself is that I knew we were right for each other when we first met. We are well suited and, regardless of whatever happens in this amazingly dramatic life of mine, I don't want to imagine life without him.

So what happens next for James and myself? Could it be Vegas? TV shows? Film of my life? *Benidorm* TV series? Who knows? What I can tell you is that my life has been nothing short of dramatic so far, and somehow I don't think that will ever stop being the case.

APPENDIX I

JOE'S CHARITIES

JOE LONGTHORNE works tirelessly to raise funds on behalf of a number of charities. Since 2012 he has also launched THE JOE LONGTHORNE FOUNDATION to raise funds under this name for the charities.

If you feel inspired by this book to either donate monies or go onto the Anthony Nolan Register, here are some useful contacts:

THE ANTHONY NOLAN TRUST

To become a donor you need to be eighteen-to-forty years old and in good health. The Anthony Nolan Trust specifically needs to recruit more young male donors and from ethnically diverse backgrounds.

The Anthony Nolan Trust is a registered charity. It is dependent on the public and private companies to fund its lifesaving work as it receives no government funding.

To find out more about how to join the bone-marrow register and what is involved, or simply to make a donation, please call:
020 7284 1234
www.anthonynolan.org.uk
Email: newdonor@anthonynolan.org.uk

THE TERRENCE HIGGINS TRUST
The Terrence Higgins Trust is the leading HIV and AIDS charity in the UK, and the largest in Europe.
To make a donation, please contact:
Terrence Higgins Trust, 314–320 Gray's Inn Road,
London WC1X 8DP

APPENDIX II

DISCOGRAPHY
THE ORIGINAL
RECORDINGS

JOE: HIS FIRST
RECORDINGS
(CD ALBUM)
Never previously released until
now. These were all recorded in
sessions at Fairview Studios in
Hull during 1974–1975.
  Track Listing:
1. My Life is Just Like a
  Symphony
2. Hurt
3. Crying in the Rain
4. You You You
5. I Can't Get Enough

6. Until It's Time for You to Go
7. Get Down
8. The Way We Were

FEELINGS (45 rpm SINGLE)
Released 1977. Recorded at
Arny's Shack recording studio in
Blandford, Bournemouth.
Track Listing:
1. Feelings
2. This Ol' Heart of Mine
3. The Way We Were

LIDO DE FRANCE
(45 rpm EP)
Released 1977. Recorded at
Arny's Shack recording studio in
Blandford, Bournemouth.

Track Listing:
1. Lido de France
2. Thank You for the Music
3. Joe's Song
4. Misty
5. It's Not Unusual
6. Till
7. Forever and Ever
8. The Wonder of You
9. My Way

ONLY ONCE (FIRST LP RELEASE)
Released on the ROXON label in 1980–81. Recorded at Arny's Shack recording studio in Blandford, Bournemouth.
Track Listing:
1. She Believes in Me
2. You to Me Are Everything
3. I Know I'll Never Love This Way Again
4. To Live Without You
5. Fame
6. Only Once
7. What Do You Wanna Make those Eyes at Me for?
8. Ain't No Stoppin' Us Now
9. Imagine/Woman
10. Mandy/Could It Be Magic?/I Write the Songs
11. Love on the Rocks

12. 2001/CC Rider/American Trilogy
13. I Never Dreamed You'd Leave in Summer

THE SINGER (SECOND LP RELEASE)
Released on the GREAT BRITAIN RECORDS label in 1986. Recorded at The Shambles recording studio in Marlow.
Track Listing:
1. When Your Old Wedding Ring Was New
2. Don't Laugh at Me
3. Hurt
4. Danny Boy
5. Just Loving You
6. You're My World
7. My Mother's Eyes
8. My Prayer
9. Answer Me
10. It's Only Make Believe
11. To All the Girls I've Loved Before
12. I'd Be a Legend in My Time
13. Love Is All
14. The End of the World

THE JOE LONGTHORNE SONGBOOK
(FIRST MAJOR LP RELEASE

ON MAINSTREAM LABEL)
Released on TELSTAR
RECORDS label in 1988.
Recorded at CBS Studios,
London; The Cottage, Cheshire;
PRT Studios, London; and The
Shambles studio in Marlow.
Platinum Seller. Reached
number sixteen in the UK
charts. Stayed on the UK chart
for twelve weeks.
Track Listing:
1. You're My World
2. My Prayer
3. Always on My Mind
4. My Mother's Eyes
5. Just Loving You
6. It's Only Make Believe
7. To All the Girls I've Loved
   Before
8. End of the World
9. It Was Almost Like a Song
10. Hurt
11. Answer Me
12. Danny Boy
13. I'd Be a Legend in My Time
14. Don't Laugh at Me
15. Love Is All
16. When Your Old Wedding
    Ring Was New

ESPECIALLY FOR YOU
Released on TELSTAR
RECORDS label in 1989.
Platinum Seller.
Reached number twenty-two
in the UK charts. Stayed on the
UK chart for ten weeks.
Track Listing:
1. I Wanna Be Where You Are
2. You're the Best Thing that
   Ever Happened to Me
3. Let's Not Lose It
4. Crying in the Rain
5. Joanna
6. Wind Beneath My Wings
7. I've Waited So Long
8. What's Going On
9. One Love in a Million
10. Seven Wonders of the World
11. Let the Heartaches Begin
12. Everybody Loves Me

WIND BENEATH
MY WINGS (FIRST
MAINSTREAM LABEL
RELEASE 45RPM SINGLE)
Released on TELSTAR
RECORDS label in 1989.
Track Listing:
1. Wind Beneath My Wings
2. Let's Not Lose It

THE JOE LONGTHORNE
CHRISTMAS ALBUM
Released on TELSTAR
RECORDS label in 1989.
Gold Seller.
Reached number forty-four in
the UK charts. Stayed on the
chart for four weeks.
Track Listing:
1. Wonderful World
2. Morning Has Broken
3. My Love for You
4. Bridge over Troubled Water
5. Christmas Song
6. Silent Night
7. Somewhere
8. Winter Wonderland
9. Christmas Time Is Here
10. I Still Love You
11. If I Never Sing Another
    Song
12. Mary's Boy Child
13. White Christmas
14. Auld Lang Syne

I WISH YOU LOVE
(FIRST RELEASE ON EMI)
Released on EMI RECORDS
label in1993.
Reached number forty-seven
in the UK charts. Stayed on the
chart for four weeks.

Track Listing:
1. Young Girl
2. Lady Blue
3. So Deep is the Night
4. If I Only Had Time
5. Mary in the Morning
6. Say it with Flowers
7. Where Are You Now
8. Runaway
9. Over and Over
10. True Love
11. My Funny Valentine
12. Never Say Never
13. Walk in the Room
14. I Wish You Love

LADY BLUE
(45 RPM SINGLE)
Released on EMI RECORDS
label in 1993.
Track Listing:
1. Lady Blue
2. Say it with Flowers

YOUNG GIRL
(JOE'S FIRST EVER 45RPM
CHART SINGLE)
Released on EMI RECORDS
label in 1994.
Reached number sixty-one in
the UK charts. Stayed on the
chart for two weeks.

Track Listing:
1. Young Girl
2. I Wish You Love
3. Do I Care?

PASSING STRANGERS
(45 RPM SINGLE, WITH LIZ
DAWN)
Released on EMI RECORDS
label in 1994.
Reached number thirty-four
in the UK charts. Stayed on the
chart for four weeks.
Track Listing:
1. Passing Strangers
2. Midnight in Paris

LIVE AT THE ROYAL
ALBERT HALL
Released on EMI RECORDS
label in 1994.
Reached number fifty-seven in
the UK charts. Stayed on the
chart for two weeks.
Track Listing:
1. Mary in the Morning
2. If I Only Had Time
3. What's Going on
4. Unchained Melody
5. It's Not Unusual
6. To All the Girls I've Loved
Before

7. Pop Star Medley (Daniel, I Just
Called to Say I Love You, Stand
by Me)
8. This Is My Life
9. I Believe I'm Gonna Lose You
10. Rock Medley (Whole Lotta
Shakin', Great Balls of Fire)
11. Life on Mars
12. The Lady is a Tramp
13. Perfect Love
14. You're the First, the Last, My
Everything
15. Wind Beneath My Wings
16. Matt Monro Trilogy (Born
Free, Portrait of My Love,
Born Free)
17. If I Never Sing Another
Song
18. Somewhere (Instrumental)

REFLECTIONS
Released on TELSTAR
RECORDS label in 1999.
Track Listing:
1. Mack the Knife
2. We Don't Cry Out Loud
3. How Do You Keep the Music
Playing?
4. Always Something There to
Remind Me
5. I Will Drink the Wine
6. Midnight in Paris

7. Perfect Love
8. On the Sunny Side of the Street
9. I Believe I'm Gonna Love You
10. The Long and Winding Road
11. Love Letters
12. One for My Baby
13. You Will Be My Music

14. You're the First, the Last, My Everything
15. When a Child is Born
16. Crazy
17. The Man that Got Away
18. I've Got You Under My Skin
19. Midnight in Paris
20. Great Balls of Fire
21. American Trilogy

JOE LONGTHORNE LIVE IN CONCERT
Released on RITZ MUSIC GROUP label in 2001. Concert recorded in Aberdeen.
Track Listing:

1. MacArthur Park
2. As If We Never Said Goodbye
3. Mary in the Morning
4. River Stay Away from My Door
5. He Ain't Heavy, He's My Brother
6. To All the Girls I've Loved Before
7. Something
8. Big Spender
9. I (Who Have Nothing)
10. Delilah
11. Sweet Caroline
12. Mack the Knife
13. Love Is All

YOU & ME
(JOE'S FIRST ALL-NEW STUDIO ALBUM FOR A DECADE!)
Released by UNION SQUARE MUSIC in 2008.
Track Listing:

1. Let Me Try Again
2. On Days Like These
3. September in the Rain
4. Welcome to My World
5 Concrete and Clay
6. The Shadow of Your Smile
7. Help Me Make It through the Night
8. It's Impossible
9. Smile
10. Les Bicyclettes des Belsize
11. Love is in the Air
12. If
13. Jean
14. Rose Garden

15. Cycles
16. You & Me
17. When You Were Sweet Sixteen
18. You'll Never Find
19. Funny How Time Slips Away

LADY BLUE
(a whole album of Joe's own songs)
Released by Joe Longthorne in 2012
Track Listing:
1 Lady Blue (Longthorne, Dunstall)
2 Joanna (Longthorne, Mason)
3 Wave Breaking Over Me (Longthorne, Dunstall)
4 I Wish You Love (Longthorne, Dunstall, Osborne)
5 Do I Care (Longthorne, Dunstall)
6 I Still Love You (Longthorne, Dunstall)
7 Seven Wonders of the World (Longthorne, Dunstall)
8 Never Say Never (Longthorne, Dunstall)
9 Where Are You Now (Longthorne, Dunstall)
10 Over and Over (Longthorne, Dunstall)

11 True Love (Longthorne, Dunstall)
12 I've Waited So Long (Longthorne, Mason)
LIVE Bonus Track: Midnight in Paris (Longthorne, Winters, Holiday)

There have been many compilation releases, as well as several limited edition live recordings, but here we have tried to keep to the main studio or general release live recordings.

More details of these and Joe's video and DVD releases are available on www.joelongthorne.com and www.tmpromotions.co.uk

APPENDIX III

VIDEOGRAPHY/
DVD-OGRAPHY

THE SINGER
Year: 1989
Released by: TELSTAR
1. Just Like Magic
2. Joanna
3. All by Myself
4. One Love in a Million
5. You'll Never Walk Alone
6. I'm So Excited
7. Wind Beneath My Wings
8. Everybody Loves Me
9. Don't Give Up
10. He Ain't Heavy, He's MyBrother
11. Heartache Tonight
12. If I Never Sing Another Song
13. My Love for You
14. Bridge over Troubled Water
15. You're the Best Thing that Ever Happened to Me
16. Dancing in the Street
17. Almost Like a Song
18. Somewhere

THE VERY BEST OF JOE LONGTHORNE
Year: 1991
Released by: TELSTAR
1. My Girl
2. I Who Have Nothing
3. Forever Man
4. April Showers

JOE LONGTHORNE

5. California, Here I Come
6. American Trilogy
7. I Love You Because
8. Reach Out I'll Be There
9. Somewhere over the Rainbow
10. I Can't Stop Loving You
11. Try a Little Tenderness
12. Let the Heartaches Begin
13. Unforgettable
14. The Best of Times
15. 1-2-3
16. If I Loved You
17. Dancing in the Street
18. I Get Around
19. I've Waited So Long
20. Rock 'n' Roll Medley
21. I Get the Sweetest Feeling
22. Say it with Flowers
23. The Heat Is On
24. The Impossible Dream

LIVE IN CONCERT
Year: 1994
Released by: EMI
Recorded at: Opera House, Blackpool
1. Somewhere
2. Crazy
3. If I Only Had Time
4. It's Not Unusual
5. Till

6. To All the Girls I've Loved Before
7. Whole LottaShakin'
8. Great Balls of Fire
9. Daniel
10. I Just Called to Say I Love You
11. Stand by Me
12. Say it with Flowers
13. If I Never Sing Another Song
14. Falling in Love Again
15. This Is My Life
16. The Man that Got Away
17. Sweet Caroline
18. It's Now or Never
19. Nessun Dorma
20. When You're Smiling
21. Hello Dolly
22. You're the Best Thing that Ever Happened to Me
23. Could It Be Magic
24. Wind Beneath My Wings
25. Unchained Melody
26. If I Loved You
27. Somewhere (Instrumental)
28. I Wish You Love
THIS RECORDING HAS NOW BEEN SUPPLEMENTED BY '93 DIRECTOR'S CUT
Released by: CLEARVIEW
In addition to the original

footage this now includes two
other songs:
You're the First, the Last, My
Everything
You'll Never Walk Alone
It also includes an additional 30
minutes of footage.

LIVE AT THE ROYAL
ALBERT HALL
Year: 1995
Released by: PMI
1. Mary in the Morning
2. If I Only Had Time
3. Whole Lotta Shakin'
4. Great Balls of Fire
5. Unchained Melody
6. It's Not Unusual
7. Till
8. Daniel
9. I Just Called To Say I Love You
10. Stand by Me
11. Say it with Flowers
12. This Is My Life
13. Sweet Caroline
14. Life on Mars
15. I Believe I'm Gonna Love You
16. It's Now or Never
17. The Lady is a Tramp
18. Perfect Love
19. Wind Beneath My Wings
20. Born Free

21. If I Never Sing Another
    Song
22. Somewhere
23. You'll Never Walk Alone

A MAN AND HIS MUSIC
Year: 1996
Released by: POLYGRAM
1. Somewhere
2. Stormy Weather
3. The Long and Winding Road
4. Midnight in Paris
5. All the Way
6. Delilah
7. Big Spender
8. I've Got You Under My Skin
9. You Will Be My Music
10. One for My Baby, and One
    More for the Road
11. Don't Cry Out Loud
12. So Deep is the Night
13. American Trilogy
14. How Do You Keep the
    Music Playing?
15. For All We Know
16. You Belong to Me
17. Release Me
18. What Kind of Fool Am I?
19. You're the First, the Last, My
    Everything
20. When Your Old Wedding
    Ring Was New

21. Somewhere
22. Turtle Nights

THE ULTIMATE
COLLECTION
Year: 1997
Released by: TELSTAR
1. Somewhere
2. I Saw Her Standing There
3. He Ain't Heavy, He's My Brother
4. I Who Have Nothing
5. I Get a Kick Out of You
6. Joanna
7. Dancing in the Street
8. Put the Weight on My Shoulders
9. Say it with Flowers
10. You're the Best Thing that Ever Happened to Me
11. I'm Gonna Make You Love Me
12. The Impossible Dream
13. Bridge over Troubled Water
14. Let the Heartaches Begin
15. Wind Beneath My Wings
16. American Trilogy
17. One Love in a Million
18. I'll Never Love This Way Again
19. Try a Little Kindness
20. You'll Never Walk Alone

21. Till
22. My Girl
23. Don't Cry Out Loud
24. Somewhere over the Rainbow
25. 1-2-3
26. Runaround Sue
27. Great Balls Of Fire
28. Oh Boy
29. That's Alright

THE GENIUS OF JOE
LONGTHORNE
Year: 2002
Released by: VCI
Recorded at: Southport
1. Introduction
2. As If We Never Said Goodbye
3. Mary in the Morning
4. If I Only Had Time
5. Perfect Love
6. I've Got You Under My Skin
7. When a Child is Born
8. You're the First, the Last, My Everything
9. Delilah
10. Till
11. Big Spender
12. I Am What I Am
13. Love is in the Air
14. Don't Cry Out Loud
15. Copacabana

16. Life on Mars
17. I Left My Heart in San Francisco
18. Love Is All
19. Great Balls of Fire
20. Unchained Melody
21. I Will Drink the Wine
22. You'll Never Know
23. American Trilogy

JOE LONGTHORNE … with Love
Year: 2004
Released by: Clearview
Recorded at: Sheffield City Hall
1. Macarthur Park
2. As If We Never Said Goodbye
3. Mary in the Morning
4. River Stay Away from My Door
5. As I Love You
6. I Wanna Be Where You Are
7. Don't Cry Out Loud
8. Big Spender/Something
9. Delilah
10. Is This the Way to Amarillo
11. Hello
12. Sweet Caroline
13. To All The Girls I've Loved Before
14. You're the First, the Last, My Everything

15. I Believe I'm Gonna Love You
16. What Kind of Fool Am I?
17. For the Good Times
18. Life on Mars
19. The Man that Got Away
20. It's Now or Never
21. 24 Hours from Tulsa
22. Nessun Dorma
23. American Trilogy
24. Once upon a Song

JOE'S BACK
Year: 2005
Released by: CLEARVIEW
1. Play On
2. People
3. If I Loved You
4. Mack the Knife
5. As I Love You
6. Where Are You Now?
7. Too Much Too Little Too Late
8. Amarillo
9. Mary in the Morning
10. Big Spender
11. Delilah
12. I Who Have Nothing
13. Quando Quando Quando/ The Last Waltz
14. It's Now or Never
15. You're the First, the Last, My Everything

315

16. Just the Way You Are
17. Born Free
18. Love is in the Air
19. Hello Again
20. Sweet Caroline
21. I Believe I'm Gonna Love You
22. You'll Never Know
23. One Man Woman
24. The Lady is a Tramp
25. My Way
26. Woman
27. Music
28. Always Stop to Cry
29. Can You Feel the Love Tonight?
30. Roll over Beethoven
31. Great Balls of Fire
32. Unchained Melody
33. American Trilogy

LIVE IN PARADISE
Year: 2005
Released by: CLEARVIEW
Recorded at: THE PARADISE
ROOMS, BLACKPOOL
1. Overture
2. People
3. If You Love Me
4. Mary in the Morning
5. As I Love You
6. Mack the Knife

7. What I Did for Love
8. For Once in My Life
9. You'll Never Know
10. Where or When
11. I Left My Heart in San Francisco
12. The Lady is a Tramp
13. My Way
14. So Deep is the Night
15. Crazy (performed by Joe's sister, Lizzie)
16. I Wanna Be Where You Are
17. If I Loved You
18. Quando Quando Quando/ The Last Waltz
19. Born Free/Portrait of My Love
20. You're the Best Thing that Ever Happened to Me
21. If I Never Sing Another Song

LIVE FROM THE LONDON
PALLADIUM
Year: 2006
Released by: CLEARVIEW
1. When Your Old Wedding Ring Was New
2. Somewhere
3. People
4. For Once in My Life
5. If You Love Me

6. Mary in the Morning
7. Mack the Knife
8. As I Love You
9. Big Spender
10. Till
11. Love is in the Air
12. Hello Again/Sweet Caroline
13. The Lady is a Tramp/My Way
14. You'll Never Know
15. When a Child is Born
16. You're the First, the Last, My Everything
17. Just the Way You Are
18. The Impossible Dream
19. For the Good Times
20. If I Never Sing Another Song

IF I NEVER SING
ANOTHER SONG
Year: 2008
Released by: VEGAS
Documentary film featuring Joe
on tour
Performances include:
1. As If We Never Said Goodbye
2. I've Got You Under My Skin
3. American Trilogy
4. Hello Again
5. As I Love You
6. My Way
7. My Mother's Eyes

8. Somewhere
9. I Believe I'm Gonna Love You
10. You're the Best Thing that Ever Happened to Me
11. Mary in the Morning
12. Woman
13. Sir Duke
14. Lately
15. Can You Feel the Love Tonight?
16. That's What Friends Are For
17. If I Never Sing Another Song

THE YOU & ME TOUR
Year: 2008
Released by: VEGAS
Documentary film featuring Joe
on tour
Performances include:
1. Somewhere
2. Mack the Knife
3. My Way
4. Something
5. If You Love Me
6. The Impossible Dream
7. If I Never Sing Another Song
8. Don't Cry Out Loud
9. Mary in the Morning
10. Can't Smile Without You
11. The Lady is a Tramp
12. As I Love You

13. Just the Way You Are

14. Love is in the Air

Also includes Joe's Variety Club of Great Britain award ceremony for his Lifetime Achievement Award

JOE LONGTHORNE SINGS TO THE GODS

Year: 2008

Released by: VEGAS

Recorded at: KOURION AMPHITHEATRE, CYPRUS

1. Overture

2. Somewhere

3. For Once in My Life

4. Let Me Try Again

5. Love is in the Air

6. September in the Rain

7. If

8. To All the Girls I've Loved Before

9. Delilah

10. Big Spender

11. Something

12. Hello

13. Sweet Caroline

14. Born Free

15. Can't Smile Without You

16. You're the First, the Last, My Everything/Just the Way You Are

17. I Left My Heart in San Francisco

18. When a Child is Born

19. Piano Medley: Georgia on My Mind/Imagine/Whole Lotta Shakin'/Great Balls of Fire

20. Wind Beneath My Wings

21. If I Loved You

22. So Deep is the Night

23. You're the Best Thing that Ever Happened to Me

24. What Kind of Fool Am I?

25. The Lady is a Tramp

26. My Way

27. In the Ghetto/The Wonder of You/American Trilogy

28. If I Never Sing Another Song

There have been three DVDs of A YEAR IN HIS LIFE, produced in 2004. These contain footage of BBC/ITV interviews and concert footage.